STALIN'S FALCONS

EXPOSING THE MYTH OF SOVIET AERIAL SUPERIORITY OVER THE LUFTWAFFE IN WW2

STALIN'S FALCONS

EXPOSING THE MYTH OF SOVIET AERIAL SUPERIORITY OVER THE LUFTWAFFE IN WW2

DMITRY ZUBOV

STALIN'S FALCONS

First published in Great Britain in 2024 by
Air World
An imprint of
Pen & Sword Books Ltd
Yorkshire – Philadelphia

ISBN 978 1 39909 567 9

A CIP catalogue record for this book is available from the British Library.

Typeset by SJmagic DESIGN SERVICES, India.
Printed and bound in the UK by CPI Group (UK) Ltd.

Pen & Sword Books Limited incorporates the imprints of Atlas, Archaeology, Aviation, Discovery, Family History, Fiction, History, Maritime, Military, Military Classics, Politics, Select, Transport, True Crime, Air World, Frontline Publishing, Leo Cooper, Remember When, Seaforth Publishing, The Praetorian Press, Wharncliffe Local History, Wharncliffe Transport, Wharncliffe True Crime and White Owl.

For a complete list of Pen & Sword titles please contact

PEN & SWORD BOOKS LIMITED
George House, Units 12 & 13, Beevor Street, Off Pontefract Road,
Barnsley, South Yorkshire, S71 1HN, England
E-mail: enquiries@pen-and-sword.co.uk
Website: www.pen-and-sword.co.uk

or
PEN AND SWORD BOOKS
1950 Lawrence Rd, Havertown, PA 19083, USA
E-mail: uspen-and-sword@casematepublishers.com
Website: www.penandswordbooks.com

Contents

Introduction

> You have failed our country, our Red Army. You will not deign to release Il-2s in sufficient quantities until now. Our Red Army needs Il-2 aircraft now like air, like bread. Shekman[1] gives one Il-2 a day, and Tretyakov[2] gives one, two MiG-3. This is a mockery of the country, of the Red Army. We don't need MiGs, but Il-2. If Aviation Plant No. 18 wants to get rid of the country by giving one Il-2 a day, then it is cruelly mistaken and will suffer punishment for this. I ask you not to put the government out of patience and I demand that you produce more Il-2s. I'm warning you for the last time. Stalin.[3]

It was this angry telegram on 23 December 1941 that put an end to the production of the MiG-3, the most numerous of the 'New Type' fighters at the time of the German attack on the USSR. Another promising fighter, the LaGG-3, only survived its competitor for six months, although it did not disappear without a trace like the MiG-3. After replacing the engine,

1 Matthew Shekman, Director of the Voronezh Aviation Plant No. 18. The plant was founded in the city of Voronezh in 1930 to implement Stalin's largescale plans for the development of the Soviet aviation industry. However, due to lack of resources and complete managerial chaos, the construction of the plant was delayed for almost ten years. In 1939 mass production of Il-2 ground-attack aircraft began at Voronezh Aviation Plant No. 18. In connection with the disaster at the front caused by the rapid German advance, on 10 October 1941 Aviation Plant No. 18 was evacuated to the city of Kuibyshev (now Samara). There, in the production workshops built by Gulag prisoners, Director Matthew Shekman and employees of the evacuated Aviation Plant No. 18 tried to re-launch production of Stalin's beloved ground-attack aircraft, the Il-2.

2 Anatoly Tretyakov, Director of the State Aviation Plant No. 1 (Moscow) since February 1941. In the autumn of 1941, due to the approach of German troops, Plant No. 1 was evacuated to the city of Kuibyshev (now Samara).

3 RGASPI. Foundation 558. Inventory 11. Case 151. Sheet 57.

Director of Aviation Plant No. 18, Matthew Shekman.

this aircraft was converted to the La-5. And only the Yak-1 fighter was produced without significant changes until 1944. However, despite Stalin's praise, the Yak-1 was not better than its competitors. It continued to be mass-produced only as a result of the intrigues of its creator Alexander Yakovlev, who became one of the leaders of the Soviet Aviation Industry by the will of Stalin.

The inexpediency of simultaneous production of three fighter models at once (Yak-1, LaGG-3 and MiG-3) with approximately equal characteristics was obvious to everyone who had the appropriate competence. However, Stalin, the only person in the USSR who determined the direction of development of the Red Army Air Force, was in a strange state of indecision. He avoided choosing a single fighter model for mass production and returned to this question only after the terrible defeat of the Soviet Red Army Air Force by Luftwaffe aircraft in 1941. Stalin's indecision turned into serious problems for the Red Army Air Force long before the German attack on the Soviet Union.

Serial production of the Yak-1, LaGG-3 and MiG-3 fighters in the first half of 1941 ended in a natural failure. Despite attracting huge financial and organizational resources, the Soviet aviation industry could not ensure the implementation of the plan for the numbers of fighters produced. Such incredible haste led to the quality of production of fighters of the 'New Type'[4] being completely unacceptable, even by the standards of Red Army Air Force. Such modest results, obtained at the price of refusing to release the I-16 fighter, which was well in production, did not correspond in any way to Stalin's grandiose plans for the development of Soviet aviation.

What made the 'Red Lord' at the end of 1938 feverishly look for a replacement for the I-16, the mass production of which was mastered with great difficulty by the young Soviet Aviation Industry? For what reason was the most massive fighter, which was actively used in all military conflicts

4 With this phrase, Stalin distinguished the Yak-1, LaGG-3 and MiG-3 from fighters of the 'Old Type' I-16, I-15, I-153 in official documents.

Director of State Aviation Plant No. 1, Anatoly Tretyakov.

of the 30s and made the 'Stalin's falcons' famous all over the world, declared obsolete by Stalin and was discontinued? Were fighters of the 'New Type' better in their characteristics than the good old 'Rat'?[5]

The answers to these and many other questions cannot be obtained without a deep analysis of the destructive influence of the criminal Stalinist regime on all stages of planning, designing, manufacturing and operating combat aircraft in the USSR in the second half of the 1930s. For many years it was impossible to do this because of the total closeness of sources and the deliberate replacement of facts with stupid propaganda clichés, the author of which was Stalin himself. Despite the gradual opening of archives, this topic still remains poorly explored, which means that it is subject to the negative influence of both Soviet and modern versions of myths and everyday misconceptions.

The development of the Red Army Air Force in the period 1934-1941 became a kind of mirror reflecting all the vices of the Stalinist state system, which caused the total failure of Soviet fighter aircraft in the confrontation with the Luftwaffe. However, the traditional historical approach to the analysis of this period, which focuses on various technical and statistical aspects of the development of the Red Army Air Force, has significant drawbacks. It gives only a superficial picture, leaving unanswered the true reasons for the deplorable state of Soviet fighter aviation. The attempts of historians to give a qualitative analysis of the actions of key characters who determined the strategy and tactics of the Red Army Air Force, primarily Stalin, lead to an incorrect interpretation of their motives in the spirit of the popular everyday concept of 'Fatal Decisions'.

In this book, the author would like to draw readers' attention especially to the social and psychological aspects of the development of Stalin's Red Army

5 'Rat' was the nickname for the I-16.

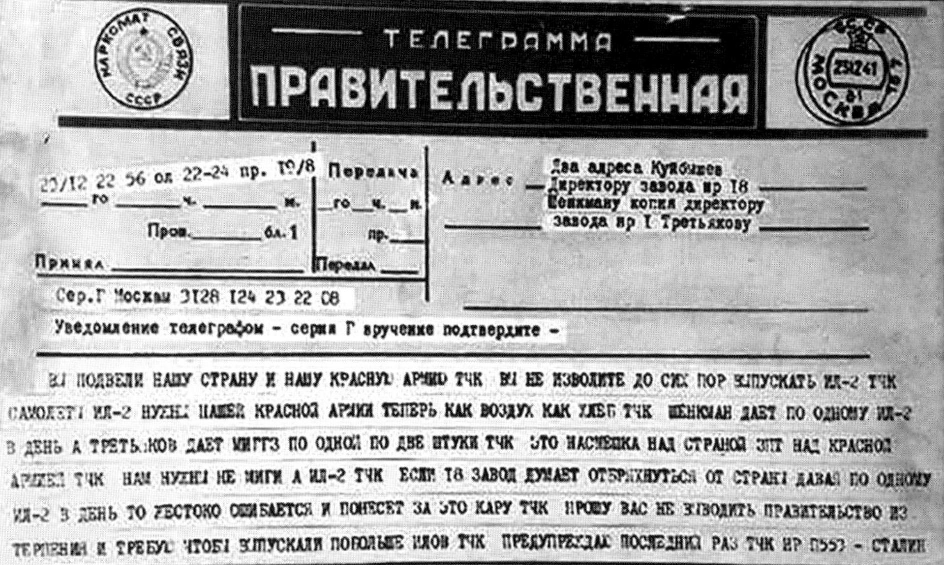

НАРКОМАТ СВЯЗИ СССР

ТЕЛЕГРАММА
ПРАВИТЕЛЬСТВЕННАЯ

23/12 22 56 ол 22-24 пр. 19/8
Передача
Адрес — Два адреса Куйбышев
Директору завода нр 18
Шенкману копия директору
завода нр 1 Третьякову
Пров. бл. 1
Принял
Передал
Сер.Г Москвы 3128 124 23 22 08
Уведомление телеграфом - серия Г вручение подтвердите -

ВЫ ПОДВЕЛИ НАШУ СТРАНУ И НАШУ КРАСНУЮ АРМИЮ ТЧК ВЫ НЕ ИЗВОЛИТЕ ДО СИХ ПОР ВЫПУСКАТЬ ИЛ-2 ТЧК
САМОЛЕТЫ ИЛ-2 НУЖНЫ НАШЕЙ КРАСНОЙ АРМИИ ТЕПЕРЬ КАК ВОЗДУХ КАК ХЛЕБ ТЧК ШЕНКМАН ДАЕТ ПО ОДНОМУ ИЛ-2
В ДЕНЬ А ТРЕТЬЯКОВ ДАЕТ МИГ3 ПО ОДНОЙ ПО ДВЕ ШТУКИ ТЧК ЭТО НАСМЕШКА НАД СТРАНОЙ ЗПТ НАД КРАСНОЙ
АРМИЕЙ ТЧК НАМ НУЖНЫ НЕ МИГИ А ИЛ-2 ТЧК ЕСЛИ 18 ЗАВОД ДУМАЕТ ОТБРЫКНУТЬСЯ ОТ СТРАНЫ ДАВАЯ ПО ОДНОМУ
ИЛ-2 В ДЕНЬ ТО ЖЕСТОКО ОШИБАЕТСЯ И ПОНЕСЕТ ЗА ЭТО КАРУ ТЧК ПРОШУ ВАС НЕ ВЫВОДИТЬ ПРАВИТЕЛЬСТВО ИЗ
ТЕРПЕНИЯ И ТРЕБУЮ ЧТОБЫ ВЫПУСКАЛИ ПОБОЛЬШЕ ИЛОВ ТЧК ПРЕДУПРЕЖДАЮ ПОСЛЕДНИЙ РАЗ ТЧК НР П553 - СТАЛИН

Stalin's telegram of 23 December 1941.

The text of Stalin's telegram was turned into a pretentious slogan that hung on the wall in the assembly workshop of ground-attack aircraft Il-2s at Aviation Plant No. 18.

Air Force. Such an approach can provide new opportunities for a logical explanation of chronic failures in the design and production of aircraft. The designers, managers, technologists and workers of the aviation industry who created fighters and 'Stalin's falcons', who flew and died in them, were part of the totalitarian state created by Stalin. His personal vices contributed to the cultivation of hostility and intolerance in Soviet society, stimulated the constant search for external and internal enemies, to whom responsibility for the troubles and misfortunes of the half-starved population of the Stalinist Empire was shifted. Disunity, sometimes hostility, has become a perverted form of relations between many state structures responsible for the development of the Red Army Air Force. The reverse side of the total state supervision of many bureaucratic structures over the activities of the Soviet Aviation Industry enterprises was complete lack of control. Stalin's absolute planning turned into complete chaos and confusion. A lot of groups reflecting the divergent interests of the military, top management in the aviation industry, leading aircraft designers, and directors of aircraft plants locked in a deadly battle for the attention of 'Red Tsar'. In order to understand who won in this continuous struggle, and why, a deep psychological analysis of the motives of the main actors of these events is necessary.

Assembly of ground-attack aircraft Il-2s at Aviation Plant No. 18.

A column of workers and engineers of Voronezh Aviation Plant No. 18 at a festive demonstration on 7 November. End of the 1930s.

Gulag prisoners at the construction of auxiliary premises of Aviation Plant No. 18 in the city of Kuibyshev.

Stalin and his closest servants, mid-1930s.

Chapter 1

Stalin's favorite 'brainchild'
The childish delight of a narrowminded 'Great Leader'

On 1 May 1935, a cool spring morning, an important event for all Soviet people takes place on a huge square surrounded by the medieval towers of the Moscow Kremlin and other fancy buildings reflecting the megalomania of the Russian tsars. There are only two days a year (1 May and 7 November) when a pompous Bolshevik ritual is carried out – a military parade combining the pomp of Orthodox worship with a Roman military triumph. This event, sacred to the paranoid Bolshevik sect, was supposed to demonstrate to external and internal enemies the full power of the 'Red Empire'.

On the rostrum of a squat granite structure, the Mausoleum, on the underground level of which there is a sarcophagus with the body of Vladimir Lenin, is a group of nondescript people. The people gathered in the square can only see their shoulders and heads. However, all Soviet citizens know that in the centre of the podium is the great leader of all peoples: Joseph Stalin. This little man with a moustache, dressed in a very modest shabby military overcoat and a military cap, is outwardly expressionless and grey. He is emphatically modest in behaviour and appearance. Nothing distinguishes him from the crowd of his confidants. However, every Soviet worker and peasant knows perfectly well what Stalin really looks like. A giant image of 'Red Tsar', where he is represented by a tall, black-moustachioed handsome man, is available for viewing from all sides of Red Square. His portrait is printed in every Soviet newspaper; monuments are already appearing on every city square, where he is depicted together with the founder of the 'Red Empire', Vladimir Lenin.

At this moment a grandiose theatrical action is unfolding on the square. The ranks of cadets of higher and secondary military educational

Military parade on Red Square.

institutions, pathetically mincing a step, are replaced by armed detachments of the working people of Moscow. Then comes the turn of archaic cavalry squadrons, ridiculous horse-drawn machine guns ('tachanka'), horse-drawn artillery and even soldiers on bicycles. Behind the infantry squares of the marching troops, columns of military equipment rush: numerous armoured vehicles and towed guns. Then more than 500 light and heavy tanks passed through Red Square, clanking their tracks.

All this carefully directed action, for the preparation of which huge amounts of money have been spent in a hungry and impoverished country, is carried out only for one person on earth – 'Great Leader' Joseph Stalin. Meanwhile, habitually inspecting the endless columns of rumbling military equipment and rows of fanatically marching and galloping Red Army men on horses the 'Red Tsar' got bored. He had already seen all this pretentious action many times. The impressive flight over Red Square of 800 aircraft of different types is already perceived by him as a familiar routine. Even the armadas of huge angular TB-3 bombers that slowly sailed through the sky of Moscow no longer make the same enthusiastic impression on Stalin. Sometimes the suspicious and distrustful 'Red Lord' exchanges remarks with his loyal servants, who are hanging on his every word. 'Is he happy with

Joseph Stalin and Kliment Voroshilov at the rostrum of the Mausoleum welcome the participants of the military parade, mid-1930s.

T-28 tanks passing through Red Square during a military parade on 7 November 1938.

today's parade?' A whirlwind rush through the heads of the organizers of the magnificent performance, who are anxiously peering at Stalin's frowning face. Someone from the leader's entourage, feeling the growing irritation of the 'Red Tsar', has already begun to assume which of the organizers of the failed parade will be sent to rot in Gulag, and who will be shot. However, detractors from among Stalin's retinue were too hasty with conclusions. In reality, the organizers of the 1935 aviation parade will be shot only in 1937.

Ah, today the faithful servants have prepared an original surprise for their evil 'Red Lord'. At the final part of the parade, when no one expected to see something new, five bright red I-16 fighters roared over Red Square on a low-level flight almost at the level of the rostrum. Having flown to the very end of Red Square, they, effectively rotating the whole group, sharply lifting their blunt noses, almost vertically screwed into the sky. This unplanned joint flight of the latest Soviet fighters produced a stunning effect on Stalin. Usually very emotionally restrained in public, the 'Great Leader' suddenly began to clap his hands loudly from the childish delight that seized him. The servants standing on the podium next to Stalin breathed a sigh of relief and also began to applaud vigorously, supporting their 'Master'.[1]

1 As Stalin was unofficially called by his entourage.

Dog breeder sappers on bicycles at a military parade on 1 May 1938.

The hero of the parade of 1935, an ugly plane with an unusually short blunt-nosed fuselage, which caused such vivid emotions in the leader, was not a novelty for Stalin and had already been demonstrated to him once. However, the first demonstration of the I-16 at the Frunze Central Aerodrome, located on the northern outskirts of Moscow, was met by Stalin rather coldly and suspiciously. Then the organizers of the presentation of the aircraft also tried very hard to make a favourable impression on the 'Red Tsar'. They put pilot Valery Chkalov in the cockpit of an experimental fighter, who soon became the main 'Stalin's Falcon'. However, the carefully prepared presentation clearly failed. Due to the terrible quality of the production of a fighter, the demonstration flight almost ended in disaster. However, the experienced Valery Chkalov was able to carry out the aerobatics of the faulty aircraft so confidently that none of the distinguished guests at the airfield noticed the problems. After landing, Chkalov had to show all his natural charm to get Stalin's consent to mass production of this dangerous and technically incomplete aircraft.

Meanwhile, the story of the brilliant display of the five I-16 fighters at the parade on 1 May 1935 was continued. After the speech, the pilots of the

The hero of the parade of 1935, the I-16, an ugly plane with an unusually short blunt-nosed fuselage.

I-16, hardly restraining their excitement from performing a risky manoeuvre in front of Stalin himself, returned to the airfield. They did not know the reaction of the 'Red Dictator' to their circus performance and anxiously discussed the details of the aerobatics that they performed over Red Square again and again. Unexpectedly, an aide-de-camp of Stalin's closest friend and devoted servant, People's Commissar for Defence of the Soviet Union (Minister of War), arrived at the airfield: Kliment Voroshilov. The pilots froze in anxious expectation, fearing immediate arrest and despatch to prison. However, this time they were not waiting for the execution, but a reward from Stalin himself. Voroshilov's adjutant presented each confused pilot with the badges of extraordinary military ranks and a cash prize – five thousand rubles each! Moreover, soon Kliment Voroshilov himself called the I-16 fighter base airfield and the commander of the five fighters, 'Stalin's Falcon' Vladimir Kokkinaki, for a telephone conversation. Over the phone, Voroshilov solemnly announced, 'Comrade Stalin is delighted with the skill of the pilots and asks them to fly over Moscow again.'

Stalin's 'Red Five'[2] flew over the Moscow streets several times, demonstrating aerobatics. Planes flew in different parts of the city, and later

2 'Red Five' was an aviation aerobatic group created by order of Stalin in 1934.

a legend was even born that on 1 May 1935, several 'Red Fives' flew over Moscow.

After such an emotional event, the extremely suspicious, but equally naïve, Stalin finally believed in the superiority of the Soviet fighters and the highest skill of the 'Stalin's Falcons' piloting them. However, time would tell how deeply wrong was the 'wisest of the wise'.

Communist Mordor for workers and peasants

The scale of the demonstration of military equipment at the Stalinist parades is amazing and raises a logical question about from where in the agrarian Russia inherited by the Bolsheviks from the tsar they killed an extensive industry capable of producing aircraft and tanks in such huge quantities came? To answer this question, it is necessary to understand the psychology of the Bolshevik leaders.

The young Soviet Republic renounced its obligations on huge debts for the supply of weapons by the allies in the First World War and became an international outcast. The long civil war and total terror of Vladimir Lenin drained Russia of blood and put its population on the verge of physical

'Red Five'

extinction. The gang of Bolsheviks, who mercilessly dealt with internal 'enemies', thoroughly prepared for the fight against external 'enemies', which for them was actually the whole world. However, the populist ideas of communism in practice turned into a complete economic collapse. The abolition of money and a complete ban on even small businesses turned into ruin and the collapse of everything. Infantry and numerous cavalry, 'hardened' in battles with their own people, were absolutely insufficient for an ambitious battle for a world revolution. Urgent measures were needed to turn impoverished Russia into a forge of modern weapons. However, international isolation closed the Bolsheviks' access to Western technologies.

The founder of the Soviet Union, Vladimir Lenin, was a convinced Germanophile and hated total Russian backwardness. Almost from the first days of coming to power, he dreamed of the industrialization of Russia and the creation of a powerful military industry. It was he who, during his short time in power, laid the foundations for the total industrialization and

Father of the 'Red Empire', Vladimir Lenin, and his 'son', Joseph Stalin.

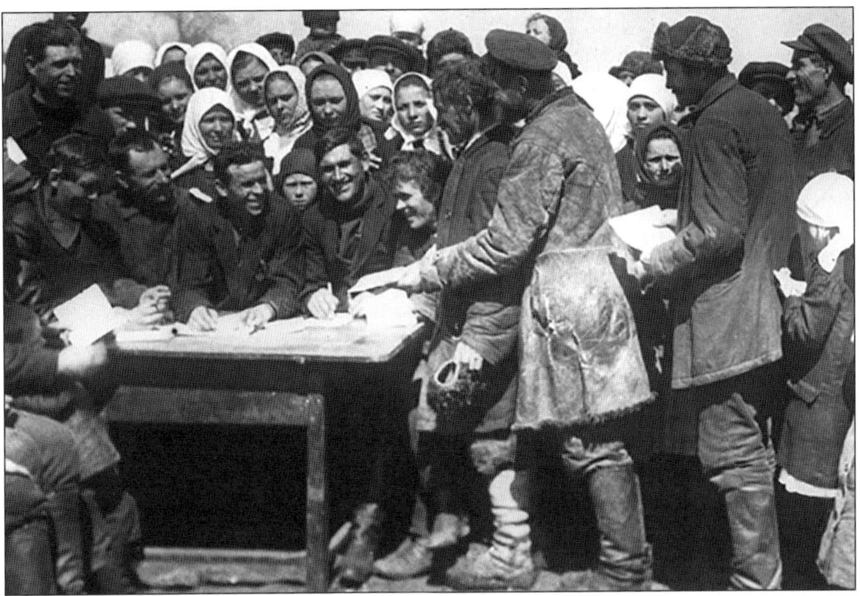

Peasants enroll in kolkhoz (collective farms), early 1930s.

militarization of the Soviet Union by robbing his own people and turning them into slaves of the communist system. The values taken away from the population and the tsarist gold inherited by the Bolsheviks allowed Lenin to establish the first, so far informal and strictly secret, contacts with Western business. Many European companies, especially German ones, were ready to turn a blind eye to the official ban on interaction with the criminal Bolshevik regime for a generous reward. However, by 1923, the neurosyphilis that Vladimir Lenin had suffered from for many years had passed into the terminal stage. The disease quickly deprived the Bolshevik leader of his mind and brought him to the grave. His young successor and 'spiritual son' Joseph Stalin, who by the end of the 1930s had concentrated absolute power in his hands, immediately began to implement the plans of his 'spiritual father'.

However, with similar immorality and pathological cruelty, there was one important difference between Lenin and Stalin. Vladimir Lenin was a brilliantly educated intellectual and the son of a high-ranking tsarist official. He was fluent in several European languages and lived in forced emigration in Europe for many years. Joseph Stalin was the son of a shoemaker, who never finished the meagre education of a rural priest. Moreover, the intellectual abilities of the future 'Red Tsar' were extremely limited. As Stalin seized absolute power, the development of Russia began to obey the peculiarities of the character of this intellectually limited psychopath-fanatic.

The new society of universal equality and freedom, proclaimed by the Bolsheviks on the ruins of the Russian Empire, turned out to be a chimera. Under the red flag the former pathological social structure of tsarist Russia was hidden; the role of the former tsarist aristocracy was transferred to a new, already Bolshevik 'aristocracy'. All other segments of the population were completely deprived of all rights and freedoms against the background of propaganda and populist slogans. The Bolsheviks turned almost all the 'citizens' of the USSR into slaves and divided them into a number of castes. The Gulag prisoners who were doomed to death were the most disenfranchised, and a small group of Soviet officials and party bosses became the most privileged caste. The Red 'aristocracy', which at the same time were members of the religious sect of the Bolsheviks, was a mixture of different social strata of the former tsarist Russia. The thin social stratum of Soviet engineers and aircraft designers was one of the most prosperous social groups. However, many of them, having fallen out of favour with the suspicious 'Red Tsar', were declared 'enemies of the people' and thrown into NKVD prisons. By order of Stalin, a huge uneducated peasant population was forcibly driven into collective farms, *kolkhozes*, where they

Stalin's military industry.

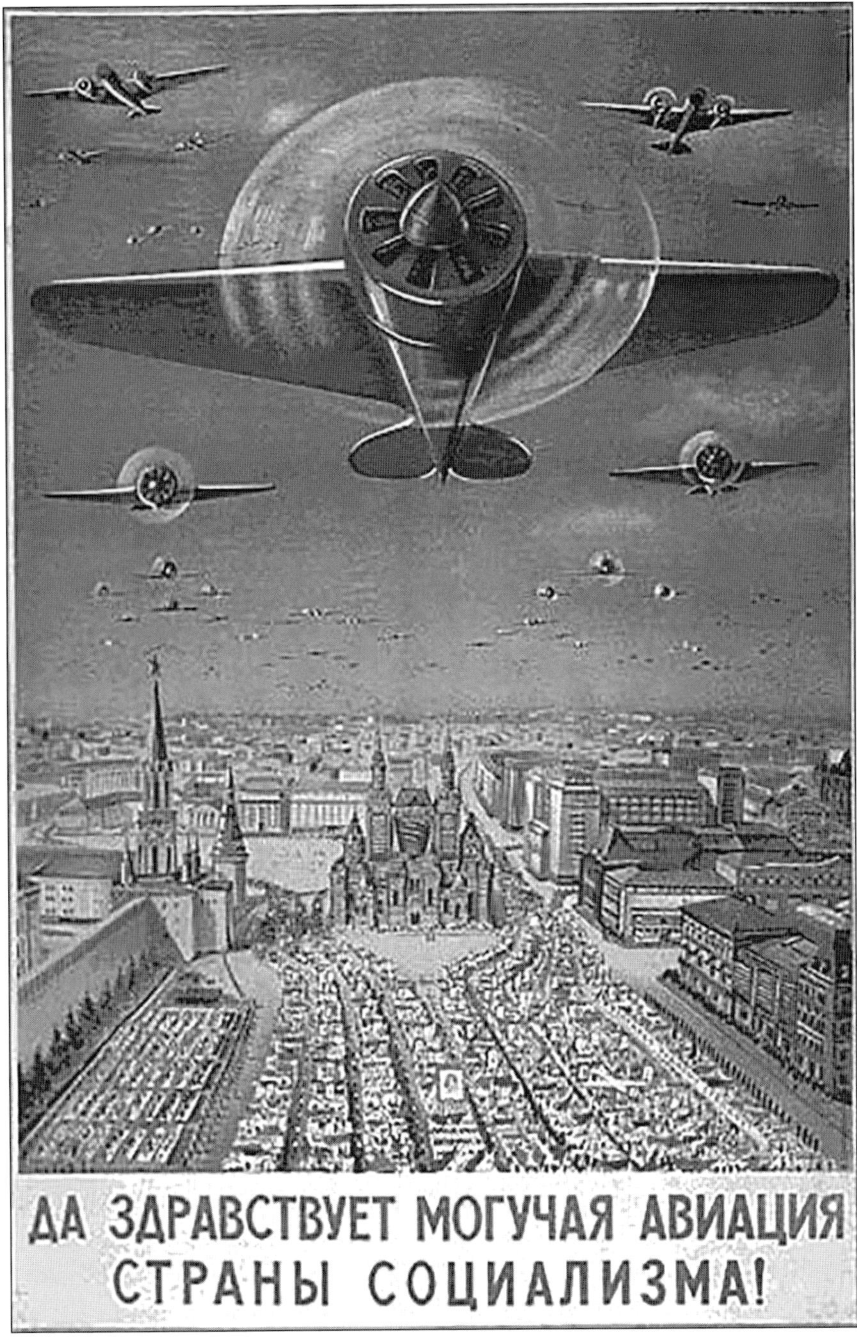

Propaganda poster glorifying Stalin's aviation.

Stalin at the end of the 1920s.

cultivated the land with the help of technologies of the eleventh century. The most enterprising peasants were exiled to Siberia, where most of them were doomed to certain death from starvation. The growing army of workers, recent peasants, who received only primary school education, unsuccessfully tried to fulfill Stalin's impossible plans.

Thus, at the beginning of the 1930s, the features of the communist Mordor began to form rapidly. It was based on the key features of the Stalinist character, namely total fear, turning into horror; bloody cruelty, turning into terror; general secrecy, turning into manic suspicion and universal unquestioning submission to a single leader, turning into deification and slavish worship. The life of any Soviet 'citizen' was in the hands of the ruthless Stalinist repressive machine. The living conditions in the Soviet Union corresponded psychologically to the conditions of the Dark Middle Ages and obscurantism. And over all this emerging 'Evil Empire', the NKVD, the sleepless eye of the Communist Party, and therefore Stalin personally, was constantly supervising.

Only in such appalling conditions of terror and universal submission, was the incapable manager and psychopath Stalin able to begin implementing his sinister militaristic plans. Future colossi of Stalinist industry, including numerous aviation plants, suddenly began to appear in the swamps and ravines.

Stalin's 'Great Break'

Solving the problem of the lack of financial resources for the development of industry and the extremely poor and uneducated population, teetering on the verge of hunger, required reasonable approaches and a long-term transformation of the structure of society. However, the intellectually limited fanatic Stalin, who knows no doubts, cut it with one blow, like a Gordian knot. 'Red Tsar' declared that the main task of the new planned economy was to build up the military power of the state at the highest possible pace.

Industrialization was elevated by Stalin to the status of an absolute, the highest goal, for the realization of which all means were good. Soon, ‘Red Tsar’ announced the first five-year plan (1 October 1928-1 October 1933), pathetically presenting it as a set of carefully thought-out and real tasks. In a hungry country, it was necessary to create new industries, increase the production of all types of products and start producing new complex military equipment. At the initial stage, this was achieved by re-distributing the maximum possible amount of resources taken from the starving population for the needs of industrialization.

Stalin, being a loyal student of Lenin, began to use the resource that was abundant in Russia in the 1930s, namely the lives and slave labour of the large submissive population of the Soviet Empire. He carried out the industrialization of the Soviet Union virtually with fire and sword, sacrificing millions of lives of his own people. At the same time, he generously paid European and American companies, robbed gold from the half-starved population for the supply of Western technologies and equipment vital for industrial development.

Based on Stalin’s crazy plans, the number of factories that the Bolsheviks inherited from tsarist rule had to be increased tenfold. Since the Russian aviation industry was in its infancy, and the Bolsheviks only dreamed of

Stalin in the cockpit of the prototype Polikarpov I-5 fighter.

largescale production of aircraft, it was necessary to create it almost from scratch. In the early years of the Stalinist regime, Moscow became the main centre of aircraft construction. Later, almost the entire huge country was entangled in a network of Soviet aviation industry enterprises.

However, the foreign equipment paid for by the lives of the population was used extremely inefficiently. Often machines bought for gold rusted for years in the open air. The expensive equipment installed in the new factories was operated by unskilled workers using such barbaric methods that it soon failed. There was an acute shortage of qualified workers, certified engineers and experienced production organizers everywhere. 'Red Tsar' imposed cruel medieval methods of industrial management based on total intimidation. Imminent death threatened everyone who expressed the slightest doubt about the effectiveness of primitive methods of creating a military industry.

Total economic planning was chosen as the main means of implementing ambitious plans. However, 'Red Tsar' did not trust Russian economists and

Red Army Air Force in action.

specialists in planned development and suspected them of wanting to harm his 'brilliant' plans. Therefore, Stalin, a loyal student of Lenin, gave orders to hire foreign specialists – in fact, the main external enemies of communism. The primitive Marxist and leader of the proletariat made insidious plans to destroy his external enemies with the help of weapons produced in factories and according to drawings designed by their own hands. Copying Western ideas and experience, something that was categorically denied in the era of the late Stalin, was not only not hidden at the initial stage, but was also actively promoted.

The Great Depression contributed to the implementation of Stalin's plans to create industry on a scale never seen before for Russia. American companies, suffocating from overproduction with a total reduction in consumption, gladly agreed to co-operate with the exotic Red Russia, which paid generously for their services in gold. The American architectural firm Albert Kahn Associates Inc. was chosen as a strategic partner for the design of the communist 'paradise'. This company had proved in practice the possibility of rapid design and construction of industrial enterprises at the factories of Henry Ford. The pace of their work was just what was needed for the implementation of Stalin's industrialization. It took a week for the Albert Kahn specialists to prepare working drawings, and the buildings of industrial enterprises were built in just five months. From 1929 to 1932 the American company designed and organized the construction of more than 500 industrial facilities in the USSR: tractor plants in Stalingrad, Chelyabinsk, Kharkiv; automobile plants in Moscow, Nizhny Novgorod; mechanical workshops in Chelyabinsk, Lyubertsy, Podolsk, Stalingrad, Sverdlovsk; steel mills and rolling mills in Kamenskoye, Kolomna, Kuznetsk, Magnitogorsk, Nizhny Tagil, Verkhny Tagil, Sormovo and other cities.

Among the great construction projects were numerous enterprises of the Soviet aviation industry. In a short time the largest aviation and aircraft engine plants were built in the European part of Russia (Moscow, Gorky, Voronezh, Kazan). If the expansion of the number of aviation plants was to be based on some minimal experience in the design and production of aircraft in the Russian Empire, then the situation with the creation and production of aircraft engines was quite bad. Indigenous aircraft engine designers and especially aircraft engine plants simply did not exist in Russia before the beginning of the 1930s. Along with the purchase of ready-made foreign aircraft engines, a more radical practice of buying entire plants for the production of aircraft engines abroad became widespread. By the end of the

An exemplary plant of the Stalinist military industry.

1930s Stalin ordered everyone to forget about the foreign origin of aircraft engines; from then all of them suddenly became Soviet and suddenly had Russian 'creators'.

In 1932 a catastrophic famine broke out in the USSR. Despite the deaths of millions of people, Stalin's government continued semi-legal co-operation with companies from Western Europe, primarily with Germany. German firms provided loans to the USSR under the guarantees of their government, and the USSR, as the customer, placed the allocated funds in Germany. In the middle of the 1930s, French firms also became partners of the Soviet Union. Only the United Kingdom refused on principle to initiate technical co-operation with the criminal communist regime of Stalin.

Under the mask of the production of peaceful products, the true purpose of tractor, automobile, aviation and mechanical industries was hidden. Unrestrained militarism was the basis for the new Red 'Evil Empire', which Stalin created on the ruins of rotten tsarist Russia. The basis of the economy throughout the entire existence of the Soviet Union was preparation for war.

Servants 'Red Lord' on winged things

The results of Stalin's industrial 'miracle', achieved by the middle of the 1930s at the cost of total hunger and the death of a part of the population, did not at all satisfy the greedy 'Red Lord'. In April 1935 the Council of Labor and Defence approved a new, even more ambitious plan for the development of the Soviet Air Force for 1935-1937, which provided for:

> the increase of Soviet Aviation by three times(!); the accelerated development of Soviet heavy bomber aviation and the re-equipment of Soviet fighter aviation with more modern models; the introduction of qualitatively better types of aircraft and engines; the transformation of the Red Army Air Force into a powerful type of armed forces that solved independent operational tasks and fully ensured close interaction with the ground forces and the fleet.[3]

Thus, Stalin demanded even greater sacrifices from the ruined people to implement his grandiose plans. This was a natural consequence of the fact that the character of the 'Red Lord' combined the symptoms of megalomania and pronounced sadism. Stalin had the characteristic symptoms of a psychopath-fanatic. He always set impossible tasks and demanded their fulfilment at any cost. 'Red Tsar' believed that the people under his control should do the impossible. Stalin was convinced of the effectiveness of administrative and command methods of managing the economy, built on the fear of cruel punishment. This barbaric approach to management was fully shared by the loyal servants of 'Red Tsar'. Uneducated, incompetent, intellectually limited, Stalin surrounded himself with even more stupid and narrow-minded people who were ready zealously to carry out all his orders. However, the situation with the execution of unrealistic orders of the 'Red Lord' was very difficult. If, thanks to a happy coincidence, the task was completed, then Stalin attributed the victory to himself. If, as most often happened, the task ended in failure 'Red Tsar' burst into a torrent of anger and immediately began searching for the perpetrators, who were subject to painful torture and execution.

3 Russian Air Force. Unknown documents (1931-1967), Moscow, Publishing house 'Bulletin of the Air Fleet', 2003, pp. 33-5.

To triple the production of aircraft in the conditions of an inefficient planned system, it was necessary to constantly expand, increase the number and repeatedly reserve the production capacities of the Soviet aviation industry. The huge bureaucratic system created for these purposes was forced to plan in every detail, and then constantly monitor the activities of everyone, even the smallest enterprise of the aviation industry. Delighted with falsified statistical reports, insatiable and absolutely incompetent in the field of economics, 'Red Lord' set new impossible tasks, directly coming from his night fears. Concerned about the availability of aircraft factories located in the European part of Russia and future enemy bombing attacks, Stalin demanded the expansion of industrialization far to the east of the vast country. By his order, the construction of numerous aviation plants began not only in the densely populated European part of Russia, but also in Siberia and even in the Far East. The narrowminded and incompetent Stalin did not consider the fact that the wild and undeveloped territory located beyond the Ural Mountains had no industrial and transport infrastructure, nor any qualified workers. Following his will, aircraft factories were built in Irkutsk, Novosibirsk and even in Komsomolsk-on-Amur in a short time. As of 1 January the Stalinist aircraft industry had eighteen enterprises with a total production area of 57,3600 square metres, which employed 151,907 workers. At these plants 5,932 machine tools, mainly imported, were used for the serial production of aircraft.[4]

In the statistical reports sent to the leader, things were going brilliantly in the Soviet aviation industry. The scale of production of various types of aircraft had been growing steadily. In the 1930s, over 6,500 I-15, I-15bis and I-153 fighters and about 9,000 I-16 fighters were built. By the end of 1939 Stalin's aviation industry included a huge number of plants of various profiles:

- Aviation plants – 31
- Aircraft engine plants – 7
- Aviation instrument-making plants – 6
- Aviation aggregate construction plants – 3
- Aviation metalworking plants – 4[5]

4 Kostyrchenko G.V., From 'The history of the formation of the Soviet aviation industry', *Aviation Industry*. 1988. No. 12.

5 Ibid.

In addition to industrial plants, four state research institutes were created: the Central Aerohydrodynamic Institute (TsAGI), the Central Institute of Aviation Motors (TsIAM), the All-Russian Institute of Aviation Materials (VIAM), and Giproniiaviaprom, designed for research and experimental design works.

However, the reality was very far from beautiful figures. The fear of brutal reprisals stimulated the Soviet bosses to engage in repeated overestimation of the figures of products made. Planning specialists, on the basis of these unrealistic indicators and in an effort to please Stalin's insatiable military 'appetite', laid down a further multiple increase in the production of fighters. In the end, when the truth was revealed, the plant directors and engineers were executed, but others came in their place and the vicious circle of distortion of reality was repeated again and again.

Another major problem for the Soviet aviation industry was the appalling quality of mass-produced fighters. The planes built in huge numbers were more dangerous for the pilots who flew them than for the enemies of the Soviet regime. The accident rate grew at an incredible pace. The reason for this problem was the people who designed and produced Stalin's planes.

The huge ambitions of the young 'Red Empire' in the field of aircraft construction did not correspond at all to the level of education of the population. Before the revolution of 1917, several thousand people a year received higher technical education in the Russian Empire. The bloody terror and civil war launched by the Bolsheviks destroyed the weak Russian industry and weakened the few engineering personnel. Many Russian engineers emigrated. For example, the well-known Russian aircraft designer, and later world-famous helicopter designer Igor Sikorski, was forced to leave for Europe, and then the United States, due to persecution by the Bolsheviks.

At the end of the 1920s, the Bolsheviks, experiencing an acute shortage of their own aircraft designers, were forced to invite foreign specialists. Gradually, based on Western experience, the training of Russian aviation engineers began. Initially they were engaged only in copying German, French and British aircraft. However, in the conditions of the Soviet totalitarian regime, the support of talented aircraft designers and the promotion of innovations in the USSR with external similarity to Western aeroplanes, led to a perverted form of development. The basis of Western industrial development was the desire to create a new product that could bring commercial profit in the face of fierce competition. In the Soviet Union, the criterion for the success of a new engineering product was the praise of Stalin. Therefore, by the end of the 1930s, the main skill of the Soviet aircraft designer was not revolutionary achievements in the design of the aircraft, but the ability to please the leader with a new 'wonder weapon', allegedly surpassing all Western contemporaries.

Such a perverse approach in technical creativity was based on the ideology of communism, which categorically rejected the very idea of intellectual abilities and competence. The founding father of the 'Red Empire', Vladimir Lenin, believed that a cook could run the state, and a peasant in *bast* shoes could design aeroplanes. However, being an intellectual, he clearly separated populist statements from real life and never tried to implement this delusional idea in practice. Almost all of Lenin's associates, like him, were highly educated. The founder of the USSR tried to attract career tsarist officers to the leadership of the Red Army, and certified engineers to design military equipment. Under Stalin, the situation changed diametrically. 'Red Lord' did not understand the essence of technical education. He hated smart and talented people, whom he considered dangers to the maintenance of his own power. The shoemaker's son Stalin, guided by personal sympathies, preferred to support the 'specialists' fanatically devoted to him. This is why there were so many crooks and self-taught people who could only read and write with difficulty, or had no education at all, among the Soviet 'engineers'. In the 1930s a little experience working under the guidance of a foreign aircraft designer or a former tsarist engineer was quite enough to create your own design bureau.

According to statistics, in the USSR at the beginning of the 1930s a graduate of a technical institute became the chief designer in five years. Soon a whole galaxy of Stalin's young designers appeared, whose abilities and competence caused great doubts. The dynamics of the growth of the number of aircraft design bureaux is also amazing. In 1935 there were eight of them, in 1936 fourteen, in 1937 twenty-four, in 1938 twenty-six and, finally, in 1939 thirty. At much the same time, the total number of aircraft designers who worked in numerous aircraft design bureaux increased from 1,370 to 3,166 people in 1936-1939.[6] It was then that a naive legend appeared about the superiority of Russian aircraft designers and, accordingly, about

6 Kostyrchenko G.V., From 'The history of the formation of the Soviet aviation industry', *Aviation Industry*, 1988, No. 12.

Stalin in the circle of his closest servants, mid-1930s.

the technical perfection of their products. This Stalinist myth, a primitive fruit of Soviet propaganda, continues to sound contrary to the facts, and is still very popular in the Russian Federation.

Stalin's main fear

Like any mentally limited dictator, Stalin was obsessed with military power, and considered himself a military man. At the same time, his physical characteristics – lack of height, asthenic physique and a paralyzed left arm – clearly contradicted his ambitions. The reverse side of Stalin's physical inferiority complex was his love for military aviation. No military parade could be held without the flight of fighters over Red Square. The youngest son of the leader also did not accidentally become a military pilot. However, Stalin, as well as the Soviet aviation industry created by his order, had one serious drawback. The admirer of aviation and the 'father' of 'Stalin's Falcons' was pathologically afraid of flying! The facts show that 'Red Lord' had only flown on an aeroplane twice in his long life.

The bloody dictator Joseph Stalin was obsessed with fears throughout his life. One of the most powerful phobias was an attempt on his life.

Among the many possible ways that 'enemies of the people' could choose to carry out the murder of the head of the USSR, the paranoid Stalin especially singled out an aviation disaster. The fact is that young aviation, especially in such a technologically backward country as Soviet Russia, was very unsafe. Aviation disasters, accompanied by the deaths of Soviet officials and party functionaries, were not uncommon in the USSR of the 1920s and 1930s. Most often, it was impossible to determine the cause of the accident. The impressionable Stalin, who valued his own life very much, preferred excessive security measures. He not only never used the services of air transport himself, but also categorically banned his closest servants from flying. This rule was unshakable until the beginning of the Second World War, which became for Stalin the most terrible shock of his entire life. He was so confident in his brilliant foresight and ability to outplay Hitler in big political games that the 'unexpected' German attack plunged him into a months-long stupor.

It was this terrible shock, from which he did not recover until the end of his days, that forced 'Red Tsar' to break his firm rule in a critical situation and make a plane flight twice. This alarming event took place in 1943, when Stalin went to the Teheran Conference to meet with colleagues in the anti-Hitler coalition – the British Prime Minister Churchill and the American President Roosevelt. We will only note that the leader unpatriotically chose the ultra-reliable American Douglas DC-3 for the flight, and not the Soviet Li-2 (Douglas DC-3, produced in the USSR under licence). By the way, Stalin's flight on the Baku-Teheran route was accompanied by twenty-seven fighters. However, even absolute safety did not save the 'Red Tsar' from the agonizing fear that accompanied this extreme air journey.

It must be admitted that Stalin's fears were not in vain. In particular, his beloved Soviet fighter aviation became the biggest disappointment in his life. The abominably designed and even worse manufactured Soviet aircraft became a vivid proof of the complete inefficiency of the communist system.

Chapter 2

Fighter I-16. 'Rat' for Stalin
The typical fate of a Stalin's aircraft designer

November 1929. Moscow. Butyrskaya prison.

A small room with steel bars on the windows. Poorly-dressed women are sitting on a dirty bench, with bundles of food on their knees. They are patiently waiting for a short meeting with their doomed husbands who have fallen into the bloody clutches of the OGPU. Suddenly, a prison guard in a military uniform shouts out the name 'Polikarpov'. One of the women gets up and fussily follows the guard into another room, but without windows. There are two old shabby chairs and in the middle of the table sits an investigator in the uniform of an OGPU officer. Soon the guard introduces a haggard man in torn clothes into the room. His hands are habitually folded behind his back, he looks absently and indifferently at the ground. This is the future 'King of Fighters', Nikolai Polikarpov, who was sentenced to death without trial by firing squad. During his time in prison he has already come to terms with his fate and got used to constant calls for interrogations. He does not know where and why he was brought from a narrow, smelly prison cell. Nikolai Polikarpov is so depressed and indifferent to what is happening to him that he barely noticed his tearful wife in the room. She anxiously examines her husband, whom she has not seen for many days. Several important details catch the eye and are remembered for a lifetime. Polikarpov is pale and unshaven. Being in a dirty and cramped cell, where 'enemies of the people', who were sentenced to death on ridiculous charges, lay and sat on the floor, deprived him of strength. The knees of his dark trousers are completely white from prison dust. This is the result of constant prayers in a dirty prison corner, waiting for a meeting with God. The son of a priest, Nikolai Polikarpov is a very religious person and perhaps it was constant prayers that helped him survive the inhumane horror of Stalin's prison. Hardly had the husband and wife, who had not seen each other for many days, exchanged a few words

Aircraft designer Nikolai Polikarpov with his employees against the background of the P-1 aircraft, early 1920s.

than the investigator sitting at the table waved his hand, and the guard roughly pushed Polikarpov out of the room for prison visits.

Polikarpov's wife described the terrible experience of finding the famous Soviet aircraft designer in Stalin's dungeons, which miraculously did not end in death for him. In a few years Stalin would make him his favourite, and therefore the only designer of fighters. 'Red Lord' will award Nikolai Polikarpov the highest orders of the Soviet Union, bestow all sorts of benefits and provide fantastic conditions for the creation of aircraft. However, the talented aircraft designer would pay dearly for his devoted service to Stalin. During his long period of dominance among Soviet aircraft designers, Nikolai Polikarpov could not create a single successful fighter, and the deadly horror of the Red tyrant remained with him until the last day of his life.

Corruption of the soul aircraft designer

In 1892, in a remote village located in the very centre of the European part of the Russian Empire, the first-born male, the future support of the family, was born into the family of a rural priest. Intellectually gifted by nature, the boy was lucky enough to grow up in an atmosphere of reverence not only for religion, but also for education. Father Nikolai Polikarpov traditionally combined the position of a priest with teaching work. However, unlike most rural priests, he was a talented educator and organizer of public education in the remote Livensky district of the Orel province.

The education of young Nikolai, which was initially carried out in a typical theological seminary for the son of a priest, then continued at the Saint Petersburg Polytechnic Institute. For the dense Russian Empire, where the majority of the population was illiterate, such a path from the village to the metropolitan institute was the lot of the chosen. This rare event testifies to the greatest abilities of Nikolai Polikarpov and his desire for self-realization. The efforts of the talented young man were supported by relatives, and, first of all, by the head of the family. Nikolai Polikarpov's father had to spend all his modest savings to pay for his son's expensive education at an elite capital institute.

During his studies (from 1911 to 1916) at the shipbuilding Faculty of the Saint Petersburg Polytechnical Institute, Nikolai Polikarpov became interested in aviation and at the same time began to master the 'Course of Aviation and Aeronautics'. The young man, who was purposeful but burdened with a large tuition fee, combined training in two specialties at once with work as an engineer at aviation plants in Saint Petersburg.

In 1914 the First World War began and clearly showed the total technical backwardness of the Russian Empire. The stupid Tsar Nicholas II, suffering constant defeats from the Germans, was ready to allocate huge funds for the development of various kinds of 'wonder weapon'. One of the promising areas for creating such technical innovations, which promised an early victory in a lost war, was aviation. Russian aircraft enthusiasts finally got the opportunity to implement their bold ideas. The most famous among them was the brilliant young aircraft designer Igor Sikorski, who at that time held the position of chief engineer of the aviation department (Saint Petersburg) Russo-Baltic Wagon Factory.[1]

1 Russo-Baltic Wagon Factory was established in 1869 in the city of Riga (Russian Empire) as a branch of the German-Dutch company Van der Zypen und Charlier, which produced railway cars. In 1910 an aviation workshop was established in Riga which, in 1912, was moved to St Petersburg. The head of the workshop, Mikhail Shidlovsky, hired Chief Engineer Igor Sikorski in April 1912, and the workshop was transformed into the aviation department.

Nikolai Polikarpov, taken while working at Russo-Baltic Wagon Factory.

Sikorski needed talented assistants and Nikolai Polikarpov, while still a student, was attracted to work in his team. The shortage of Russian Empire aviation specialists was very great. As a result, after graduating from the institute, Polikarpov was released from compulsory military service. Sikorski almost immediately appointed him head of production of S-16 fighters. Later, Polikarpov, who proved his design abilities in practice, was engaged in the modernization of the S-16 fighter and the Sikorski Ilya Muromets four-engine bomber, and also participated in the design of new fighters: S-18, S-19 and S-20.

After the Bolsheviks came to power, the convinced monarchist Igor Sikorski offered his talented employee a joint emigration. Citing the inability to leave his family, Polikarpov refused Sikorski's offer and remained in Soviet Russia. Young and ambitious aircraft designer Polikarpov felt that, under the Bolsheviks, new prospects for independent creativity were opening up for him. Sikorski was only three years older than him, but he had already achieved world fame. Perhaps Nikolai Polikarpov, who was distinguished by independence, was tired of being in the shadow of his young teacher.

On the Dark Side

After his emigration, the name Sikorski, who hated the Bolsheviks, was banned in the Soviet Union. And, here is his former student Nikolai Polikarpov, who went to co-operate with the criminal red regime, receiving unlimited opportunities for rapidly building a career. By the beginning of the 1930s, he was the most famous Soviet aircraft designer of fighters.

Let's consider only the most important steps in the development of his successful career. In the 1920s Polikarpov was engaged exclusively in copying Western aircraft from the First World War, mainly British. Despite the propaganda of the Bolsheviks, it was not possible to organize any indigenous design of aircraft at that time in Soviet Russia. In 1923 Nikolai Polikarpov received his own design bureau and aviation plant from the Bolsheviks. Igor Sikorski, who wandered around the world, could only dream of such opportunities for technical creativity. Under the leadership of Polikarpov, production of replicas of Nieuport XVII C. 1, Nieuport XXI, Nieuport XXIII, Farman F. 30A fighters, Sikorski Ilya Muromets bombers, etc. began. All the materials used in the construction of aircraft, as well as engines, had to be bought in the West for gold.

The main difficulty for Polikarpov was in unsuccessful attempts to achieve acceptable aircraft manufacturing quality from unskilled workers. In this doomed effort, the ardent 'patriot' and aircraft designer found common language with representatives of the new Russian government. The Bolsheviks were staunch supporters of the superiority of red fanaticism over the intelligence and technical culture of the hostile West. Many aircraft parts that could not be manufactured in Russia, due to the lack of qualified specialists, Polikarpov had to simplify and modify. At the same time, the quality of aircraft manufacturing remained extremely low. 'Russian' planes were much inferior to their Western prototypes. It was also necessary to take into account the fact that in the middle of the 1920s Western firms went

Aircraft designer Igor Sikorsky at the Ilya Muromets aircraft assembly workshop.

far ahead, and Polikarpov in Russia could hardly organize the production of archaic wooden aircraft from the time of the First World War. However, the Soviet leaders were happy with these modest results. Despite the ambitious plans, there was simply nothing but a few dozen British and German aircraft, captured during the civil war, in the Red Army Air Force. For that reason the Bolsheviks were ready to spend huge amounts of money even on the production of frankly outdated and poorly manufactured aircraft.

In 1924 Polikarpov creates a copy of the British de Havilland DH 9A light bomber and reconnaissance aircraft, a 1916 model, that received the Soviet name R-1 (Reconnaissance aircraft 1). It became the first Soviet aircraft produced in a large series. However, before launching production of the R-1, a young Soviet aircraft designer had to solve a very important problem. The fact is that the first copies of the British machine were made from American seaside spruce, which was distinguished by the best strength indicators and the absence of knots. But there were not enough funds to buy this high-quality material in huge quantities in half-starved Russia. However, the patriot Polikarpov found an acceptable solution to this acute problem. For the first time, he proposed making aeroplanes from Siberian pine, which turned out to be much worse in quality, but was more affordable. However, Polikarpov had to recalculate the entire design of the R-1 reconnaissance aircraft. In addition to replacing the main material, he

Sikorsky S-16 fighter.

Nieuport XXIII fighter.

simplified the design, reducing the total number of parts by a third. Thus, the Soviet R-1 aircraft was a degraded copy of the British one, while a pirated copy of the American Liberty L-12 aircraft engine was installed on its serial copies. Such 'improvements' made by Polikarpov did not have the best effect on the flight qualities of the aircraft, but ensured mass production, which the Bolsheviks so dreamed of.

Fortunately, Polikarpov did not always have to study and reproduce bad copies of the aircraft of the beginning of the First World War. Sometimes he got his hands on innovative designs that were significantly ahead of their time. Polikarpov was most impressed by the German Junkers D.I. fighter accidentally captured by the Bolsheviks. The young aircraft designer, who was used to dealing with wood and aircraft fabric, was struck by the revolutionary design of this aircraft. The Junkers D.I. was one of the first all-metal aircraft that caused surprise among its contemporaries. The innovative German aircraft was a monoplane with a low wing arrangement. Its frame was made of aluminium pipes, the skin is made of duralumin. The design included a wing centre section with detachable wings connected to a short fuselage. Perhaps this particular aircraft turned out to be the prototype for the future I-16. However, before the creation of this beloved Stalin's Polikarpov fighter, there was a long way to go.

Meanwhile, the rapid increase in the fleet of Soviet aircraft sharply raised the problem of creating a simple and reliable training aircraft. In 1927 Polikarpov designed the U-2 training aircraft, which quickly gained wide recognition in the nascent Red Army Air Force. The successful design of a light and cheap multi-purpose aircraft had been a demand for several

Starting the engine on the reconnaissance aircraft Polikarpov R-1.

decades. The U-2 played a major role in the training of pilots in flight schools and flying clubs (Stalin's *Osoaviakhim*: The Society for the Assistance of Defence, Aircraft and Chemical Construction). This aircraft was produced in the USSR in various modifications until 1954, becoming one of the most popular aircraft in the world.

Stalin, who had concentrated absolute power in his hands by the end of the 1920s, needed serial fighters that were not inferior to Western models. In February 1928 Polikarpov presented to the Soviet military a wooden fighter-semi-plane I-3 with a German BMW VI engine. Although the fighter did not show any phenomenal flight characteristics, it was simple and cheap to produce. For that reason the I-3 was hastily adopted and mass-produced until 1934, becoming the main fighter of the Red Army Air Force of the beginning of the 1930s.

In September 1928 Polikarpov developed the R-5 multi-purpose aircraft, an enlarged two-seat copy of the I-3 with the same BMW VI engine. The aircraft began to be mass-produced from the beginning of 1930 and soon became the 'workhorse' of the Red Army Air Force. At about the same time Polikarpov began designing a new I-6 fighter with the Gnome-Rhône Jupiter engine, the French version of the British single-row piston radial engine, in which the features of the future I-16 were already noticeable. However, in order to become the 'King of Fighters' Polikarpov must win in the fight against many dangerous competitors.

'Enemies of the people' behind the drawing board

In 1929, when Stalin turned 50, his power over the huge 'Red Empire' became unlimited. However, the Bolshevik tyrant was not satisfied with either the country that he inherited from the tsar, or the numerous submissive people. Stalin wanted to turn the agrarian Soviet Union into a country of giant factories including factories producing countless armadas of combat vehicles. The new generation of Soviet people was to become an unstoppable avalanche, a steel boot, crushing the bourgeois countries of Western Europe and, subsequently, the whole world. The era of Stalin's 'Great Break', the most tragic time in the history of the USSR, had come. The entire population of a huge country was preparing to sacrifice itself to the gigantic ambitions of the 'Red Lord'.

Meanwhile, the quality of Soviet fighters designed by Polikarpov and produced at Soviet aviation plants continued to remain very low. One aviation accident followed another. Stalin, who longed for the accelerated industrialization of a poor country, could not admit that the reason for the terrible quality of Soviet aircraft was the vicious state economy created by him, which deprived citizens of motivation to work. Following his pathological nature, 'Red Lord' explained all the problems with the machinations of internal enemies who needed to be discovered and executed. A large-scale hunt for 'witches' began throughout the country.

On the evening of 24 October 1929, Soviet aircraft designer Nikolai Polikarpov was arrested by the OGPU.[2] He was charged with a whole bunch of ridiculous accusations. The narrow-minded Stalinist executioners remembered his co-operation with the enemy of the Bolsheviks, Igor Sikorski, and accused him of 'participating in a counter-revolutionary wrecking organization'. All the facts of the Polikarpov plane crashes were explained by sabotage and deliberate harm to Stalin's aviation. In a short time, many aircraft designers and employees of the Soviet aviation industry were arrested and sentenced to death on similar charges.

2 OGPU – Joint State Political Directorate – Stalin's secret police.

Pilots at the R-1 aircraft, 'Our answer to Chamberlain'.

For more than a month, Nikolai Polikarpov was in Butyrskaya prison awaiting execution along with other former Soviet aviation specialists, and now 'enemies of the people'. However, Stalin's servants, who led the Soviet aviation industry, realized with horror that they were preparing to shoot almost all aircraft designers of the USSR. Realizing that in this case they would have to answer for the failure of Stalin's ambitious plans, they hurried to cancel the execution. However, they also could not admit that the Stalinist OGPU made a mistake and slandered innocent Soviet citizens. Finally, Stalin's servants found a 'brilliant' solution, which was then widely practised throughout the existence of the criminal Soviet regime.

On 30 November 1929 the deputy chief of the air force of the Red Army, Yakov Alksnis, known for his cruelty and extreme intellectual limitations, met with 'enemies of the people'. The doomed aircraft designers were surprised to hear from a Stalinist servant that their executioners were ready to give them a chance to atone for their 'guilt' before the 'Red Lord'. In a pathetic form, Yakov Alksnis called on them 'to give their mind and strength to create in the shortest possible time a fighter that would surpass the planes of potential enemies'.[3] Driven to despair, the aircraft designers were forced to agree to become Stalin's slaves in exchange for their lives.

In December a special design bureau was organized at Butyrskaya prison under the unofficial technical leadership of 'enemy of the people' Dmitry Grigorovich.[4] 'Enemy of the people' Nikolai Polikarpov became his deputy. All administrative posts were occupied by employees of the OGPU Economic Department. In January 1930 the special design bureau was transferred to the territory of Aviation Plant No. 39 (Moscow). There, Stalin's slaves began to live and work in a special hangar, called the 'Inner prison'. Soon, the special design bureau was renamed Central Design Bureau OGPU No. 39.

As a result of hard work, Polikarpov, together with other 'enemies of the people', created a light manoeuvrable biplane fighter, the I-5. On 29 April 1930 the I-5 first took to the sky. Soon, according to the test results, it was adopted by the Red Army Air Force. Serial production of the fighter continued until 1934. The I-15 and I-153 biplane fighters became a further development of the I-5.

Meanwhile, the investigation into the case of 'enemies of the people' entrenched in the Soviet aviation industry, had been completed. On 18 March 1931 the OGPU board sentenced Nikolai Polikarpov to ten years in Stalin's Gulag, and confiscation of property, accusing him of espionage, counter-revolutionary activities and undermining the Soviet aviation industry.

On 6 June 1931 a closed review of aviation equipment was held at the Frunze Central Aerodrome, attended by Joseph Stalin, People's Commissar for Military and Navy Affairs Kliment Voroshilov (Minister of War) and Chairman of the Supreme Soviet of the National Economy (Minister of Industry) Sergo Ordzhonikidze. 'Enemy of the people' Polikarpov presented to the distinguished guests the I-5 fighter designed in the 'Inner prison'. The demonstration flight of the new aircraft was performed by 'Stalin's Falcons' Valery Chkalov and Alexander Anisimov. Stalin really liked the new manoeuvrable biplane and its creator, who showed full loyalty to the 'Red Tsar' with all his appearance.

---

3 Khvoshchevsky G.I., Pages of the history of Aviation Plant No. 39 named after Menzhinsky: *from Moscow to Irkutsk: a chronicle and documentary history*, Irkutsk, Publishing house of LLC Printing house Irkut, 2012.

4 Dmitry Grigorovich (1883-1938), a representative of the older generation of Soviet aircraft designers and creator of the first Russian seaplanes and flying boats. In the service of the Bolsheviks, he was engaged in designing fighters.

Engine repair of training aircraft, Polikarpov U-2.

On 28 June 1931 the OGPU board decided to consider the sentence against Polikarpov conditional and, on 7 July, the All-Union Central Executive Committee (the government of the USSR), on Stalin's personal instructions, decided to grant amnesty and release some of the arrested aviation specialists, including Nikolai Polikarpov.

In 1932, after the creation of the I-15 fighter, Aviation Plant No. 84, located in the city of Khimki near Moscow, was allocated specifically for Polikarpov. Soon he headed the design bureau, located on the territory of this plant.

Further, the career of the forgiven 'enemy of the people' began to develop rapidly and reached its culmination in the late 1930s after receiving the unofficial status of 'King of Fighters'. However, the vindictive 'Red Lord' preferred to always leave opportunities for pressure on even his the most loyal subjects. Until the end of his days, the 'King of Fighters' continued to be under the supervision of Stalin's special services. The Polikarpov criminal case was officially closed only in 1956, twelve years after the death of the aircraft designer and three years after the death of Stalin.

The Birth of Stalin's 'Rat'

1 October 1934. Moscow. The Kremlin. Stalin's office. Dead of night. Stalin is sitting alone at his desk and sorting through the papers that were brought to him during the day. Most of the loyal messages did not arouse his interest. Finally, he got to the papers from the Main Department of Aviation Industry People's Commissariat of the Defence Industry of the Soviet

Serial training aircraft, Polikarpov U-2.

Union. He frowns, things are not going very well in his beloved aviation industry. Stalin picks up the report of the Head of the Main Department of Aviation Industry, George Korolev. It says: 'I inform you that the I-16 fighter of Aviation Plant No. 39 with the Wright Cyclone engine gave a speed of 430km/h at an altitude of 3,000 m, putting us in first place in the world in fighters.'

A grimace of surprise appears on Stalin's face. He carefully re-reads the report again, picks up the phone in his hand and demands that the secretary on duty immediately connect him with George Korolev.

There is a terrible commotion in the Main Department of Aviation Industry. A sleepy night attendant urgently calls the home of the head of the Main Department of Aviation Industry. His wife, awakened by the call, tries to explain to Korolev, who does not understand anything from a dream, that Stalin will now talk to him on the phone. With shaking hands, Korolev picks up the phone. A minute later, a quiet, sinister voice with a Georgian accent, familiar to all Soviet people, is heard on the phone:

'And, do you know, Comrade Korolev, that the world speed record is 500km/h and it does not belong to the Soviet Union at all?' Korolev can't utter more than one word out of excitement. Stalin continues:

'Organize a demonstration flight of a fighter. I personally want to take a look at it. I give you one month to prepare!'

'Yes, Comrade Stalin!', the only thing that the frightened head of the Main Department of Aviation Industry, George Korolev, could say. The receiver was hung up on the other end of the line.

In the Main Department of Aviation Industry, the feverish preparation of a new aircraft for showing to Stalin begins. The Polikarpov Design Bureau is making noise like a disturbed hive. Several prototypes of the I-16 fighter are being prepared for a responsible demonstration flight. Technicians and specialists from the pilot production are trying urgently to eliminate a huge list of defects in the design of the fighter. The work goes on day and night. Everyone understands perfectly well that it is impossible fully to prepare an experimental aircraft in such a short time and they are waiting with bated breath for a risky demonstration flight in front of Stalin himself.

'We really need it, Comrade Stalin!'

At the beginning of November 1934 Stalin's motorcade arrived at the Frunze Central Aerodrome, located on Khodynka Field, on the outskirts of Moscow. This airfield was a special site where experimental and serial aircraft created at design bureaux and produced at aviation plants in Moscow were usually tested. From the luxurious black limousines, Stalin

Repair of a Polikarpov R-5 aircraft.

The first copy of the R-5 aircraft on state tests at the Red Army Air Force Research Institute, Autumn 1928.

and his most trusted servants cheerfully got out: People's Commissar of Heavy Industry (Minister of Industry) Sergo Ordzhonikidze, Chairman of the Central Control Commission of the Communist Party of the Soviet Union Lazar Kaganovich, People's Commissar of Food Industry (Minister) Anastas Mikoyan and a number of others. The distinguished guests were greeted timidly by the aviation chiefs and escorted to a special wooden podium. Stalin immediately demanded to be shown a new record-breaking I-16 aircraft in the air.

A short, stocky pilot, who would become the most famous 'Stalin's Falcon', Valery Chkalov, sat in the cockpit of an experimental fighter. He confidently lifted the I-16 into the air. Those sitting on the podium watched with interest an unusual sight – raising the landing gear of a fighter. The fact is that all the fighters that were demonstrated to Stalin earlier had rigidly fixed landing gear. The new Polikarpov high-speed fighter was one of the first Soviet fighters equipped with a retractable landing gear. It was made according to a reliable scheme in the form of two three-rod pyramids. The tail support was made in the form of a crutch – only on the last series of I-16 was a small duralumin wheel with a diameter of 150mm installed. The landing gear was raised and released using a mechanical lever on the right side of the cockpit. However, the technologically simple and, therefore, reliable design turned out to be extremely difficult to use in reality. To move the landing gear, the pilot had to make an average of forty-four turns with the handle of a mechanical winch. In order to twist the handle, it was necessary to exert almost superhuman muscular efforts. Even physically very developed – he had worked as an assistant to a blacksmith – Chkalov performed the operation of lifting the landing gear with great difficulty. Moreover, this heavy physical operation had to be performed continuously, otherwise the winch cables jammed and the landing gear remained in a half-released state. In addition, the pilot had to turn the handle with his right hand, and at the same time control the aircraft with the left. Thus, in order not to lose control of the aircraft, the pilot, in fact, needed a third hand and incredible luck!

However, this time the strong hands of the blacksmith did not let Chkalov down and he completely raised the landing gear. A specially prepared demonstration of the capabilities of the new fighter began with the performance of spectacular aerobatics. For Valery Chkalov, who was used to testing experimental aircraft, flying the new I-16 in front of Stalin required all his piloting skills. The fact is that Polikarpov, designing a new aircraft, deliberately made it very unstable. The aircraft designer proceeded from a reasonable premise that an unstable aircraft would be significantly more manoeuvrable. However, in reality, in addition to good manoeuvrability, there was a very dangerous tendency to stall the aircraft in

Polikarpov I-5 fighter before take-off from Frunze Central Aerodrome, 1933.

Polikarpov I-15bis fighter on ski landing gear.

a spin. To survive, the pilot had to be trained in the technique of effectively removing the capricious I-16 from spin. At the same time, he had to keep his cool even near the ground, otherwise the fighter's instability threatened disaster and death. Chkalov, who had made many flights on the I-16, had studied closely the deadly features of the Polikarpov novelty. His reviews regarding the flight qualities of the aircraft were not enthusiastic. As for composure, this famous Soviet pilot was by nature completely devoid of fear in the air. In this quality, Valery Chkalov was very similar to another master of aerobatics, the German First World War pilot Hermann Göring, who later became chief of the Luftwaffe.

The demonstration programme was executed perfectly by Chkalov. All attempts of the aircraft to stall into spin were parried instantly by the experienced pilot. The American engine installed on the experimental Russian fighter worked without interruption. Finally, it was time to land. But this time Chkalov was waiting for the expected, but extremely unpleasant surprise. The capricious landing gear of the I-16, as usual, got stuck as it dropped from the wing. From his experience, the 'Stalin's Falcon' knew that it was possible to solve the problem with the help of overload. Chkalov performed several spectacular dead loops and the landing gear finally came out and stood on the locks. After that, the I-16 landed safely at the airfield.

Experimental fighter TsKB-12 (I-16) with Wright Cyclone SR-1820-F-3 engine.

The high-level viewers, who did not understand anything about aviation, did not notice any problems and regarded Chkalov's desperate attempts to save his life as part of the demonstration programme.

After the plane landed the suspicious Stalin, who did not trust any of his servants, wished to personally meet the brilliant pilot. He was once again playing his favourite game of checking and rechecking his entourage. Interviewing the present pilots of the plant and the Red Army Air Force Research Institute, Stalin was interested in their opinions about the new fighter. All the respondents praised the plane.

Stalin asked the aviation specialists who surrounded him, 'So, do we need such a plane?'

Everyone answered in chorus, 'We really need it, Comrade Stalin!'[5]

Although Stalin was well aware of the characteristics of the I-16 and had personally ordered its mass production a year earlier, he was still afraid of being deceived by his subordinates. 'Red Lord' naively believed that simple engineers and pilots would tell him the whole truth about the true state of affairs. It should be noted that, by that time, officially and unofficially, about

5 Maslov M.A., *Fighter I-16. Skittish 'Donkey' of 'Stalin's Falcons'*, Moscow, 'Yauza', 'Collection', EKSMO, 2008. p.21.

twenty experienced pilots had tested the I-16 in the air. They knew about the flaws in the design of the aircraft and the low quality of its manufacture. However, none of those present dared to tell the cruel 'Red Leader' that the fighter created by his order had turned out to be a blatant failure. The reason for such a unanimous silence of aviation specialists was not only fear of Stalin: engineers and pilots were hostages of this project and their material wellbeing, and perhaps even their lives, depended on the recognition of the I-16 as suitable for mass production.

Stalin's big plans and low production culture

Although the decision to mass produce the I-16 was made on 22 November 1933, the real, and by no means mass, but in fact piece production of fighters unfolded only in the second half of 1934. During the year, a small series of fifty was collected at Aviation Plant No. 39 in Moscow. In 1935 the production of the I-16 at the aircraft factory was limited to only a few intended exclusively for testing.

Stalin chose Aviation Plant No. 21 in the city of Gorky as the main location for the production of the I-16. This plant was built in 1930-32 on

Test pilot Valery Chkalov in the cockpit of a TsKB-12 (I-16) with a Wright Cyclone SR-1820-F-3 engine and three-blade Hamilton Standart propeller.

Chkalov and Stalin.

the western outskirts of the city and was originally planned by 'Red Lord' as a large factory for the production of fighters. Although all the residents of the city guessed what kind of products were made at the plant hidden behind a high fence and disguised by trees and bushes, it was declared secret according to the stupid Stalin's tradition.

Twenty-nine-year-old Evgeny Miroshnikov was appointed the first director of Gorky Aviation Plant No. 21. Paradoxically, despite his youth, the director belonged to the older generation of factory workers. The fact is that, for the numerous aviation plants built in record time, Stalin's servants bought the latest foreign machine tools for gold but were unable to train qualified workers for their maintenance. The Bolsheviks, who were prone to disastrous adventures, believed that the illiterate youth, drugged by communist propaganda, would be able to replace experienced skilled middle-aged workers. As a result of such a failed personnel policy, by 1934 the share of young, untrained personnel aged 18-22 years at Gorky Aviation Plant No. 21 was over 70 per cent. The qualifications of young workers and engineers were either completely absent or extremely low. Most received an initial specialized engineering and technological education directly in the production process or at short-term courses organized at the factory. All these circumstances could not but affect the organization of mass production of the new I-16 fighter. Despite the fact that the plant's management was informed about the plan to produce 225 new fighters in March 1934, by the end of the year only forty-one of the I-16 were produced. Even these several dozen aircraft were assembled in the conditions of an incredible *Shturmovshchina*[6] and were of terribly low quality.

According to the record of 6 December 1934, the official representative of the customer (Red Army Air Force) at Aviation Plant No. 21, Nikolay

6 *Shturmovshchina* – a common Soviet practice of frantic overtime work at the end of a planning period in order to fulfil the planned production target. The practice usually gave rise to products of poor quality at the end of a planning cycle.

Zhukov, rejected the acceptance of five aircraft based on a long list of defects. For example, in the defective statement for aircraft No. 42114 the following shortcomings are indicated:

> weak gas tank mounting, sawdust in the engine, cables jam, traction is not attached, there is no sight bracket, the glass is cracked, the reloading of machine guns is stuck.[7]

In this regard, a technical meeting was held at the plant to eliminate defects and meet the requirements of the Red Army Air Force Research Institute. Of a total of forty-one aircraft produced by Aviation Plant No. 21 in Gorky in 1934, fifteen were completely unusable.

Stalin's Kiss

On 2 May 1935, the day after the military parade on 1 May, an inspection of aviation equipment was held at the Frunze Central Aerodrome, intended personally for Stalin. Valery Chkalov also took part in demonstration flights of the I-16. After landing, admiring the skill of piloting, Stalin publicly kissed the pilot who landed, who was young enough to be his son and talked to him for some time. The 'Red Lord' was not lucky with his own sons, who inherited his natural vices. The narrow-minded Stalin, who saw in his own sons only a distorted reflection of his own shortcomings, constantly unconsciously searched for and, of course, found his 'real' sons among the young military men.

First Director of Gorky Aviation Plant No. 21, Evgeny Miroshnikov.

On 5 May 1935 pilot Valery Chkalov was awarded the Order of Lenin, the highest government award, 'for repeatedly showing exceptional courage and courage in testing new aircraft

7 GU TSANO Foundation 2066, Inventory 9, Case 51, Sheet 17.

designs'.[8] From this moment on, the 30-year-old Chkalov became the most famous 'Stalin's Falcon' and, in fact, the godson of Stalin.

The wave of Stalin's 'love' also affected the forgiven 'enemy of the people' Nikolai Polikarpov. Simultaneously with Chkalov, the aircraft designer was also awarded the Order of Lenin 'for outstanding services in creating new high-quality aircraft designs'.[9] After the official recognition by Stalin, Polikarpov received almost unlimited material and human resources from the state. He had at his disposal the most numerous design bureau in the USSR and many aviation plants. For several years Polikarpov practically monopolized the sphere of creating new fighters, reconnaissance aircraft and training aircraft. He did not need to have entrepreneurial talents; the whole power of the Stalinist administrative and command system was in his hands. For his loyalty to Stalin, he received huge privileges (a personal car, which was extremely rare in the Soviet Union, a luxury apartment with servants), accommodation in the capital.

However, the 'love' of 'Red Tsar' was as pathological as he was. A few years after his triumph, Nikolai Polikarpov lost Stalin's trust, which actually meant the end of his brilliant career as 'King of Fighters'.

3,000 defects in the design of the aircraft

With all the difficulties, in 1935 the serial production of Stalin's favourite fighter was still delayed. During the year, more than 500 I-16s were produced at Gorky Aviation Plant No. 21 by 'heroic' efforts. To fulfill Stalin's ambitious plans by at least 50 per cent, the young director of the plant, Evgeny Miroshnikov, and his team of engineers and technologists showed miracles of improvisation. It was extremely difficult to achieve this at an unfinished plant, in the absence of the necessary equipment and a shortage of not only qualified personnel, but even low-skilled workers. The price of such an achievement was extremely high and was subsequently paid for by the lives of hundreds of Soviet pilots who died in the I-16 disasters. Hungry for world domination, Stalin did not pay attention to the absolute unpreparedness of the hastily created Soviet Aviation Industry for mass production of aircraft.

---

8 Resolution of the All-Union Central Executive Committee of 5 May 1935 'On awarding comrades Polikarpov N.N. and Chkalov V.P.', *Izvestia*, 6 May 1935 (No. 106), p. 1.

9 Ibid.

The engineers and managers of Gorky Aviation Plant No. 21 in 1936.

The entire aircraft production planning system was entangled in a web of pathological lies. The planned figures of the design capacity of the plants, taken entirely from Stalin's paranoid delirium, did not correspond in any way to the real deplorable state of the aviation plants that were not fully complete.

In the summer of 1933 Stalin wrote to his devoted servant People's Commissar for Military and Navy Affairs (Minister of War) Kliment Voroshilov:

> In terms of tanks and aircraft, apparently, the industry has not yet managed to properly re-equip itself in relation to the new (our) requirements. Nothing! We will push and help her to adapt. The whole point is to keep well-known industries (mainly military) under constant control. They will adapt and will perform the programme, if not by 100%, then by 80-90%. Isn't that enough?[10]

Under the pressure of the pathological features of his character, Stalin lost completely the ability to distinguish between truth and falsehood.

10 Mukhin M.Y., *Aviation industry of the USSR in 1921-1941*, Moscow, Nauka, 2006, p. 114.

He believed that pressure, intimidation and political propaganda could more than compensate for the lack of raw materials, workers and machine tools. Any discrepancy between illusions and reality caused Stalin's furious anger, which escalated into another attack of bloody terror.

Meanwhile, the 'adventures' of the I-16 fighters of the first batch continued and reached another crisis. The fact is that the new aircraft had to be checked and accepted by the official representative of the customer (Red Army Air Force). Formally, these people were not connected with the plant and were responsible for the quality of the aircraft adopted by the Red Army Air Force. However, reality has shown that the young director of the plant, Evgeny Miroshnikov, in full accordance with the Bolshevik attitude, could do the impossible. For the management of Gorky Aviation Plant No. 21, with the help of deception, intrigue, psychological pressure and direct bribery, it was possible to drag most of the defective fighters through 'strict' military acceptance. A new stage of experimental operation in military conditions, full of difficulties and disasters, had begun for the I-16.

Formal military tests of ten I-16s took place in the 34th Aviation Squadron (commander Captain Chivel) of 56th Aviation Brigade Kiev Military District in the period from 16 May to 21 November 1936. For this purpose, specially selected fighters were used with the least number of defects, manufactured by Gorky Aviation Plant No. 21 with the following serial numbers: 52104, 52110, 52111, 52117, 52120, 52122, 52125, 52128 and 5217. Despite careful selection and special work to eliminate defects, out of ten aircraft participating in the tests one aircraft suffered a shift in the fuel tank in flight. By the way, the shift of the fuel tank and the breakage of the fuel hoses, as a result of which dozens of litres of fuel were poured on the pilot's feet, became a typical defect for the I-16 fighter. With this problem, the 'engineers' of Gorky Aviation Plant No. 21 'struggled' with varying success for several years.

Although the other I-16 fighters participating in the tests remained formally intact, and did not kill their pilots, they demonstrated a huge number of large and small defects. Soon after several serious accidents, a commission was created by order of the test manager, which carefully studied the new fighters. As a result, fifteen defects were found that were dangerous for flights and forty-two defects that reduced the combat capability of fighters. So, for example, on all aircraft, the canvas wing skin peeled off, and the control brackets of the tail crutch cables came off.[11]

11 GU TSANO Foundation 2066, Inventory 9, Case 171, Sheet 43.

Stalin's kiss.

Similar complaints began to arrive at Gorky Aviation Plant No. 21 and from other military units that had recently been re-equipped with the I-16. Pilots complained about the displacement of gas tanks, violation of landing-gear adjustments, broken pipes, brackets, broken control knobs, pulling out screws and rivets, broken shafts, machine guns clogging with dust etc.[12] As a result, deputy Director of the Central Aerohydrodynamic Institute (TsAGI) Andrey Tupolev even wrote a letter to Director of the Gorky Aviation Plant No. 21, Evgeny Miroshnikov, pointing to an unacceptably large number of defects. According to estimates of the design bureau at Gorky Aviation Plant No. 21, by the end of 1937 more than 3,000 changes were made to the design and equipment of the I-16 fighter.

According to the results of military tests, the following conclusions were made about the flight qualities of the I-16 fighter:

> Take-off on the I-16 with the M-25 engine is complicated, the aircraft has a large take-off and a tendency to turn left when running along the runway. Piloting at low altitudes requires

12 GU TSANO Foundation 2066, Inventory 9, Case 171, Sheet 33.

> increased attention from the pilot, because the aircraft quickly loses speed with a slight tug of the handle and breaks into spin.
>
> At medium and high altitudes, the development of piloting does not present any special difficulties...
>
> Landing on I-16 is difficult. It rushes over the ground for a long time, a high landing speed, a large and unstable mileage with an arbitrary change in direction.[13]

However, after the end of the I-16 military tests, new defects that were deadly for pilots would be revealed in the aviation units that received fighters manufactured by Gorky Aviation Plant No. 21.

At high speed, the I-16 crashed into the ground and exploded

December 1936, the neighbourhood of the city of Bobruisk. The 142nd Fighter Aviation Brigade Byelorussian Military District, based here, had recently received a new I-16 fighter. The weather for many days was clear, the most favourable for flights, but very frosty. The pilots of 142nd Fighter Aviation Brigade methodically mastered the technique of piloting a new, very capricious aircraft in control. The next training take-off passed without incident. Nothing foreshadowed trouble. Suddenly, the pilots watching the flight from the ground noticed that the fighter sharply lifted its nose and went up almost vertically. There was clearly some kind of trouble with the plane or the pilot. After a while, the I-16 began to fall, tail down. Then the plane abruptly turned nose down and entered a vertical dive. At high speed, the I-16 crashed into the ground and exploded. Experienced pilots who watched the tragedy unfold in the air were amazed at the apparent lack of attempts by the pilot to take the plane out of the spin and save his life. After examining the wreckage of the plane and fragments of the pilot's body lifted from the crater at the crash site, the commission was not able to determine the specific cause of the disaster. The personnel were already used to frequent accidents and catastrophes of the I-16, so they considered the incident an ordinary accident.

---

13 Maslov M.A., *Fighter I-16. Skittish 'Donkey' of 'Stalin's Falcons'*, Moscow, 'Yauza', 'Collection', EKSMO, 2008, p. 31.

However, a few days later, two similar disasters occurred. Two experienced pilots were killed in one day. Witnesses rushed to the crash site of one of the planes. The body of the pilot was found away from the wreckage of the fighter, scattered by the explosion for tens of metres. He was lying twenty metres from the crash site, holding in his right hand a fragment of the control handle of the aircraft.

The loss of three planes at once for an unknown reason with the death of the pilots turned out to be an emergency. Information about the constant disasters of the I-16 reached Stalin. A commission from the Red Army Air Force department, including representatives of the Nikolai Polikarpov design bureau, was immediately sent to Bobruisk. A long-term investigation of a series of aviation accidents had begun. Even for an amateur in the field of aviation, it was obvious that three experienced pilots could not lose consciousness almost simultaneously while piloting the I-16. However, the high commission from Moscow behaved very strangely from the beginning of its work. All documents about the I-16 disasters were immediately classified. Assumptions about design errors or manufacturing defects timidly expressed by representatives of 142nd Fighter Aviation Brigade were immediately rejected as deliberately false.

Valery Chkalov, his wife, and aircraft designer Nikolai Polikarpov.

The commission authoritatively stated that the aircraft was tested by the best 'Stalin's Falcon', Valery Chkalov, and the production of the fighter was approved by Stalin himself! Therefore, it was criminal to doubt the technical serviceability and correctness of the design of an aircraft that the great 'Father of Nations' liked! Further the Moscow 'experts' began to repeat more and more persistently that the reason for the flight accidents that ended in the deaths of pilots was the wrong method of their training. Having blamed the command of 142nd Fighter Aviation Brigade for the disasters, who did not teach their subordinates to fly their favourite Stalin's fighter, the Moscow bosses left for the capital.

However, in 1936, Stalin's repressions had not yet reached their climax. Many Red commanders were alive who retained at least a grain of critical thinking. Therefore, after the departure of Stalin's commission and the categorical prohibition of the Moscow authorities to doubt the design and quality of the manufacture of the I-16, an unofficial investigation of disasters continued. The chief engineer of 142nd Fighter Aviation Brigade, Ivan Prachik, after some time accidentally discovered the true cause of a series of disasters on the I-16. When checking the control system of the fighters standing in the cold hangar, he began to move the control handle vigorously, as is usually the case in the air when performing aerobatics. Suddenly,

A typical picture of the 'operation' of the I-16 'Rat' fighter in military regiments.

the metal handle broke into pieces with a crack, like a dry wooden stick. Stunned by his unexpected discovery, Ivan Prachik consistently checked the control handles of several I-16s standing nearby. With sharp movements of the control handle in the cold, its destruction occurred every time. Further investigation showed that in winter weather conditions, at temperatures well below zero Celsius, the load on the control handle increased significantly. Perhaps this was due to icing of the cables and thickening of the lubricant. During long flights at high altitudes, where the temperature in the open cockpit of the I-16 was significantly below zero, the brittle metal alloy from which the control handle was made was destroyed, which led to fighter crashes.

The scandal with the defective control handles I-16 could no longer be hidden, as well as thousands of other complaints that were received by aviation plants. Thus, the management of Gorky Aviation Plant No. 21 had to urgently start production of new control handles of the fighter, tested for strength in low temperature conditions. Urgent replacement of control handles continued throughout 1937. A total of 2,025 new sets were sent to military units, followed by an order for another 250 sets. The control handles of the newly released I-16s were appropriately modified and strengthened.

However, the pilots' confidence in the new fighter was seriously undermined. Things completely unheard of happened. 'Stalin's Falcons' refused to fly in the deadly planes even after the replacement of defective control levers. The situation was saved by the commander of 142nd Fighter Aviation Brigade, Kombrig (Colonel) Evgeny Ptukhin. For several days he came to the aircraft parking lot together with the technicians, got into the first fighter that caught his eye and performed aerobatics over the airfield. The personal example, better than any other, inspired confidence in the pilots that flying on the I-16 is not always deadly. The subsequent fate of this famous 'Stalin's Falcon' turned out to be typical for the top commanders of the Red Army Air Force. On 23 February 1942, hero of the Spanish Civil War Lieutenant General Evgeny Ptukhin was shot on charges of plotting against Stalin.

They climb from everywhere, like Rats!

The Spanish Civil War became a kind of testing ground where all sorts of scoundrels suffering from megalomania, including Franco, Mussolini, Hitler and Stalin, realized their dream of turning aviation into an independent branch of the armed forces. The difficult situation in which the troops of republican Spain got into forced Stalin urgently to send military assistance to the friendly regime. In October 1936 the first batch of I-16s, thirty-one aircraft, accompanied by pilots of the 1st Aviation Brigade, was delivered to the Iberian Peninsula.

Before the advent of the latest Soviet fighters, German Ju 52 bombers operated over Madrid with almost impunity. Moreover, in order to morally influence the residents of the Spanish capital, they flew at the heights of the roofs of houses, without feeling the slightest threat from the republican air defence. It was during the repulse of the raids on Madrid that the I-16 received its unpleasant nickname of 'Rat', which then stuck to it for many years. A popular legend says that, during the attacks of the Soviet I-16, one of the pilots of a Ju 52 shouted over the radio 'Saliande Todas partes como ratas!' – 'They climb from everywhere, like Rats!' After the appearance of the I-16, the calm flights of the Ju 52s over Madrid stopped. It must be admitted that while the I-16 resisted outdated fighters of German and Italian production, it showed itself quite satisfactorily. However, the 'Rats' losses were very large. In December 1936 alone, the Soviet Special Brigade lost seven I-16s in combat, and several more aircraft crashed as a result of accidents.

At the beginning of 1938, the final turning point in favour of the Nationalists came in the skies of Spain. With the appearance of early modifications of the German Bf 109 fighter, Soviet fighters began to suffer catastrophic losses. Even the most combat-ready Republican squadrons, including the Soviet Special Brigade, which had I-16 fighters in service, were no longer able to resist successfully the latest German fighters. In the summer and autumn of 1938, the losses of the republican aviation were very high and it was on the verge of defeat. During August 1938 eight I-16s were lost in combat and three more crashed in accidents. In September 1938 combat losses amounted to seventeen 'Rats', two more fighters were lost in disasters and one was captured by the nationalists. Thus, the collisions in the skies of Spain showed that Soviet fighters in all respects lost to the latest models of the German aviation industry.

Planes produced by 'Wreckers'

The ominous year of 1937 was one of the peaks of Stalin's repressions. Against the background of the secret executions of tens of thousands of

I-16 Type 5 fighter aircraft of the Republican Spanish Air Force.

Soviet citizens, the implementation of the ambitious plans of the 'Red Tsar' continued. The mastering of the new promising I-16 fighter in military units was associated with permanent disasters. Moreover, the number of flight accidents naturally increased as the number of fighters produced increased. Despite the atmosphere of general fear and total secrecy, the most egregious disasters of the I-16 could not be hidden. In the spring of 1937 a new series of mysterious aviation accidents began in the military units operating the 'Rats', which ended with the deaths of the pilots. This time the cause of the disasters was a fatal defect in the wings. In aircraft with the factory numbers 521999, 5210229, 5210243, when performing an ascending barrel roll, the wing consoles[14] broke off. These aerobatics were not performed on earlier I-16s, so at first the fact of destruction was attributed to the performance of barrel rolls, accompanied by large overloads of the wingtips. In full accordance with Soviet tradition, the Moscow commission once again declared 'bad' pilots and their 'frivolous' commanders to be the culprits for the disasters. Since no actions were taken to study the wing defect and change the production, Gorky Aviation Plant No. 21 continued to produce defective killer fighters of Soviet pilots in large quantities.

In May 1937 four disasters were officially recorded in the military units of the Red Army Air Force, the cause of which was the destruction of wing consoles. The investigation of the circumstances of the flight accidents showed that the deceased pilots did not expose their aircraft to exorbitant

14 Wing panel I-16 (detachable wing console) attached to wing centre section.

loads. Thus, a sudden separation of the wing consoles on the I-16 could occur even in horizontal flight. However, another Moscow commission again tried to hush up the cause.

The commanders of the military unit were insistently instructed that no one would allow the rhythmic production of Stalin's favourite fighter to be stopped because of some dead pilots – 'hooligans'. The higher authorities ordered those pilots who regularly violated instructions when piloting an 'excellent' Soviet fighter to be suspended from flights and put on trial. Pilot errors, in their opinion, were the only cause of constant emergencies. However, the fight against 'hooligan pilots' started in military units did not bring any results. 'Stalin's Falcons' continued to die during regular flights on the I-16. The pride of Soviet fighter aviation, the 'beautiful plane', continued to be produced in increasing quantities with deadly defects. However, it was the sending of the I-16 as an aid to the republican Spain, torn apart by the civil war, that finally allowed us to shed light on the true causes of the 'mysterious' disasters. Soon, due to a defect in the wings, several Soviet volunteer pilots and several Spaniards died. Unlike dozens of their own citizens who died, it was not possible to hide the deaths of the Spanish pilots. Reports of disasters finally reached Stalin. The anger of the 'Red Lord' was terrible! An order was issued for an immediate investigation of the true causes of aviation accidents and severe punishment of those responsible.

Workers with a poster calling for judging 'Wreckers'.

The commissions for the investigation of disasters in the Soviet Union and Spain found very similar destruction when examining aircraft. Almost all the crashed I-16s were found to have a tear in the skin of the end section of the wing's leading edge, as well as the destruction of the fastening of the wing ribs at the aileron hitch nodes. The reason for the disasters was very banal – insufficient structural strength. The scandal with the death of pilots in Spain intensified and letters finally flowed to Moscow describing the details and scale of the revealed problem with the I-16 wings. Soviet representatives in Spain in their messages to Stalin indicated that these planes were made by 'Wreckers'. They complained that, due to the destruction of the wings, pilots Lesnikov, Moseyko, Burov, Orzhanov, as well as the squadron commander of the I-16 'Stalin's Falcon', Konstantin Kolesnikov, were killed in flight.

On Stalin's personal instructions, inspections of the newly released I-16 aircraft began. Now the commission did not include employees of Polikarpov, but, on the contrary, employees of the Tupolev Design Bureau who were in conflict with the 'King of Fighters' were sent. The investigators received unlimited powers, including the right to open the defective wing consoles. What the members of the commission saw there struck their imagination. Inside the opened wing, an incorrect adjustment of the internal braces was found, the duralumin skin was fastened not with rivets, but with temporary clips; duralumin scraps, fabrics, metal washers and other foreign objects were found inside the wing. Now the pilots finally understood the strange noise and rumble that sometimes came from the wing over the roar of the engine. The scale of the damage was huge! For example, in the Byelorussian Military District, after an inspection of eighty-five I-16s produced in 1936-1937, forty-six were declared unfit for flight!

The scandal with the I-16 wings flared up with incredible force. On 18 May 1937, the first meeting was held in Moscow, the topic of which was the development of measures to eliminate the defect of the 'Rat' wings. This important event was attended by all interested parties: employees of the Polikarpov Design Bureau, the management of Gorky Aviation Plant No. 21 and representatives of the Red Army Air Force command. During the meeting, it was recognized for the first time that during the inspection of emergency fighters the grossest manufacturing defects were found. In 1937 this wording meant that the Gorky Aviation Plant No. 21 working gang were 'enemies of the people'. Fortunately for the employees of the Polikarpov Design Bureau, the commission's conclusions did not mention anything about chronic defects in the design of the fighter. Although the frightened Moscow bosses could not but admit the fact of gross violations in the production of the aircraft, they were not interested in the growth of the scandal around the I-16. All the parties who took part in the meeting bore their share of responsibility for dozens of disasters of Stalin's favourite fighter and the deaths of Soviet pilots. As a result, the official version was adopted, which stated that the 'excellent' I-16 fighter has some minor shortcomings that need to be eliminated immediately.

On 20 May 1937 the next meeting was held, at which a detailed work plan was adopted to replace the 'Rat' wing consoles. At first it was proposed to carry out this work directly in military units. For this purpose, it was necessary to organize special factory brigades and send them to the places the fighters were based. By the way, this is how they had to solve the problem of replacing the wing consoles of the I-16s in Spain. However, given the huge number of 'Rats' located in military units on the territory of the USSR, they decided to do this work in stationary conditions, on several aviation plants.

At Gorky Aviation Plant No. 21, the management was puzzled by the problem of how, without reducing the pace of production of the I-16, to urgently produce a huge number of new wing consoles. To replace the wings on all previously manufactured fighters, it was urgently necessary to produce 2,742 sets (i.e. two detachable wing parts, port and starboard). It was not possible to cope with such a fantastic task by the forces of Gorky Aviation Plant No. 21 alone, so Novosibirsk Aviation Plant No. 153 and Aviation Plant No. 153 (Tushino, near Moscow region) were involved in this work. In total, this grandiose work continued until the middle of 1938. By this time, 2,829 sets of reinforced wings were manufactured and sent to the military districts operating the I-16. Serial I-16s with reinforced wing console design began to be produced at Gorky Aviation Plant No. 21 in May 1938.

However, Stalin did not forgive his servants for the grandiose failure of his favorite fighter. He wanted blood!

The 'guilty' were found and executed!

In 1937 it seemed to Stalin that grandiose plans to turn the USSR into one continuous military plant were close to implementation. However, numerous facts of failures of new models of weapons that he personally approved, in particular the I-16 aircraft, became a terrible blow for him. 'Red Tsar',

Japanese fighter Ki-27, Mongolia, summer of 1939.

of course, could not admit that the main reason for the total failures was himself. The suspicious leader believed that 'traitors' and 'deceivers' were to blame for this by preventing the implementation of his brilliant plans. Thus, the Stalinist executioners from the NKVD had their hands free for the arrests and executions of revealed 'enemies of the people'.

Of the high-ranking officials involved in the fate of the I-16, the first victim of terror was Deputy People's Commissar for Defence of the Soviet Union (Minister of War) and Chief of the Air Force of the Red Army Komandarm 2nd rank (Colonel General) Yakov Alksnis. On 23 November 1937 he was removed from all posts, expelled from the Communist Party and arrested on charges of creating a mythical 'Latvian fascist organization' in the Red Army. During the investigation under torture, Yakov Alksnis pleaded guilty and on 28 July 1938 was sentenced to death. The next day, the sentence was carried out at a special Kommunarka shooting ground south-west of Moscow.

The next victim of Stalin's anger naturally became the Director of the Gorky Aviation Plant No. 21. On 3 February 1938, Evgeny Miroshnikov was arrested by NKVD officers. During the interrogations, unable to withstand the torture, he confessed that he was a member of a 'counter-revolutionary organization', whose goal was to disrupt the production of aircraft by 'wrecking' and, of course, 'the fight against the Soviet government'. On 7 September 1938, Evgeny Miroshnikov, who had managed Gorky Aviation Plant No. 21 since its construction and had a huge impact on the fate of the I-16 fighter was sentenced to capital punishment. On the same day, he was shot at the Kommunarka shooting ground.

During the 'thorough' investigation, Stalin's executioners declared a number of other high-ranking employees of Gorky Aviation Plant No. 21 'enemies of the people'. They were immediately arrested and executed after a short investigation. Thus, in addition to the pilots who died in the disasters, the failed I-16 fighter also took a large number of managers, engineers and production organizers to the grave.

I-16 vs Ki-27

In 1938, the first two-week conflict occurred between Soviet and Japanese troops in the Lake Khasan area. Tension on the border between the protectorate of the USSR Mongolia and the protectorate of Japanese Manchuria continued to grow. Two 'Evil Empires', who sought to spread to the whole globe, could not divide a piece of desert territory between them in any way. Periodically, skirmishes took place between the advanced posts of the Russians and the Japanese, both sides accusing each other of border violations.

The situation became particularly acute in the spring of 1939. After a series of clashes with the Russians, provoked by Japanese troops, Japanese aircraft appeared in the air over territory formally belonging to Mongolia. From that moment on, Soviet aviation also entered the conflict. Thus, there was another opportunity to test the 'improved' I-16 fighter.

However, the 'new' Nikolai Polikarpov fighter, released in 1938, again proved to be bad. The problems that were finally 'eliminated' after the shooting of 'enemies of the people' returned in a strange way. Soviet pilots again began to complain that it was impossible to fight in such a 'fighter'. When trying to engage in battle with the Japanese, numerous cases of engine problems were noted, forcing the 'Stalin's Falcons' to go to forced landings. Again, the hood of the fighter was filled with oil from a faulty lubrication system.

In May 1938 both combat and technical losses were very high. Information about the new failure of the I-16 reached Stalin. 'Red Lord' ordered that his loyal servant People's Commissar for Defence of the Soviet Union (Minister of War) Marshal of the Soviet Union Kliment Voroshilov urgently needed to understand the reasons for the failure and immediately correct the situation in Mongolia.

After Stalin's personal intervention, a feverish re-organization of the Soviet aviation group began, which lasted until 17 June 1938. All troops on the territory of Mongolia were now merged into 1st Army Group, and the aviation group intended for air support of the troops became known as the Air Force 1st Army Group. The command of Soviet aviation in Mongolia was assigned personally to the 'Stalin's Falcon' General Yakov

The shameful war with Finland. The pilot of the I-16 reports to his commander on the results of the departure.

Smushkevich. Together with him, a large group of experienced Soviet pilots who had fought in Spain arrived. Also, to strengthen the Air Force 1st Army Group, a large group of I-16 fighters was transferred urgently from the interior of the Soviet Union. By 20 June 1938, there were 151 fighters of various types, including ninety-five I-16s, as part of 22nd Fighter Aviation Regiment and 70th Fighter Aviation Regiment.

However, in the course of numerous air battles, this entire armada of fighters under the leadership of Yakov Smushkevich did not show itself in the best way. From 22 May to 15 September the Japanese shot down eighty-seven 'Rats'; another twenty-two I-16s crashed as a result of accidents and catastrophes. The Japanese also lost sixty-two Nakajima Ki-27s with another thirty-four severely damaged and later written off. The overall score was not in favour of the I-16. At the same time, it should be borne in mind that the Nakajima Ki-27 fought not only with the 'Rats'. Thus, given the large numerical superiority of the Soviet pilots, it can be stated that the confrontation in the air ended with Japanese victory. However, Japan's attempt to expand the borders of the empire ended in complete failure. Despite the heavy losses of people and equipment on both sides, the borders between the two 'Evil Empires' had not changed.

Stalin decided that the Soviet Union had become the winner in the war with Japan, so, after the conflict ended, a propaganda campaign was launched to glorify the valiant 'Stalin's Falcons'. The main Soviet ace of Khalkhin Gol was proclaimed as pilot Senior Lieutenant Viktor Rakhov from 22nd Fighter Aviation Regiment, who, according to official data, won eight personal and six group victories on the I-16. Six personal and thirteen group victories were won by squadron commissar Arseny Vorozheikin from the same regiment. The commander of 22nd Fighter Aviation Regiment, Major Grigory Kravchenko, squadron commander Senior Lieutenant Vasily Trubachenko and assistant squadron commander Lieutenant Ivan Krasnoyurchenko had five victories each. A real shower of awards fell on the 'Stalin's Falcons' who distinguished themselves in the battles. At the same time, it is worth noting that the accounting of downed aircraft specifically in this conflict was conducted very poorly, and on both sides. The Japanese overestimated their success sometimes by 5-7 or more times. 'Stalin's Falcons' exaggerated their victories about the same way.

On 17 November 1939, Stalin awarded Yakov Smushkevich the title of Hero of the Soviet Union for the second time for the successful command of aviation in Khalkhin Gol. Two days later he was appointed Chief of the Air Force of the Red Army. On 4 April 1940, Yakov Smushkevich was awarded the title of Komandarm 2nd rank, and on 4 June the title of Lieutenant General. In August 1940 he was transferred to the position of Inspector-General of the Red Army Air Force, and in December of the same year became Assistant Chief of the General Staff of the Red Army. The brilliant career of another beloved 'son' of Stalin, made thanks to the I-16, was suddenly interrupted by a new generation of Soviet fighters. For the failure of the programme to re-arm the Red Army Air Force with fighters of the 'New Type' and, in fact, for deceiving the 'father', Smushkevich fell out of favour with Stalin. On 8 June 1941, he was arrested by NKVD officers on charges of participating in a 'military conspiratorial organization'. Allegedly, on the instructions of this 'organization', Smushkevich carried out work 'aimed at defeating the Republican Spain, reducing the combat training of the Red Army Air Force and increasing the accident rate in the Soviet Air Force'. On 28 October 1941, by order of People's Commissar (Minister) of Internal Affairs Lavrentiy Beria, Yakov Smushkevich was shot in the village of Barbysh, Kuibyshev region.

Despite the 'victory' in the war with Japan, the enterprises that produced fighters, primarily Aviation Plant No. 21 in Gorky, were literally inundated with complaints about the quality of the aircraft. The usual vicious circle of endless improvements and changes in the design of the I-16 fighter continued. The measures taken to optimize production and the endless struggle to improve the quality of the I-16 again led to nothing. The new leaders of Stalin's aviation industry, who took the place of the executed, for the sake of preserving their own lives, showed miracles of lies and resourcefulness to prove the effectiveness of their work to the 'Red Lord'. In the end, the problem of the failed fighter was solved by itself, when in 1939 Stalin decided that the I-16 simply exhausted the resource of improvement and finally became obsolete. For the new commanders of the Red Army Air Force and the leaders of the Soviet aviation industry, another alarming period had come in their senseless activities. They were already preparing for the suspicious Stalin a whole set of 'new' fighter models to replace the 'old' 'Rat'. However, in 1939, there was still nothing to replace the I-16.

The shameful war with Finland

Having finished the showdown with the eastern 'Evil Empire', Stalin turned his 'all-seeing eye' to the western 'Evil Empire' – Germany. However, unlike Japan, Stalin had a 'strong' mutual love with Hitler. Having shared

The consequences of the accident of the I-16 fighter during taxiing on the take-off field, 18 March 1941.

Poland with 'fraternal' Germany, 'Red Tsar' wanted an equally brilliant continuation of the restoration of the lands of the former Russian Empire. The occupation of the Baltic States did not cause any problems for the Soviet Union. After that, it was naturally Finland's turn. The Soviet Union, in an ultimatum, first demanded that the Finnish government conclude a so-called 'mutual assistance agreement', which actually meant a peaceful occupation. And then he demanded it give up part of the Finnish territory 'for the security of Leningrad'. However, to Stalin's surprise, the Finns refused. Enraged the 'Red Lord' gave the Red Army an order to capture the obstinate Finland. On 30 November Soviet troops crossed the border, and SB high-speed bombers and long-range Ilyushin DB-3 bombers carried out airstrikes on several Finnish cities, including the capital Helsinki.

According to the plan of the Red Army Air Force management, the main task of the I-16 was to escort Soviet bombers, which were completely defenceless from attacks by Finnish fighters. For example, on 6 January, Lieutenant Jorma Sarvanto in a Fokker D. XXI single-handedly shot down six twin-engine Soviet Ilyushin DB-3 bombers at once. As a result of the attack, twenty-two members of their crews were killed, and only two pilots were saved.

However, the I-16s were unable to escort bombers over long distances due to their short range. Airfields for Soviet fighters, as a rule, were located far from the front line, and the fighters consumed almost half of the fuel just to reach the combat area. In addition, the fuel consumption of the I-16 engine in winter conditions was significantly higher than in summer. The problem could only be solved by external fuel tanks. Feverish tests of external fuel tanks on the I-16 began in March-April 1939. However, the excessive haste and self-confidence of aircraft designers led to a failure. The fact is that the cylindrical and flat tanks with a capacity of 100 litres, suspended under the fuselage, shifted the centre of gravity of the aircraft too far back. As a result, during take-off, the chronically unstable I-16 fell heavily on its tail, which could cause a disaster.

A new solution to the problem of the limited range of 'Rats' was proposed by aircraft designers at Gorky Aviation Plant No. 21. After studying the experience of the first battles on Khalkhin Gol, they developed a suspension scheme for external fuel tanks under the wings of the I-16. This is how the external fuel tanks were located on the Japanese Nakajima Ki-27 fighter. The shortage of aluminium forced aircraft designers to choose fibra – pressed cardboard, impregnated with a special chemical composition to give strength – as a material for the manufacture of external fuel tanks. However, as it turned out later, although the use of external fuel tanks did not interfere with the take-off of the I-16, it created a new dangerous problem. It was not possible to solve the problem of simultaneous separation of external fuel tanks from the wings when they are reset. This led to the fact that, at the time of dropping the external fuel tanks, the extremely unstable I-16 inevitably stalled into a spin, which also threatened disaster.

However, most of the I-16s that fought in Finland never received either fuselage or underwing external fuel tanks. This was due to the terrible organization of the logistics and various technical problems. Thus, using only the fuel supply in the internal tanks, the 'Rats' were unable to fulfil their main task of escorting the bombers.

On 13 March 1940 an armistice was signed between the Soviet Union and Finland. Despite the fact that little Finland lost the war to the military colossus of the Soviet Union, the 'victory' turned into a huge international disgrace for Stalin's empire. And the latest campaign with the participation of 'Rats' ended in complete failure. The main indicators of the weak effectiveness of Soviet fighters were the low losses of Finnish aviation and huge losses of Soviet bombers. In total, 113 high-speed SB bombers were shot down, and another twenty-seven were 'missing'. Forty-one SBs were damaged seriously and required factory repairs. Non-combat losses amounted to seventy-two high-speed SB bombers, and total losses amounted to 253 aircraft. As for the other twin-engine bombers, the Ilyushin DB-3s, their losses amounted to ninety-one, of which only fifty-six were shot down by Finnish fighters. Thus, in total, the Red Army Air Force lost 334 bombers over Finland. The total losses, according to various sources, ranged from 554 to 582 aircraft of all types. The exact number of I-16 fighters shot down in combat, alas, is still unknown.

The Finnish air force lost seventy-one aircraft and the Swedish volunteer group lost another six aircraft. At the same time, the number of fighters lost for combat reasons was thirty-three, including fourteen Gloster Gladiators, eleven Fokker D. XXIs, three Bristol Bulldog Mk IVAs, three Fiat G. 50 Freccias, one Morane-Saulnier M. S. 406 C1 and one Hawker Hurricane.[15]

Old, but not useless!

The passionate 'love' between Stalin and Hitler allowed Soviet aircraft designers in 1939 to get access to German aviation technologies. Extensive co-operation between the 'fraternal' peoples included trips of Soviet designers to aviation plants in Germany. Also, with the gracious permission of the Führer, it was possible to buy and then carefully examine several samples of the latest German aircraft. When, at the end of 1939, stunned by the scope and quality of the German aviation industry, the creator of the I-16, Nikolai Polikarpov, returned from a trip to Germany, he found that Stalin had stripped him of the unofficial title of 'King of Fighters'. He was waiting for the arrest and execution, but the 'good' Stalin decided to postpone the massacre for a while, hoping to still use Polikarpov's abilities in designing new aircraft.

15 Zefirov, M.V., *Aces of the Second World War: Luftwaffe Allies: Estonia. Latvian. Finland*, Moscow, AST, 2003, p. 158.

Experimental I-16 No. 1021681 with external tanks. Gorky Aviation Plant Airfield No. 21., 1939.

The brainchild of Polikarpov repeated the fate of its creator. A new generation of fighters in 1939-1940 could not be created. Therefore, the industry continued to produce the already outdated, but not yet useless I-16. A total of 2,208 'Old Type' fighters were produced in 1940. At the beginning of 1941, by order of Stalin, the production of the I-16 was discontinued. However, Gorky Aviation Plant No. 21 had, for a long time, to carry out a lot of work on repairing and eliminating design flaws on previously released 'Rats'.

In the summer of 1941, the insidious Hitler was the first to betray his 'partner' Stalin, and the whole power of the Luftwaffe fell on Stalin's aviation. The defeat of 'Stalin's Falcons', most of which were still flying the I-16, was crushing. However, the Soviet pilots fought back as best they could. It was during the collapse of the Red Army Air Force that the suicidal tactics of air ramming, approved by Stalin, appeared. On 22 June 1941, Ivan Ivanov made the first ram on the Eastern Front of the Second World War in an I-16. As a result of Ivanov's suicide attack, an He 111P-4 'G1+AL' from 3./KG 55 'Greif' was shot down south of the city of Dubno, the entire crew of which was killed.

By the way, 'Rats' continued to be used almost until the very end of the war with Germany, but chiefly in second- and third-line roles. Moreover, despite the claims of 'obsolescence', the I-16 proved itself during the battles of 1941-1942 to be no worse than the 'more advanced' LaGG-3, MIG-3 and Yak-3 fighters that replaced it. However, this conclusion does not indicate the advantages of the I-16, but the egregious vices of fighters of the 'New Type' that replaced 'Rats'.

The failed dream of a psychopath

For the period from 1934 to 1942, together with the training aircraft UTI-4 (I-16 Type 15), the total number of I-16s produced was 10,292. Thus, the 'Rat' is the first fighter in the world to be manufactured on such a large scale. The main condition for mass production with an acute shortage of aluminium was the composite construction of the fighter (wood, duralumin, steel) with a predominance of wood and materials based on it (plywood). For six and a half years of production, eight main and many small-scale types of Stalin's favourite fighter were manufactured. Such a variety of modifications is not connected with success at all but, on the contrary, with endless attempts to correct the inherent defects of the design and production of the I-16. For several years of fruitless efforts, all the components of the aircraft repeatedly passed through a vicious circle from poor-quality design to poor-quality manufacturing, and then through numerous attempts at improvements, leading to new problems. During this time, six engine types were replaced on Stalin's favourite fighter. Landing gear, armament, wing centre section and wings, cabin equipment, etc. were repeatedly 'improved'. In the process of endless modernization of the I-16 aircraft, its flight weight increased significantly (from 1,345 to 1,900kg). The specific load on the wing, take-off and landing speeds increased and the rate of climb worsened significantly. At the same time, the main problem of the I-16, a monstrous accident rate, had not been eliminated. The fighter was a set of irremediable shortcomings. The Soviet aviation industry, swollen as if by leaps and bounds, was able to produce a fighter in gigantic quantities only by sacrificing its quality.

During the long-term operation, the pilots simply got used to the I-16 and adapted. The irremediable vices of the plane were accepted as an inevitable evil. Soviet aviation still had nothing else. All the time of use, the aircraft continued to collect a plentiful harvest of victims of its technical disaster. The participation of I-16s in many wars also did not bring it fame. All the Stalinist military companies frankly failed. 'Rat' was constantly missing something: speed, then a powerful motor, then good weapons, then a range of action, and so on.

Nikolai Polikarpov was able to fulfil Stalin's dream of a mass fighter and this was the reason for the failure of aircraft designer and his brainchild. The I-16 is a striking example of weapons created to please the vicious motives of a psychopath who seized power through terror and created a criminal state. 'Rat' suffered from the same vices as its customer, namely, indiscriminately killing everyone who came into contact with it. Under the conditions of the Stalinist state, creativity, intelligence, organizational talents and production culture were destroyed and replaced with stupid subordination, outright stupidity and the desire to please the leader. It is for this reason that the talented aircraft designer Nikolai Polikarpov could not create anything but a flying disaster over many years of work. The I-16 fighter remained a flying disaster until the end of its days.

Chapter 3

A new fighter for a new war
Death and oblivion of Stalin's favourites

A frosty morning on 15 December 1938. Moscow. Frunze Central Aerodrome. On the airfield is the prototype of the 'Super Rat' (I-180), which differs from its predecessor I-16 by use of a new powerful engine, a licensed copy of the star-shaped 14-cylinder French Gnome-Rhône 14K Mistral Major. A large group of mechanics is bustling around the experimental aircraft. The aviation bosses standing nearby look very concerned. There were serious reasons for such a nervous situation that developed on the eve of the first flight of the prototype. After the failure of the I-16, Stalin began to have great doubts about everyone who was responsible for the development and production of new combat aircraft. The aviation bosses and the 'King of

'Super Rat' (I-180).

Fighters' had only one chance to restore their reputation. Everyone present at the tests of the prototype of the new fighter knew perfectly well what Stalin was doing with those who did not meet his expectations.

Valery Chkalov at the zenith of glory.

'Super Rat' (I-180) was created in an extraordinary hurry. The plane was supposed to be ready for the unofficial sixtieth birthday of the almighty 'Red Lord'. Stalin was personally interested in the progress of the work, creating a permanent hysteria amongst aviation bosses at all levels. The preliminary design of the new aircraft was ready in February 1938 and, by the beginning of December, the first 'Super Rat' was 'ready'. The I-180 prototype, assembled in a hurry, had a huge number of significant malfunctions (for example, 190 defects were detected on 2 December). Of particular concern was the modernized engine, the victim of risky attempts by Soviet engineers to squeeze additional power out of an excellent French engine. However, for experimental Soviet aircraft, such an emergency condition before the flight was considered the norm. The aviation bosses did not consider design flaws and poor-quality assembly of the prototype an obstacle to performing a test flight. The new bosses of Soviet aviation, who replaced their predecessors who had already been shot, dreamed of repeating the old trick of 1935 with a spectacular presentation of a new fighter to Stalin.

It is no coincidence that the high honour of lifting the first example of the I-180 into the air again fell to the most experienced tester, and Stalin's favourite, Valery Chkalov. By the end of 1938 this main 'Stalin's Falcon' was at the zenith of his glory. Valery Chkalov had everything that a Soviet person could dream of: a luxury apartment in the centre of Moscow, a car and even a private plane while the village where Stalin's favourite was born was renamed Chkalovsk in 1937. However, no matter how much fame and power this outstanding Soviet pilot possessed, he was only a slave to the base desires of the 'Red Lord'.

On 1 December 1938 Chkalov was urgently called back from leave to conduct tests of the new I-180 fighter. Despite the interrupted leave, the work that the elite 'Stalin's Falcon' was supposed to do did not involve much stress. Only one full-fledged flight was planned for a beautiful report to Stalin. Valery Chkalov was supposed to receive a huge fee for it. Further, Nikolai Polikarpov intended to transfer the aircraft for long-term tests to another 'Stalin's Falcon' – Stepan Suprun. He was less well-known, which meant he was more suitable for this dangerous job. However, from the very beginning, nothing went according to plan. Three times (7, 10 and 12 December) Chkalov tried to take off in the 'Super Rat', but each time there was a serious breakdown that left the plane on the ground. After each attempt, the I-180 was hastily repaired, hoping for a miracle.

Finally, on the 15th, the take-off took place. Experienced Chkalov confidently lifted the 'Super Rat' into the sky and, after making the first circle over the airfield at an altitude of 100 to 200 metres, continued the flight with a climb. Known for his obstinate character, 'Stalin's Falcon' habitually violated the flight task prescribed by Polikarpov and took an experimental plane on a risky flight over the Moscow region. The official Soviet version of the crash does not contain a description of the purpose of the Chkalov flight. However, unofficial information says that he wanted to fly near Stalin's country residence (Kuntsevo Dacha). Perhaps Chkalov

Aircraft designer Nikolai Polikarpov at the beginning of the 1940s.

A Bf 109 B fighter with a Jumo 210 D engine, captured on 4 December 1937 after an emergency landing on the territory of republican Spain, on tests in the USSR, summer of 1938.

knew that a big fan of aviation was there and, hearing the noise of the engine, would certainly look at the new fighter from the window of his office. By the way, very short curtains were hung on the windows of the Stalin residence by order of the 'Red Lord', which were conducive to such unplanned observations. The fact is that the paranoiac Stalin was terrified that an assassin might hide behind the curtains.

The dangerous plan almost succeeded. A dashing flight near Stalin's country residence took place, and a satisfied Chkalov was already returning to the airfield. However, when at a distance of only 1.5 kilometres from the runway, the Super Rat's engine stalled suddenly. The Polikarpov fighter, known for its instability, immediately dropped to the left and began to fall rapidly. Valery Chkalov, who repeatedly got into extreme situations on various experimental aircraft, was not at a loss. At the last moment, he leveled off the I-180 and tried to make an emergency landing. If 'Stalin's Falcon' had not violated the Polikarpov flight mission, and continued to test the 'Super Rat' over a huge airfield, he had every chance to land the plane with minimal damage and stay alive. However, Chkalov was falling over a densely built-up area. At the site of a possible forced landing there were wooden houses, sheds and the territory of the motor depot construction company called 'Moszhilgosstroy', a small state-owned enterprise surrounded by a high wooden fence. The experienced 'Stalin's Falcon' steered the plane towards a small space free of buildings. However, at the last moment, the I-180 caught on electrical wires, hit the right wing on an electric pole and, turning around, crashed into a pile of wood waste. The wooden fuselage of the fighter broke in half from the impact of a huge force, and Chkalov was thrown out of the cockpit for ten to fifteen metres along with the tail part of the aircraft. However, even with such a catastrophe – not the first in his life – Chkalov had every chance of surviving. There was no fire, and he was not injured seriously. But, unfortunately, Valery Chkalov hit his head on a metal rail that just happened to be at the crash location. Stalin's Falcon was still alive when the workers of the Moszhilgosstroy motor depot construction company removed him from the wreckage and sent him to the hospital in the back of a one-and-a-half-ton truck. Meanwhile, everyone who was at the airfield, waiting for Chkalov's triumphant return of, saw the crash of the I-180 and froze with horror. The test managers' last hopes melted away when the message came that Valery Chkalov had died in Botkin Hospital.

The crash of the prototype of the 'Super Rat' had terrible consequences. All the people involved in the death of Stalin's favourite were arrested immediately. Only aircraft designer Nikolai Polikarpov remained at large and even tried to continue his work on the I-180. However, from that moment on, his life changed radically. Aircraft designers, who had previously greeted Polikarpov respectfully and recorded his every word, suddenly began to avoid contact with him. Such a radical change in the behaviour of others is easy to explain. Under the conditions of Stalin's terror, every Soviet citizen, guided by the instinct of self-preservation, tried to cut off all ties not only with 'enemies of the people', but also with their relatives and even acquaintances. All the 'enemies' of the

I-16 Type 10 at Tamtsag-Bulak airfield, Mongolia.

'Red Lord' immediately disappeared not only from life, but also from memory. Their images in photos were painted over with black ink, pages from books that mentioned them were cut out and destroyed. However, in the case of Nikolai Polikarpov, the bloody machine of Stalin's terror for some reason failed. Such 'mercy' on the part of Stalin's executioners looks especially strange against the background of the fact that, by 1938, all Polikarpov's recent competitors, including aircraft designers Andrei Tupolev and Vladimir Petlyakov, had been in a special Stalin prison for several years and even their names were banned.

Poster glorifying Stalin.

However, being free turned out to be a terrible torture for Nikolai Polikarpov. One can imagine the nightmarish psychological state of the former Stalinist favourite, accustomed to everyone's attention, which no one noticed for two long months. Yesterday's subordinates and junior colleagues literally shunned Polikarpov as if he were a leper. Only the bravest friends in the darkest corridors of the design bureau whispered to him that his days were numbered. Depressed by such an oppressive atmosphere, the aircraft designer resigned himself to his fate. Polikarpov stopped coming to his design bureau and again began to find solace in deep prayer. Work on the I-180 was stopped. Thus, aircraft designer Nikolai Polikarpov, who angered his master, literally turned from 'King of Fighters' into a kind of Tolkien's 'Ghost king'!

Finally, after two months of waiting for arrest and execution, Polikarpov, deprived of his beloved job, was suddenly returned from the 'world of shadows'. One night Stalin called him and told him in a gentle voice that he was not to blame for anything. Next, 'Red Lord' invited his faithful servant to go on holiday and rest, and then continue working on improving 'Super Rat'. However, after this terrible nervous shock, Polikarpov never returned to his former working state. Despite the optimistic plans and orders to deploy serial production, the completion of the I-180 fighter ended in complete failure. During the tests, 'Super Rat' set a kind of record for destroying the famous 'Stalin's Falcons'. In addition to Valery Chkalov, another victim of the I-180 was the experienced test pilot Thomas Suzi, who died in the crash of the second prototype of the 'Super Rat'. In September 1940, People's Commissar of Aviation Industry Aleksey Shakhurin finally ordered the long-term painful work on the creation of the I-180 to stop.

Nikolai Polikarpov continued to work, but only a pitiful shadow remained of the former talented and purposeful aircraft designer. Several experimental models of fighters developed by him at the beginning of the 1940s also proved unsuccessful. The time of 'King of Fighters' had passed irrevocably. Stalin had new favourites, and he paid less and less attention to his devoted 'Nazgul' ('Ghost king', adjutant Lord of Darkness). The psychologically broken aircraft designer continued the quiet 'life' of the ghost until his death in 1944.

The echo of the war from distant Spain

The last phase of the Spanish Civil War became a terrible new blow to Stalin's shattered confidence in the success of Soviet fighters and the skill of the 'Stalin's Falcons' piloting them. Favourite 'Rats' suffered a complete collapse in confrontations with the latest Luftwaffe fighter. Soon the Bolsheviks had new evidence of the indisputable superiority of the German aviation industry in their hands. In March 1938, a captured Bf 109 B, seized after an emergency landing in Spain, was delivered to the Red Army Air Force Research Institute. In total, during the Spanish Civil War, two Bf 109 B fell into the hands of the Republicans. One was shot down by Soviet pilot Alexander Gusev. Despite the damage, the Bf 109 B landed on its belly and was sent to the USSR for study. After repair of the German fighter, 'Stalin's Falcon' Stepan Suprun conducted a series of test flights. The conclusions of the flight test report noted:

> The Messerschmitt aircraft successfully combines speed and simplicity in piloting techniques and stability. It is necessary to implement such a combination for high-speed Red Army Air Force fighters. In flight, the controlled stabilizer on the Bf 109 B made it possible to remove loads from the pilot's control handle in all modes. The aircraft has a good combination of large reserves of stability with the

Mikhail Kaganovich, Valery Chkalov and Joseph Stalin.

> simplicity of piloting techniques and a good manoeuvre ... . The aircraft can be considered a standard of stability in the class of fighter aircraft.[1]

Subsequently, a mock air battle was conducted between the captured Bf 109 B and the I-16 Type 10 – at that time the main Soviet fighter. The already outdated German fighter, manufactured in 1937, showed a confident superiority in combat over the specially prepared 'Rat' model of 1938.

'Wisest of the wise' comes into play

By the end of 1938 Stalin's suspicions that all representatives of his beloved Soviet aviation industry and the leadership of the Red Army Air Force were deceiving him were finding more and more confirmation. The intellectually limited 'Red Lord' began to be overcome by anxiety about the fate of his grandiose plans to conquer Western Europe. Although the number of fighters produced grew steadily every year, the flight characteristics were poor, and the quality of aircraft manufacturing remained terrible. In 1939, as information was received that his advertised fighters, despite

1 Yakubovich, N.V., *Aviation of the USSR on the eve of the war*, Moscow, Veche, 2006, p. 30.

People's Comissar of Aviation Industry, Mikhail Kaganovich.

the enormous efforts and resources spent, were losing outright to German and even Japanese aircraft, Stalin's disappointment increased. The question of how his 'Stalin's Falcons' would resist the aviation of the UK and France, which he considered the main enemies of the Soviet Union, began to arise more and more insistently in the head of 'Red Tsar'. Accustomed during the 1930s to regular presentations of 'wonder fighters', Stalin was waiting for his beloved aviation industry to create new aircraft to replace the failed I-16. However, the total terror organized by 'Red Lord' in 1937 turned into an unprecedented crisis and stagnation for the young Soviet aviation industry. Accordingly, things were not the best among the managers of the aviation industry, who also suffered from endless repression.

Until 1939 the production of military aircraft was under the control of the People's Commissariat of the Defence Industry of the Soviet Union. The leadership of this bureaucratic body clearly could not cope with the implementation of grandiose plans for the production of tanks, aircraft, warships and submarines. After the total failure of all areas of the military industry, by order of Stalin, Moisey Rukhimovich, People's Commissar of the Defence Industry of the Soviet Union (Minister), was arrested in 1937 and executed on 29 July 1938. The son of a locksmith, the ardent Bolshevik Rukhimovich tried sincerely to implement the utopian plans of his 'Master'. However, complete administrative and technical incompetence, combined with the destructiveness of Stalin's administrative system, did not allow the People's Commissar to achieve the grandiose indicators of industrial development which were completely invented by the main psychopath of the USSR. After the arrest of Moisey Rukhimovich in 1937, another ardent Bolshevik devoted to Stalin, Mikhail Kaganovich, was appointed to the post of People's Commissar of the Defence Industry. He had to deal with correcting the 'mistakes' of his predecessor. At the same time, in full accordance with the Bolshevik dogma, the level of educational and professional competence of the new leader did not play any role. If Rukhimovich, at least, tried to study at the Kharkiv Institute of Technology, then Kaganovich's entire education was limited to several classes of elementary school and mastering the profession of a locksmith.

On 11 January 1939 Stalin divided the People's Commissariat of the Defence Industry into four separate People's Commissariats. Mikhail Kaganovich received the position of People's Commissar of Aviation Industry (Minister). Initially, the new 'correct' People's Comissar enjoyed Stalin's boundless trust and received carte blanche to restore 'order' in the industry under his control. With the help of psychological pressure that turned into outright rudeness and threats, Mikhail Kaganovich was able to improve slightly the quantitative indicators of the Soviet aviation industry for a short time. Taking the sacred voice of 'Master' literally, the new People's Commissar began obsessively to increase the production of Stalin's favourite fighters. This trend also naturally manifested itself in Nazi Germany, where the ardent Nazi and creator of the Luftwaffe, Hermann Göring, 'correctly' understood the words of his 'Brown Lord'.

Typical day at Stalin's Design Bureau, 1930s.

The reverse side of Kaganovich's 'brilliant' leadership of the Soviet aviation industry was the total domination of the Nikolai Polikarpov I-16 and I-15 fighters, already in large-scale production, and the failure of the programme to create a new generation of aircraft. The maniacally active People's Commissar created dozens of new design bureaux, filling them with hundreds of young, but inexperienced, engineers. However, the Soviet aircraft designers could not offer Stalin anything but very strange designs for new fighters completely unsuitable for mass production. Trying to solve the problem by attracting foreign technologies, Mikhail Kaganovich sanctioned huge spending on the purchase of Western aviation components and even finished aircraft. However, none of the foreign aircraft purchased for gold could be brought to mass production. There were objective reasons for such incapacity, which were also related directly to the Stalinist repressions. Most of the few aircraft designers of the older generation, inherited by the Bolsheviks from the tsarist regime, were either in the grave (Dmitry Grigorovich), or in prison (Andrey Tupolev, Vladimir Petlyakov), or in deep depression (Nikolai Polikarpov).

The pilot work plan for 1939, presented by Kaganovich to Stalin, was filled with endless projects of archaic biplanes and modifications of already outdated aircraft models. To the sincere surprise of the leader, it turned

Chief of the Air Force of the Red Army Komandarm 2nd rank (Colonel General) Yakov Alksnis reports to People's Commissar for Defence of the Soviet Union, Kliment Voroshilov.

out that, in 1939, Soviet aircraft designers were working on only three promising fighters. These were outwardly very similar monoplane fighters with a Gnome-Rhône 14K Mistral Major engine: 'Super Rat' (I-180) from Nikolai Polikarpov, I-28 from Vladimir Yatsenko and I-220 from Alexander Silvansky. As further events showed, all three projects of promising fighters with a radial engine with a capacity of 1,100 horsepower ended in crushing failure. The older generation of Soviet aircraft designers, drained of blood by repression, could no longer satisfy Stalin's boundless ambitions.

Thus, 'Red Lord', without realizing this, once again faced the harmful consequences of his own decisions. Devoid of imagination, the bloodthirsty Stalin knew only one way to solve all the problems – personal interference in the activities of the Soviet aviation industry, the indicators of which caused him alarm. The 'Red Tsar' took up this work with his boundless fanaticism and maniacal obsession. According to Stalin's brilliant 'plan', a new generation of Soviet aircraft designers and managers would have to create fighters of the 'New Type' under his 'wise' leadership.

Soviet aviation needs to be urgently saved!

The death of Valery Chkalov led to the overflow of the cup of Stalin's patience. A new generation of fighters with a licensed French radial engine, which was supposed to replace the hopelessly outdated I-16, failed even before the start of mass production. Against the background of these events, 'Red Lord' suddenly felt that his beloved Soviet fighter aviation needed to be saved immediately!

Stalin's first step was to concentrate the resources of the distressed Soviet aviation industry. The creation of the People's Commissariat of Aviation Industry of the USSR (Ministry) helped raise the status of industrial enterprises engaged in the production of military aircraft and allowed more attention to be paid to their development.

Stalin's second step was a personnel purge – 'Chistka', which inevitably led to the informal subordination of the entire Soviet aviation industry to him. The *idée fixe* of the elderly 'Red Dictator' was the total rejuvenation of managerial personnel. The former leadership of the aviation industry, according to the leader, did not justify his 'high' trust. The main driving force of the aviation industry management reform was to be young Communists, no older than 40 years. These people were formed under the Bolshevik regime, which meant that they did not know any other 'Great Leader' except Stalin.

The 'Red Lord' could not stand any manifestations of independence from managers appointed by him. Such qualities, in his opinion, were dangerous for the 'development' of Soviet industry. He needed blind performers of his 'brilliant' plan. However, the real reason for the almost complete destruction of the older generation of Soviet managers was Stalin's paranoid intolerance towards people of his own age. He instinctively perceived them as rivals in the struggle for absolute power. It was much easier for him to cope with his fears surrounded by young people who were old enough to be his sons. However, even to his 'sons', 'wisest of the wise' never forgave the disagreement with his only 'correct' point of view.

Hostages of Stalin

It took time to implement Stalin's plan to rejuvenate the managerial personnel of the aviation industry and the 'Red Lord' had to endure more than a year of the older generation in their positions as managers. Stalin graciously treated Mikhail Kaganovich, who irritated him a lot, and actually left him as People's Commissar of Aviation Industry (Minister). Perhaps this decision was influenced by the younger brother of Mikhail Kaganovich, People's Commissar of Railways of the Soviet Union Lazar Kaganovich, who was part of the inner circle of Stalin's most loyal servants. Another important advantage of the first People's Comissar of Aviation Industry was the primitive flattery and submissiveness of the 'Master', a characteristic of his. Mikhail Kaganovich never questioned Stalin's words and tried to fulfill his slightest whim. However, the 'Red Lord' in his usual harsh manner clearly outlined to the 'temporary' People's Commissar of Aviation Industry all the shortcomings of his department and gave him only one year to eliminate problems in the industry. The main condition for maintaining the position, and possibly the life of People's Commissar of Aviation Industry, was the creation of fighters of the 'New Type' and their early introduction into mass production. Thus, from 1939, Mikhail Kaganovich was actually in the status of a hostage of Stalin. He dutifully played the role of an adviser to the 'Master' on aviation industry matters and, with his usual stupid zeal, tried to implement the most insane plans of the 'Red Lord'.

Without formally being the head of the aviation industry, Stalin concentrated in his hands the solution of all strategic questions related to the development, production and combat use of Soviet fighter aviation.

Chief of the Air Force of the Red Army, Colonel General Aleksandr Loktionov.

Although all these decisions were framed as the decisions of the Defence Committee at the Council of People's Commissioners of the Soviet Union (a commission under the government of the Soviet Union) and the orders of the People's Commissariat of Aviation Industry of the USSR, it is clear that they were solely Stalin's base desires and nothing else. All the former managers of the older generation were destroyed, and in their place were appointed representatives of the young Stalinist managerial guard, whose candidacies the 'Red Lord' chose personally. Moreover, in 1939, Stalin began to control the process of creating fighters of the 'New Type'. However, the pace of implementation of this work and the experimental developments presented did not suit him at all. 'Temporary' People's Commissar of Aviation Industry Kaganovich constantly received cruel reprimands from his powerful patron for this.

During 1939, the degree of Stalin's interference in the work of the aviation industry was steadily increasing, as reflected in a huge number of various kinds of meetings devoted to the creation of new fighters. Stalin was concerned about the problem of stimulating numerous design bureaux, especially those led by young aircraft designers. Despite the hasty announcement of the I-16 as a fighter of the 'Old Type', there were no fighters of the 'New Type' ready for mass production. The largest state aviation plant in the USSR, No. 1 (Moscow), specializing in the production of fighters, when planning work for 1939, was still forced to be content with the production of the hopelessly outdated I-153 biplane. Stalin was annoyed and frustrated by the lack of results in the work on the creation of the 'New Type' of fighters and, in this regard, constantly increased the pressure on his numerous hostages.

Money in the USSR solves all problems!

Despite the achievement of absolute power by the middle of the 1930s and the consistent destruction of all, even potential competitors, the implementation of many of the 'great' plans of the 'Red Tsar' rested on the existing inert bureaucratic system. This system, created by the Bolsheviks, at some point became so influential and pervasive that it dictated its terms even to Stalin. However, with the help of privileges on one hand and executions on the other, the 'Red Lord' learned to skillfully manipulate the Soviet bureaucracy.

The intellectually limited Stalin solved the difficult problem of finding and attracting new design and production personnel for the Soviet aviation industry roughly and straightforwardly. If Bolshevik enthusiasm alone was not enough, then it was necessary to interest young engineers and managers in money and awards. The helpful People's Commissar of Aviation Industry Kaganovich, being himself a passionate lover of privileges and luxury, suggested that Stalin create a system of awarding members of design teams and employees of the Soviet aviation industry for a special contribution to the creation of new fighters. This idea was very much liked by 'Master'. Being pathologically stingy in everyday life, the 'Red Lord' became extremely generous when it came to the implementation of his 'great' plans. According to Stalin's plan, a huge amount of money, in the amount of 100,000 rubles, with a monthly salary of 1,000 rubles for a Soviet engineer, would have to become a new incentive for fulfilling the will of the 'great' Stalin. After the approval of the 'Red Tsar' idea of bribing young engineers, in the spring of 1939 Mikhail Kaganovich presented to his 'Master' a multi-page draft of the *Regulations on Prize*. In this document, the grounds and amounts of remuneration for contributions to the development and organization of mass production of new types of aircraft were described scrupulously.

Rumours about huge cash bonuses and new opportunities for young aircraft designers, engineers and managers spread quickly enough in all organizational structures of the aviation industry. For many young engineers who languished in various lowly positions and received a very modest salary for their gruelling work, the promised fantastic bonuses became a really powerful incentive to create new aircraft projects. However, despite the formally equal conditions, only a select few who aroused Stalin's sympathy had a real chance of becoming winners in the future competition for the creation of a new 'wonder fighter'.

The main 'customer' of the new fighters

The most numerous and powerful organization in the USSR was the Red Army. This circumstance sometimes caused Stalin panic and fear. The 'Red Lord' was afraid that the army he created to gain world domination, could turn against him at any moment. The horror of a military coup forced him to monitor closely the growing influence of specific top Red Army commanders. Despite the huge scope of intervention in the activities of the Soviet armed forces, the 'Red Tsar' and his closest servants simply could not physically control the entire huge volume of military matters. Many important decisions were still made by the military independently. When Stalin's 'all-seeing eye' turned its gaze to the problems of Soviet fighter aviation, it became obvious that another conflict between the interests of the military and the ambitions of the 'Red Lord' was inevitable. The main reason for this unofficial confrontation was the right to determine the key characteristics of the future fighter.

Chief of the Air Force of the Red Army, Lieutenant General Yakov Smushkevich.

The regulations for the development, testing and adoption of new combat aircraft in the USSR in the second half of the 1930s had its own peculiarities. The formal customer of the new aircraft models was the Main Directorate Red Army Air Force, headed by the Chief of the Air Force of the Red Army. In the period of interest to us, from 1934 to 1941, four people were successively in this post: Komandarm 2nd rank Yakov

Alksnis, from June 1931 to 23 November 1937; Colonel General Aleksander Loktionov, from 23 November 1937 to 19 November 1939; Lieutenant General Yakov Smushkevich, from 19 November 1939 to August 1940; and Lieutenant General Pavel Rychagov, from August 1940 to 24 June 1941.

The fact that all these people were declared 'enemies of the people' and executed on Stalin's orders shows how dramatic this period was in the history of Soviet aviation. As he strengthened his power, Stalin interfered increasingly in the management of his beloved aviation. After the execution of Yakov Alksnis, the leadership of the Red Army Air Force began rapidly to lose independence in making key decisions concerning the development of this kind of troops. Over the next three years, Stalin replaced three people as commander of the Red Army Air Force. However, after some time the 'Red Lord' was naturally disappointed in the commanders he appointed. At the beginning of 1939, Stalin, dissatisfied with the constant failures of his aviation, took on the role of commander of the Red Army Air Force. The former holders of this position, Colonel General Aleksander Loktionov, and Yakov Smushkevich and Pavel Rychagov, who followed him, turned into passive executors of Stalin's will and his hostages. Thus, having concentrated the informal management of the aviation industry and command of the Red Army Air Force in his hands, the 'Red Lord' received full personal control over the development of Soviet aviation.

Stalin managed the development of the Red Army Air Force in his characteristic pathological manner. Completely ignoring the weak resources of the Soviet aviation industry and the limited opportunities for training qualified pilots, he immediately set impossible tasks to increase the number of aircraft. First of all, it was supposed to increase dramatically the number of fighters that were easier to produce. Stalin's already excessive interference in determining the strategy and tactics of this kind of personnel became absolute from that moment.

Thus, after the decision was made to accelerate the development of fighters of the 'New Type', it was Stalin who acted as their main customer, and the leadership of the Red Army Air Force performed only a supporting role. Such informal leadership allowed the 'Great Leader' to avoid responsibility for the monstrous mistakes that he constantly made, interference in a field whose complexity required high intelligence and competence, which he did not have. In the event of failures that became an inevitable consequence of the implementation of Stalin's arbitrary decisions, all responsibility fell on the heads of the formal leaders of the aviation industry and the leadership of the Red Army Air Force.

All resources for aviation!

The personal attention of the 'Red Lord' had radically changed the situation of Soviet aviation industry enterprises. Their number began to grow at a rapid pace, not only due to the construction of new aviation plants, but also due to the conversion of existing enterprises specializing in wood processing for the production of aircraft. In particular, for the production of all-wood fighters, many furniture factories were turned into aviation industry plants. Thanks to Stalin's attention, the amount of resources allocated to the development of the industry increased many times and reached 40 per cent of the entire military budget of the USSR by 1940.

However, in reality, the 'Red Lord' was not as omnipotent as the false Soviet propaganda reported daily in the newspapers. The inert Soviet planning system completely failed to cope with the growing appetites of Stalin. The terms of commissioning of new aviation plants grew catastrophically. Due to the lack of resources for the simultaneous construction of dozens of huge plants, the completion of most plants was stretched out for years. In the Soviet Union, by the beginning of 1940, there were virtually no fully completed aviation plants. All the key objects of the Soviet aviation industry were in varying degrees of readiness. Most of them could function only at 50 per cent of design capacity. In an especially difficult situation were aircraft engine plants, which required thousands of units of expensive imported equipment to equip them. The failure of the Red Army Air Force in the Second World War showed clearly that the enormous resources taken from the half-starved population of the USSR were spent without any noticeable effect.

Stalin 'Design Bureau'

11-13 May 1939. Moscow. The Central Committee of the Communist Party of the Soviet Union building on Staraya Square.

Many people gathered in the vast assembly hall to participate in a special meeting of the Defence Committee at the Council of People's Commissioners of the Soviet Union (commission under the Government of the Soviet Union) on the topic 'On measures to introduce new and modified aircraft into production'.

Most of them had a very vague idea of the purpose of the meeting, for which they were torn away from important matters. Dissatisfied with the slowness of his servants, Stalin gave People's Commissar of Aviation Industry

'Stalin's Falcons': Captain Stepan Suprun and Senior Lieutenant Vladimir Kokkinaki, 1938.

Kaganovich only a few days to prepare the event. However, despite the haste, the meeting was attended by representatives of all parties involved in the development, production and operation of military aircraft, only about a hundred people. The military was represented by Chief of the Air Force of the Red Army Colonel General Aleksander Loktionov, his deputy General Yakov Smushkevich, Head of the Red Army Air Force Research Institute Alexander Filin and many others. Next to them in the stuffy hall sat almost all the famous Soviet aircraft designers who worked in Moscow or in the cities closest to the capital. The older generation was represented by Nikolai Polikarpov, Sergey Ilyushin, Vladimir Yatsenko and Pavel Sukhoi. The younger generation was represented by Vladimir Gorbunov, Mikhail Pashinin, Alexander Yakovlev and many others. The meeting was led by the chairman of the Defence Committee of the Council of People's Commissioners of the Soviet Union, the narrowminded and incompetent, but infinitely loyal to Stalin, Marshal of the Soviet Union Kliment Voroshilov. In terms of its content, this formal event, apart from its scope and duration, differed little from many similar meetings that were regularly held in 1939. For three days, endless speeches with reports from the military, aircraft designers and representatives of the aviation industry continued. For example, each of the aircraft designers invited to the meeting talked about the current state of Soviet aviation and the possible prospects for its development. The most important topic for discussion, as at many previous and subsequent meetings, was the question of the development of fighter aviation. However, no real solution to this most important problem was proposed, except for empty conversations. The only result of the meeting was another statement of Stalin's thesis about the need to replace fighters of the 'Old Type' with fighters of the 'New Type' and the formal approval of the *Regulations on Prize* approved by Stalin. As a result of the meeting, in accordance with the flourishing bureaucratic procedures in the USSR, a formal commission was created from representatives of the military and the People's Commissariat of Aviation Industry of the USSR (Ministry), which was supposed to oversee the process of developing new types of aircraft.

Despite the routine, this meeting still had a strategic impact on the development of Soviet fighter aviation. However, the key events of this event took place not in the meeting room, but on the sidelines of it. The presence of the 'Red Lord' at the meeting was short. After listening to several boring reports, Stalin retired to the office next to the conference room, where he had a very important meeting scheduled.

Stalin, who did not trust anyone, personally organized the search for young promising aircraft designers. He had been looking at two young engineers for several years: aircraft designer Alexander Yakovlev and aircraft engine designer Vladimir Klimov. In fact, the three-day May 1939 meeting was just a beautiful backdrop for a meeting with the candidate already chosen by Stalin for the role of the new 'King of Fighters'. It was during this backstage conversation that the 'Red Tsar' expressed his wish to have an armada of high-speed fighters with a liquid-cooled engine and cannon armament. Thus, Stalin personally chose the general appearance and characteristics of the future fighter of the 'New Type', which determined the main trends in the development of Soviet fighter aviation for the next few years.

On the evening of 13 May, mortally tired of listening to endless reports, the participants of the meeting went to their offices, wondering what future awaited them. Although most people related to Stalin's Red Army Air Force felt vague anxiety, they did not suspect that their tragic fate was already predetermined.

At this time, in the Kremlin office, Stalin, satisfied with the implementation of his plans, smoked a pipe and made further plans to 'save' his beloved aviation. For the beloved 'Red Lord', the 'Great Break', which meant a radical change in the direction of development of Soviet aviation, had already occurred. Stalin found the people he needed and had no doubt of success. Now the 'temporary' People's Commissar of the Aviation Industry Mikhail Kaganovich was superfluous, and Stalin was looking for promising candidates to replace him.

'Science' in the service of Stalin

Meanwhile, the start of the contest to create fighters of the 'New Type' required compliance with a number of unshakeable bureaucratic procedures. Soviet aircraft designers had very limited creative freedom when working on a new aircraft. In order to receive funding for the construction of a prototype, they had to prepare an aircraft project that met fully the requirements of the customer, that is, the military. At the end of the 1930s, a special structure, the Red Army Air Force Research Institute, was engaged in the development of tactical and technical requirements, acceptance of draft designs and models of future aircraft, as well as state tests of prototypes. Military specialists of this research institute made a final assessment of the suitability of new fighters for mass production and were responsible for their adoption into service. Thus, the power of the Red Army Air Force Research Institute in this important area was almost absolute, which categorically did not suit the representatives of the Soviet aviation industry. This circumstance served as a permanent reason for severe conflicts between civil and military specialists of the Soviet aviation industry.

The Red Army Air Force Research Institute was established in 1926 as a special state structure for testing the first Soviet aircraft: Polikarpov I-1, R-1, R-3, Tupolev TB-1 and ANT-2, as well as foreign aircraft and various new aircraft weapons systems. Later, the Research Institute was re-orientated to testing and fine-tuning Soviet aircraft, as well as solving the problems of piloting aircraft in special conditions – night flights, flights in the clouds, etc. Subsequently, all newly-created aircraft and their modifications were adopted by Soviet aviation only after receiving a positive conclusion from the Red Army Air Force Research Institute. Thus, in addition to determining the strategy and tactics of the development of the Red Army Air Force, this structure performed an important function of monitoring military experts over the activities of the Soviet aviation industry.

In the 1930s, the Research Institute expanded its structure significantly. By 1931 it already had nineteen departments, each of which supervised its own separate direction. In that decade the famous 'Stalin's Falcons' served as test pilots at the Research Institute: Valery Chkalov, Vladimir Kokkinaki, Stepan Suprun, Georgy Baydukov and many others. On 1 October 1939, the Red Army Air Force Research Institute had forty-seven aircraft of various types, thirty-seven pilots, seven navigators and eighty-three aircraft technicians working there.[2]

In the second half of the 1930s the main volume of research at the Research Institute was associated with testing new and modified Polikarpov I-15, I-16, I-153, the Ilyushin DB-3 long-range bomber and SB high-speed bomber aircraft. Immediately before the German attack on the USSR, at the turn of the 1940s, the Research Institute tested prototypes of future fighters MiG-1, Yak-1, LaGG-3, the ground-attack Ilyushin Il-2, the Petlyakov Pe-2 bomber and many others.

Procrustean bed for Soviet aviation industry

On 26 August 1939 the 'Tactical and technical requirements for a single-seat high-speed fighter of the pilot construction plan 1939-1940', prepared by employees of the Red Army Air Force Research Institute, was approved by the Chief of the Air Force of the Red Army, Colonel General Aleksander Loktionov, and a member of the Military Council of the Red Army Air Force, Divizionny Komissar Philip Agaltsov.

This important document described what, in the opinion of the military, the future Soviet fighter of the 'New Type' should be:

I. Purpose of the aircraft
   High-speed single-seat fighter
II. Basic tactical requirements
   Conducting an active combat by a fighter to defeat and destroy the enemy based on the advantage in speed and power of fire. The presence of high speed is the main one.
   To perform its tasks, the fighter must have cannon and machine-gun weapons and a small supply of small-calibre bombs.

2 RGVA, Foundation 29, Inventory 34, Case 365, Sheet 160-2.

Availability of a crew reservation (partial reservation of the engine and radiator was cancelled by the Military Council Red Army Air Force).

To perform combat tasks for escorting, patrolling and in a particularly difficult situation, the suspension of additional external fuel tanks should be provided.

III. Flight and tactical requirements
1. Maximum speed at an altitude of 5,000m — 650km/h.
2. Landing speed 115-125 km/h.
3. Practical ceiling 11,000-12,000m.
4. Technical range at a speed of 0.9 maximum 600km.
5. The technical range at a speed of 0.9 maximum with full tanks with overloading of the aircraft (or with external fuel tanks) is 1,000km.
6. The turn time at an altitude of 1000 m is 16-18s.
7. The length of the run-up is not more than 200m.
8. The length of the run using flaps and brakes is 150m.

IV. Aircraft armament
A. Small arms
1. Two 12.7mm BS machine guns synchronization gear mounted on the fuselage and firing through a screw with a stock of 250 rounds each.
2. Two 7.62mm ShKAS machine guns synchronization gear, with a reserve of 100 rounds for each machine gun.

B. Bomb weapons
1. Two holders for the suspension of bombs Der-31 or two holders for the suspension of bombs Der-32 with grips outside the area swept by the screw.
2. The mechanism of emergency dropping of bombs.[3]

When developing these requirements, the specialists of the Red Army Air Force Research Institute tried to take into account the experience of analyzing the main characteristics of foreign aircraft of the class, primarily the parameters of carefully studied German fighters. However, the management of the Research Institute showed considerable imagination,

3 RGANTD (Samara branch) Foundation P-217, Inventory 3-1, Case 65.

trying to implement in the requirements the concept of a universal aircraft that is impossible in practice, suitable for performing a large number of combat missions. Well aware of the weaknesses of Soviet aviation, the military wanted to have a high-speed high-altitude fighter capable of not only destroying enemy aircraft, but also acting as a ground-attack aircraft and a light bomber. A key indicator of the sweet fantasies of the military was the maximum speed of 650km/h specified in the requirements for the fighter of the 'New Type'. Thus, the specialists of the Red Army Air Force Research Institute completely ignored the capabilities of the Soviet aviation industry for the production of such high-speed aircraft. In 1939 the speed of serial I-16 fighters of the latest modifications did not exceed 400km/h.

The dreams of the Soviet military about the 'wonder fighter' extended to the armament of the future aircraft. Although aircraft guns were mentioned in the general parameters, only two large-calibre and two small-calibre synchronized machine guns were specified when specifying the requirements. This set of weapons corresponded to a fighter with an air-cooled radial engine. Thus, in the summer of 1939, the military assumed that instead of the outdated 'Rat' (I-16), a modified version of the 'Super Rat' (I-180) of the Nikolai Polikarpov design would be adopted by the Red Army Air Force. The fact that Stalin had already chosen a different design for the new fighter and that he had other contenders for the vacant post

Test pilots of the Red Army Air Force Research Institute.

of 'King of Fighters', the military did not yet know. In addition, the only 20mm ShVAK gun created by 1939 existed only as an experimental sample.

Trying to combine their fantasies with Stalin's ambitions, the specialists of the Red Army Air Force Research Institute perceived the parameters of a fighter that paradoxically combined mutually exclusive characteristics. Since it is difficult to imagine that this document could have been adopted without the consent of Stalin, it can be assumed that the unrealistic demands of the military were acceptable to the 'Red Tsar'. He expected the Soviet aviation industry to eliminate quickly the capability gap with the Germans and considered the fantastic requirements of the Red Army Air Force to be key to another technical breakthrough in the Soviet aircraft industry. Thus, the unrealistic and contradictory requirements of the military, combined with the weakness of the aviation industry, the lack of qualified workers and the general low technical culture, doomed the ambitious programme of updating the Stalinist air force to failure in advance.

Filin vs Stalin

Based on the importance and scope of powers, the personality of the head of the Red Army Air Force Research Institute played a great role in determining the development strategy of the Soviet Air Force. In 1937, Divengineer (approximately Major General) Alexander Filin the son of a railway conductor, was appointed to the position, replacing the son of a high-ranking tsarist official Komdiv (approximately Major General) Nikolai Bazhanov. Bazhanov was executed by order of Stalin on 15 September 1938. The new Head of the Research Institute, in addition to a high level of competence, was distinguished by independence and critical thinking. However, high intellectual abilities did not prevent Alexander Filin from being a typical representative of the Stalin era. A fanatical Bolshevik, he believed in the advantages of the Soviet regime and was convinced that all the chronic vices of Soviet aviation could be overcome through the strictest control and discipline. It was these qualities of the young head of the Research Institute that for a long time aroused the sympathy of the sadistic Stalin. A strict, super-demanding character combined with manic activity made Alexander Filin an informal leader of the Soviet Air Force. In fact, it was the disciplined fanatic Filin, and not a passive hostage of Stalin, Colonel General Aleksander Loktionov, who determined the strategy and tactics of the development of the Red Army Air Force at the end of the 1930s. Being an experienced test pilot, the new head of the Research Institute knew very well the main disadvantages of the extremely unstable I-16 in flight, which killed a huge number of Soviet pilots. The idealist Filin, when creating a new generation of Soviet fighters, tried his best to avoid repeating the deadly vices of fighters of the 'Old Type'. This position as head of the Research Institute aggravated the already deadlocked situation with state tests and the deployment of mass production of a new generation of Stalin's fighters. His uncompromising struggle to fulfill the impossible requirements of the Red Army Air Force Research Institute led him to an acute conflict with Stalin's influential aircraft designers and plant managers. In the end, Filin's ambitions for a monopoly in determining the development strategy of Soviet aviation led him into an open confrontation with Stalin. Such a turn of events suggested a tragic outcome. The 'Red Lord' was in a hurry to get a new 'wonder weapon' and could not stand the obvious opposition to the implementation of his plans.

Strategic disinformation from General Petrov

June 1940. Moscow region. Kuntsevo Dacha (Stalin's country residence).

A large black car drove up to the checkpoint, from which three people got out: a tall, Stalinist favourite, Secretary of the Communist Party of the Soviet Union (Stalin's deputy in the party) Georgy Malenkov, People's Commissar of Aviation Industry, a young, slender, handsome Aleksey Shakhurin and a stately General Ivan Petrov. After a thorough search by strict security, all three visitors were taken to Stalin's office where the 'Red Lord' was waiting impatiently for them. From Malenkov's preliminary phone call, he knew about the subject of the upcoming unpleasant conversation. It was about the results of the analysis of information about the development of the German aviation industry, collected during the numerous trips of the Soviet delegation to Germany from October 1939 to May 1940.

The signing of the Molotov-Ribbentrop Pact in Moscow on 23 August 1939 opened up completely new opportunities for secretly studying the potential of the German aviation industry. Stalin, confident that he had outplayed Hitler, considered this agreement as an opportunity to purchase the latest German aviation technologies and samples of aviation equipment to create new types of Soviet combat aircraft. Such co-operation with the Nazis was especially relevant against the background of the 'moral embargo' (a ban on the sale of aviation technologies to the USSR) imposed in

General Ivan Petrov.

November 1939 by the US government in response to the Red Army attack on Finland. In addition, Stalin, who trusted no one at all, decided to test his fears about the weakness of Soviet aviation. During the preparations for the invasion of Europe, the 'Red Tsar' was very worried about the state of aviation, which, in his opinion, was to play an important role in the future success of the Red Army.

Although the delegation officially included purely civilian specialists – leading aircraft designers and specialists in the organization of production – a considerable number of the people sent to Germany were representatives of the military and NKVD agents. However, due to the fact that the 'Red Lord' did not trust even his special services, he preferred to duplicate the work of intelligence with his own agents. Moreover, the suspicious Stalin personally engaged in the selection and preparation of candidates for a trip to Germany. Each member of the delegation received a personal task from the 'Red Tsar', but the degree of importance of the instructions depended on Stalin's personal sympathy.

Forced to accept the need to send competent, but insufficiently reliable aircraft designers of the old generation to Germany, he limited himself to issuing them only general wishes within the framework of the official goals of the Soviet delegation. Only the closest and most trustworthy agents were assigned important tasks by the 'Red Lord', which clearly went far beyond the official trade agreement with Germany. One of Stalin's main agents was Brigade Engineer (Colonel) Ivan Petrov, who was personally given a secret task to assess the potential of the German aviation industry. In addition to collecting and analyzing information about the state of German industry, Petrov had to fulfill Stalin's espionage assignment – to determine the maximum number of combat aircraft that German industrial enterprises were able to produce per day. The 'Red Lord' reasonably considered Germany to be the main potential enemy that the Red Army would have to face when implementing its grandiose aggressive plans. Thus, information about the power of German industry was of crucial strategic importance in the preparation of Stalin's invasion of Europe.

The reasons for choosing the 'Master', the narrow-minded Petrov, and not the brilliantly educated and competent aircraft designer Nikolai Polikarpov, as the main agent are quite understandable. The peasant's son Ivan Petrov, who received only primary education as a child, and later became a test pilot, met fully the expectations of the 'wisest of the wise'. The complete loyalty and absence of doubts of the red spy in the genius of the 'Father of Nations' were supposed to compensate for the lack of intelligence and lack of the necessary competence in aviation.

Upon arrival in Germany, Ivan Petrov, flattered by Stalin's attention, took up the case with his usual stupid fanaticism and manic obsession. During several business trips, he visited 219 German aviation industry units, including almost all aircraft factories. At the same time, Petrov, who perceived his mission as a heroic act, later claimed in his memoirs that a Gestapo officer was following him literally from the moment he crossed the Soviet-German border. Most likely, such close attention of the Nazi special services to the members of the Soviet delegation was a clear exaggeration. Petrov, accustomed to the atmosphere of Stalinist total surveillance and denunciation, could not imagine that the Germans could ignore such an important 'spy' as him.

The official documents of the members of the Soviet delegation were prepared according to the same idiotic stereotype of total secrecy. The naive Stalinist special services took special measures to camouflage the true mission of Stalin's agents hiding under the mask of Soviet aviation specialists. According to the legend indicated in Petrov's passport, he was an engineer at the Central Aerohydrodynamic Institute (TsAGI). However, this whole idiotic masquerade turned out to be completely unnecessary. The Germans, convinced of the total superiority of German technologies and the equally total backwardness of the Russians, did not attach much importance to the obvious espionage interests of the Russians. They scrupulously fulfilled the agreement on the unhindered admission of Soviet specialists to all the places they requested. The Russian 'specialists' could not hide their surprise at German progress and with their ridiculous confused appearance and constant stupid questions caused a smile and a sense of intellectual superiority among German specialists. The Germans, while maintaining an outwardly quite respectful tone, treated the Russians like children, constantly telling them half-truths, and sowing confusion.

Not understanding the reasons for the German carelessness, Ivan Petrov was completely discouraged and was in constant anxiety and doubts, expecting early exposure and arrest by the German special services. He was

Meeting of the Soviet delegation at the Heinkel Flugzeugwerke airfield in Rostock.

sincerely convinced that the Germans were constantly deceiving the Soviet delegation by showing outdated aircraft models, and carefully hiding promising military aircraft. However, the reality turned out to be more complex than the primitive picture formed in the head of Stalin's main agent.

The only way that allowed Petrov to distract himself from fear was the processing of the extracted 'information', which was directly or indirectly related to determining the production capacity of the German aviation industry. In this 'work' he was assisted by several equally narrow-minded and suspicious assistants from among the Soviet delegation. In the evenings, locked up in a hotel, sometimes staying up late at night, Stalin's agents compared and re-checked information about German industrial capacity to produce aircraft. With each such sleepless night, the production figures of German military aircraft grew steadily. Completely confused by the Germans, who, on Göring's orders, showed them the same aeroplanes several times, the naive Stalinist agents summed up the data each time. In the end, they received absolutely fantastic figures of German aircraft production.

The last 'proof' of the incredible power of the German aviation industry was the meeting of Stalin's spies with the main bully, Luftwaffe Chief of Procurement and Supply for the Luftwaffe Generaloberst Ernst Udet. This carefree adventurer, after another solid dose of alcohol, was happy to make the Russians another victim of his empty chatter. The famous ace of the First World War, dressed in a beautiful uniform, made an indelible impression on Stalin's secret agents. At the same time, it turned out that the sympathy of the representatives of the two totalitarian regimes was mutual. The idler Udet liked the Russian 'engineers' so much, looking into his mouth with delight and catching his every word, that after an official reception at the *Reichsluftfahrtministerium* (RLM), he twice 'talked' with Stalin's agents in his own apartment. At the same time, Göring's best friend, without knowing it, brilliantly fulfilled his role in totally disinforming the Stalinist special services. Sensing the alarming interest of the narrow-minded Russians in determining the production capacity of German aviation industry, he, in his characteristic pathological manner, spun incredible tall tales to his guests. At the end of the conversation, Udet, flushed with alcohol, casually confirmed the fantastic figures of the daily production of military aircraft at industrial enterprises in Germany. And he did it with such a confident look that the narrow-minded Russian agents, with only elementary education, amazed by the unexpected 'revelations' of a high-ranking Luftwaffe official, believed every word of the pathological liar and alcoholic Udet. Thus, after Ivan Petrov's 'confidential' conversations with Göring's closest friend, his opinion about the extraordinary power of the Luftwaffe received 'official' confirmation from the *Reichsluftfahrtministerium* (RLM) itself.

After returning from Germany, Ivan Petrov prepared a special secret report, which was based on 'information' obtained from the results of personal 'observations' and confirmed by 'reliable' German sources. However, in accordance with the accepted procedure, in order to get to Stalin, the Petrov dossier needed to be checked and approved by at least two lower-level bureaucratic tiers. Initially, this 'most accurate' information about the capacity of the German aviation industry, reported at a meeting of the People's Commissariat of Aviation Industry of the USSR (Ministry), caused surprise, and even outright ridicule from the Commissariat's specialists. A special scepticism about the indicators of the number of units of daily production of German combat aircraft calculated by Petrov was expressed by the new People's Commissar of Aviation Industry, Aleksey Shakhurin. Such a 'not serious' attitude to the results of extremely risky work greatly offended the main Stalinist spy and forced him to turn to a person more 'competent' in matters of the aviation industry. This 'specialist' was Stalin's favourite Georgy Malenkov, who, by personal order of the 'Master', oversaw the Soviet aviation industry. Stalin's agent, turning to Malenkov, was not mistaken in his expectations. The fantastic report received a completely different assessment from a devoted Stalinist servant. Although Stalin's chief 'specialist' on Red Army Air Force matters, Georgy Malenkov was an absolute layman in aviation, he knew the character of his boss perfectly well and guessed accurately his reaction to the appearance of such a 'sensational' document.

Now General Ivan Petrov, in a voice trembling with excitement, reported to Stalin about the daily production of seventy to eighty combat aircraft by German industry. In conclusion, he noted that, taking into account the use of aircraft factories in Poland, Czecho-Slovakia, France and the Netherlands occupied by the Germans, the production rate would be at least 30,000 military aircraft per year or 100 aircraft per day. At the utterance of these figures, Petrov's palms, clutching the folder with the report prepared for Stalin, began to sweat treacherously. Now his life was hanging by a thread. The 'Red Lord' could well suspect Petrov of having ties with the Germans after many trips to Germany. The slightest doubt in Stalin's mind was enough for everyone who signed the report praising the power of the German aviation industry to be immediately arrested and, after excruciating torture, shot in the basements of the NKVD. However, the 'Red Lord', despite his anxiety, had not yet understood what those fantastic numbers meant. Stalin wanted to know the details, which meant that the conversation, like the life of Petrov, continued. The 'Red Tsar' began to ask Petrov questions about the sources of the information and about the method of conducting calculations. The general, pale with fear, answered the questions of the 'wisest of the wise' in a confused manner, constantly looking at his folder, which contained saving arguments proving the 'reliability' of the information.

Then Stalin turned to People's Commissar of Aviation Industry Shakhurin with the expected question: 'How many military aircraft does the Soviet Aviation Industry produce per day?'

Shakhurin quickly replied: 'Twenty-six units per day, including training aircraft.'

The 'Red Lord' said softly, 'So it's twenty-six versus eighty?'

Stalin took the folder with the documents from the trembling speaker and began to walk up and down the office in silence, as was his custom. Overwhelmed by such an indefinite reaction, the visitors froze in horror, standing at attention. Finally, Stalin stopped his anxious movements around the office, sat down at the table and, as if forgetting about those present, began to carefully read the material of the Petrov report.

Several anxious minutes passed. Stalin finished reading, closed the folder with the report, got up from the table, approached Malenkov and said in a low voice: 'We need to expand our aviation industry to this number of combat aircraft – seventy to eighty aircraft per day.'[4] None of those present

4 Petrov, I.F., 'I consider it my duty to tell you. The war began before the war', *Inventor and innovator*, 1986, No. 4, pp. 28-30, 34.

dared object to Stalin, who clearly believed in the fantastic figures from the secret Petrov report. The author of the report himself breathed a sigh of relief, realizing that today he would come out of Stalin's terrible office alive.

People's Comissar of Aviation Industry, Aleksey Shakhurin.

Just two weeks after the events described, General Ivan Petrov was waiting for a pleasant surprise. The 'Red Lord' did not forget to thank his most 'reliable' agent. On 10 June 1940, Major General Petrov, under the patronage of Stalin, took the high position of head of the Central Aerohydrodynamic Institute (TsAGI). This happened despite the fact that, in May 1940, at a meeting of the TsAGI workers activists, the majority of those present had the courage(!) to speak out against the appointment of this blatantly incompetent and simply stupid person as the head of the scientific institute.

The race under the lash of Stalin

The 'information' that Soviet agents brought from Germany clearly reflects the degree of degradation of the professional level of military specialists and representatives of Stalin's special services. The situation was aggravated by the atmosphere of general fear that had developed at all levels of management of Soviet aviation. At the end of the 1930s, in the USSR, everyone who had critical thinking and the courage to express their own opinion was either destroyed or rotted in the Gulag camps. It was this factor that prevented a critical attitude to the fantastically exaggerated data on the capacity of German aviation industry. The only person in the Soviet Union who decided what to believe and what to question was the 'Great' Stalin.

The reason why the extremely suspicious and distrustful 'wisest of the wise' did not doubt for a moment the delusional information of General Petrov is obvious. To some extent, Stalin, being a classic paranoid, was even happy to confirm his pathological fears. The image of the Soviet aviation industry, entangled in the sinister web of 'enemies of the people', formed in the pathological consciousness of a psychopath, thanks to Petrov's report once again received 'objective' confirmation. It was precisely this 'truth' that Bolshevik propaganda daily instilled in the submissive population. Numerous executions and repressions that had taken thousands of aviation industry specialists to their graves now seemed justified. The responsibility for the deepest crisis and total shortcomings of the Soviet aviation industry, which became a consequence of the vicious management of Stalin and his closest servants, now 'justifiably' fell on the shoulders of the exposed 'enemies of the people'. Moreover, it was precisely in the conditions of the collapse of the aviation industry that Stalin appeared to the Soviet people as a kind of 'saviour'. He was the only one who noticed the glaring problem of this important industry and did everything possible to solve it as soon as possible.

However, in addition to joy and conviction in his 'rightness', Petrov's gloomy report still caused Stalin a panic attack. The already manic activity of the 'Red Tsar', expressed in petty and rude interference in the affairs of the Soviet aviation industry, multiplied many times. Stalin was so concerned about the catastrophic 'lag' of the aviation industry that, in addition to endless bureaucratic meetings, he decided to visit aviation plants. Soon, accompanied by People's Commissar of Aviation Industry Aleksey Shakhurin the 'Red Lord' made several inspection trips to the largest aviation plants in Moscow and the Moscow region.[5] It was Stalin's irrational fears that made the main contribution to the creation of an unbearable atmosphere of haste and confusion that permanently accompanied the extremely ambitious programme of re-equipping the Red Army Air Force with fighters of the 'New Type'. Another factor that influenced the final result was the contradictory requirements of the military, the impossibility of fulfilling which constantly provoked an acute conflict between the Red Army Air Force Research Institute and the younger generation of Stalinist aircraft designers and production organizers.

Thus, the period 1939-1941 was the time of another tragic 'Great Break' in the history of the Red Army Air Force, which became one of the main reasons for the almost complete destruction of Soviet fighter aviation by Luftwaffe aircraft in 1941.

5 Shakhurin, A I., *Wings of Victory. Memoirs*, Moscow, Politizdat, 1990, pp. 102, 104–6.

Chapter 4

LaGG-3 – 'Flying log' or 'shadow' Bf 109

'The Three Musketeers'

January 1939. Moscow. Reception of People's Commissar of Aviation Industry Mikhail Kaganovich.

Several visitors were sitting on chairs waiting for an invitation to the office of People's Comissar, with briefcases tightly stuffed with important papers. Two of them were future aircraft designers of the new LaGG-3 fighter. Semyon Lavochkin, a subordinate of Vladimir Gorbunov, had documents with sketches of the future fighter and a sample of innovative material – 'delta wood' – in his briefcase. Finally, after a long wait, they were invited to the office of the chief. However, not two but three young aviation specialists entered the People's Commissar's office. This third was Mikhail Gudkov, senior engineer of the Main Department of People's Commissariat of Aviation Industry of the USSR, another subordinate of Vladimir Gorbunov. Tired of waiting for an audience with the People's Commissar for a long time, Gudkov, without heeding the objections of his boss, also followed Gorbunov and Lavochkin and accidentally became a participant in the presentation of the project of a new wooden fighter to the People's Commissar.

The owner of the office, Mikhail Kaganovich, a talkative lover of rude jokes, noisily greeted Vladimir Gorbunov, who was pleasant to him. The People's Comissar reacted with interest to his offer to tell him about the work that Gorbunov and Lavochkin had prepared secretly for six months. Lavochkin took out the drawings and a piece of 'delta wood' from his briefcase and spread them out on a huge table. Using all his eloquence, he explained as simply as possible to the narrowminded People's Commissar the idea of creating a wooden fighter armed with a cannon and four machine guns. Semyon Lavochkin paid special attention to the great potential of the fighter

Aircraft designer Vladimir Gorbunov.

for mass production. The design of the aircraft was made of affordable and easy-to-process wood. The attention of the childishly emotional Mikhail Kaganovich was attracted by the use of innovative material 'delta wood' in the production of the aircraft. The new structural material made it possible to replace steel, the welding of which required special equipment and highly-qualified workers, in the manufacture of spars for the wing centre section and removable wing consoles.

Charmed by the speaker's skill, Kaganovich fully approved the initial design of the new fighter and promised assistance in obtaining state funding for the project. Further, confident that Mikhail Gudkov was also working on the project, Kaganovich 'blessed' all three of those present to continue working. Inspired by the success, the young officials left the office and immediately exchanged impressions of the meeting with People's Commissar in the reception room. Gudkov, also impressed by the design of the aircraft, and having already forgotten for what reason he originally wanted to meet with Mikhail Kaganovich, asked his colleagues to accept him into the development team of the fighter. Gorbunov, interested in increasing the number of people involved in this informal work, agreed. So, quite by chance, the duo of young engineers became the Lavochkin-Gorbunov-Gudkov triumvirate. Later, the official name of the LaGG-3 fighter was formed from the initial letters of their surnames. Subsequently, for the funny habit of appearing at all official events exclusively with three young ambitious aircraft designers, they received the nickname 'The Three Musketeers' from their competitors, who had a caustic sense of humour.

Stalin's New 'Toys'

Stalin's disappointment in Nikolai Polikarpov gave a chance to a new generation of Soviet aircraft designers, who were on average ten years younger than the former 'King of Fighters'. Soon the most successful representatives of the 'youth' stood out from their environment: Alexander Yakovlev, Semyon Lavochkin and Artyom Mikoyan. The fanatical 'Red Lord' considered them to be real Soviet aircraft designers, unlike the older generation, who were inherited by the Soviet regime from the Russian Empire.

Stalin favoured the new generation for many reasons. A significant age difference allowed the 60-year-old 'Red Tsar' to psychologically treat the aircraft designers of the new generation as sons. Stalin was sometimes so carried away by his role as a father that he allowed a soft paternal tone in communicating with young aircraft designers, which was completely excluded in strictly official communication with aircraft designers of the older generation. The 'Red Lord' surrounded them with paternal care but, being a native of the Caucasus, who grew up in an archaic patriarchy, demanded unquestioning obedience from them. In addition, it should be borne in mind that Stalin was an evil and suspicious psychopath and these characteristics extended to his paternal qualities. As the tragic fate of his two native sons showed, playing the role of the 'son' of the 'Great Leader' was deadly dangerous.

Another important factor in the change of the generation of Stalin's aircraft designers was their social status and level of education. Stalin, being the son of a shoemaker, always favoured people from the social stratum of peasants and workers. It was precisely these people, to whom the Bolshevik regime opened up opportunities for self-realization, that Stalin considered the most loyal to his power. The 'Red Tsar' was very sceptical about studying at university, believing that it can be easily replaced by self-education. In such philistine views, he was very similar to his heartfelt friend Adolf Hitler. The older generation of Soviet aircraft designers, who were educated in tsarist institutes and colleges, like Tupolev, Petlyakov and Polikarpov, were psychologically distant and incomprehensible to the intellectually limited 'Father of Nations'.

Tandem of losers

A huge number of bureaucratic structures and positions were created in the Soviet Union to manage and control the aviation industry, which was developing at an incredible pace. They were occupied by yesterday's immigrants, peasants and workers, who under Stalin became a new generation of Soviet engineers and officials. Thus, the Stalinist bureaucratic system gave birth to a whole layer of young specialists, many of whom compensated for their gaps in education and lack of abilities by believing in the incredible possibilities of the Soviet system. It was to this layer of enthusiasts that the two future fathers of the new LaGG-3 fighter belonged: Vladimir Gorbunov and Semyon Lavochkin.

Each of them had different abilities and different levels of competence, but they were united by an incredible desire for success. The Stalinist bureaucratic swamp in which they got bogged down did not give any chances for the realization of their great opportunities. However, despite all the circumstances, it was young officials Gorbunov and Lavochkin who became the creators of a new fighter and overtook in this race not only young aircraft designers Mikhail Pashinin, Alexander Silvansky and others but also venerable representatives of the older generation Nikolai Polikarpov, Pavel Sukhoi and Vladimir Yatsenko. The answer to the question about the reasons for their victory lies in getting acquainted with their biography.

'We were born to make a fairy tale come true ... .'[1]

Vladimir Gorbunov and Semyon Lavochkin (real name Simon Magaziner) came from the lowest social strata of the Russian Empire. Gorbunov was born in 1903 in a village near Moscow into a very poor Russian peasant family. Lavochkin was born in 1900 in Smolensk into the poor family of a Jewish school teacher. This is where the similarity of the biographies of the two future creators of the LaGG-3 ends. However, it was the complete opposite of their characters that allowed them to win in a fierce competition for the creation of Stalin's fighter of the 'New Type'.

The relationships in the families of future aircraft designers were also fundamentally different. Semyon Lavochkin was the eldest son and the hope of his parents. Democratic relations were maintained in the family; children were brought up with a special attitude to education and culture. Despite his poverty, Semyon had his own small room with a desk, a bed and, most importantly, shelves filled with books. The head of the family did not suppress his talented son but, on the contrary, created maximum

1 The first line of the song of the 1930s, praising 'Stalin's Falcons'.

opportunities for the training and development of the future Soviet aircraft designer.

Aircraft designer Semyon Lavochkin.

The traditional patriarchy reigned in the family of Vladimir Gorbunov. The second son could not claim a high place in the family hierarchy, being in the full power of his father and older brother. However, it was this subordinate position that paradoxically contributed to the brilliant career of the future aviation engineer. The main role in Vladimir's professional life was played by his older brother Sergey. It was following the example of his brother, after graduating from *Realschule* (a type of secondary school) that Vladimir Gorbunov found himself in aviation and became an instructor pilot.

Then, also under the patronage of his brother, who by that time had become a major organizer of the Soviet aviation industry, he entered the Moscow Aviation Institute, from which he graduated in 1931. After receiving a diploma of higher education, Vladimir Gorbunov worked at the Tupolev Design Bureau. He took part in the development of drawings and the introduction into mass production of the Tupolev TB-3 and SB bombers and R-6 reconnaissance aircraft. Even the death of his older brother in a plane crash in 1933 could not stop the rapid administrative career of the future creator of the LaGG-3. In 1937, when many vacancies appeared in the Soviet aviation industry after a wave of shootings, Vladimir Gorbunov was appointed head of the aircraft department of the Main Department of Aviation Industry People's Commissariat of the Defence Industry of the Soviet Union. In January 1939, after the creation of the People's Commissariat of Aviation Industry of the USSR (Ministry), Gorbunov was transferred to the position of Head of the 4th Department of the 1st Main Department of the People's Commissariat of Aviation Industry of the USSR.

Semyon Lavochkin's path to aviation was fundamentally different and had features similar to the professional development of Nikolai Polikarpov. Since childhood, Semyon had demonstrated high intellectual abilities and phenomenal motivation to acquire new knowledge. Those qualities allowed him to repeatedly overcome the incredible difficulties that accompanied him on the way to professional success. Life in Russia throughout the twentieth century was a real test for any talented person striving for self-development. The first of the many crises that Lavochkin overcame during his long life was admission to the gymnasium. At that time, only a small percentage of the population could get an elite gymnasium education. Moreover, at the beginning of the twentieth century, anti-Semitic sentiments intensified in the archaic Russian Empire. According to the state rules, the number of Jews studying at the gymnasium should not exceed five per cent. Thus, Lavochkin's faith reduced the probability of entering the gymnasium to almost zero. However, Semyon was not only able to become one of the few who passed a strict selection and received the right to study, but also graduated from the gymnasium in the city of Kursk with a gold medal. Thus, on his own, with only some support from his family, he overcame even greater difficulties on the way to getting an education than his senior colleague Nikolai Polikarpov. The revolution of 1917 and subsequent service in the Red Army again created huge problems

Joseph Stalin and his younger son Vasily, behind whom stands the head of Stalin's personal security, Nikolai Vlasik, in 1935.

on the way to professional development and delayed Lavochkin's higher education for three years.

In 1920 the future aircraft designer entered the Moscow Higher Technical School, deliberately choosing an aerodynamic specialty. However, instead of training and long-awaited professional development, Semyon Lavochkin was expecting severe domestic difficulties and hunger. The Bolsheviks, seeking to keep power in their hands at any cost and implement their inhuman ideas, artificially created a terrible economic crisis in Russia. In their first years of 'education' Semyon Lavochkin and his fellow students had not so much to study as to wander around the Moscow region and exchange their belongings for any products from the peasants in order not to die of hunger. To ensure their existence, the half-starved students of Moscow Higher Technical School took on any, even the hardest, work. However, despite the constant threat of death from starvation and living in unheated rooms in winter, training classes at Moscow Higher Technical School continued. Under the guidance of professors pale from malnutrition, students with extraordinary enthusiasm designed and built their first aircraft from the most primitive materials.

A more favourable period for studying came after 1922 when the fanatic Vladimir Lenin temporarily changed course to create a strictly state economy and allowed small private entrepreneurship. The money abolished by the Bolsheviks re-appeared, and the economic situation of Red Russia began to improve at a fairly rapid pace. A few short years of weakening of the Bolshevik tyranny, which passed between the death of Lenin and the complete concentration of power in the hands of Stalin, contributed to the real dawn of science and culture. At that time, Lavochkin, who came from an educated background, actively participated in the cultural life of Moscow, visited theatres and went to concerts.

Due to the economic crisis, Semyon Lavochkin's studies at the Moscow Higher Technical School lasted for a very long time. However, due to the high motivation to study and the presence of highly professional professors, the level of training of a talented student was very high. After completing the theoretical course in 1927, Lavochkin was sent for an internship at the Tupolev Design Bureau to gain practical skills. After passing the initial period, the young engineer began working in the serial design department of the design bureau, dealing with the strength elements of the main components of the aircraft's structure. At that time, the first Soviet TB-1 bomber, created by Tupolev Design Bureau engineers, was being introduced into mass production at Aviation Plant No. 22 (Moscow).

Student of Moscow Higher Technical School, Semyon Lavochkin.

In 1929 Semyon Lavochkin defended his diploma and received the qualification of aeromechanical engineer. Then he went to work in the design bureau of aircraft designers Paul Aimé Richard and Henri Laville at the invitation of the Bolsheviks. At the Richard Design Bureau, Lavochkin supervised all calculations (aerodynamic and strength) and, later, at the Laville Design Bureau he gained experience in designing aircraft. The young aircraft designer not only quickly mastered the translation of technical texts from French but was soon able to talk with French colleagues without an interpreter. Hardworking Lavochkin devoted all his free time to his favourite business. In the evenings, after a long day of work, the future creator of LaGG-3 independently improved his competence. Based on the analysis of various publications of periodical literature, books and reference books, he studied the main trends in world aircraft construction. At the same time, despite the responsible work, Semyon Lavochkin's salary was very modest. He received about a tenth of what Henri Laville and other foreigners were paid for the same work. To provide for the family, the young aircraft designer had to look for an additional evening job. Fortunately, this work was connected with the design of experimental aircraft, and Lavochkin, in addition to modest fees, had a further opportunity for professional growth. The co-operation of the USSR with the French aircraft designers did not bring any practical result in the form of serial production of an aircraft. Nevertheless, interaction with representatives of the European school of aircraft engineering allowed many novice Soviet aircraft designers to gain valuable experience.

Throughout the 1930s the young aircraft designer participated in the implementation of many experimental projects for the creation of various types of aircraft, including fighters. However, Semyon Lavochkin was never able to fully realize his potential and found himself in a dead end, without a job and with no means of livelihood. The only consolation for the young aircraft designer was that he remained at large and was not shot, unlike many of those with whom he had recently worked. In this difficult situation, Semyon Lavochkin was saved by his teacher Andrey Tupolev, who got him a

Tupolev TB-1 bomber.

job in the Main Department of Aviation Industry People's Commissariat of the Defence Industry of the Soviet Union. It was there that Lavochkin met Vladimir Gorbunov, who at that time was his boss.

However, in 1938, the situation began to change. The hysteria and fear that seized Stalin, who felt the total lag of Soviet aviation, resulted in a feverish race to create a fighter of the 'New Type'. The main condition for completing the urgent task set by the 'Red Tsar' was an extremely short time for the development and launch of the aircraft into mass production. Theoretically, all aircraft design bureaux, of which there were twenty-six in 1938, could take part in the competition to create a fighter of the 'New Type'. However, in fact, only the most experienced aircraft designers, like Nikolai Polikarpov, Sergey Ilyushin or Pavel Sukhoi had a real chance to create a prototype of a new fighter. Only they had sufficient human and material resources for such a complex work.

Thus, the young losers who had been stuck in bureaucratic positions and were dying of boredom still had no hopes for the implementation of their ambitious plans.

Initiative from below

Around the middle of 1938, when Nikolai Polikarpov was feverishly working on the 'Super Rat' (I-180), the head of the department, Vladimir Gorbunov, called his subordinate Lavochkin to his office and directly suggested that he create a new fighter like the German Bf 109. He justified his idea with a favourable moment. Gorbunov, who was present at all the meetings, was well aware of Stalin's dissatisfaction with the results of air battles in Spain and of the 'Red Lord's' desire to create a new generation of fighters. In addition, both the future chief designers of the LaGG-3 knew about the characteristics of the promising Klimov M-105 engine, a further development of the Hispano-Suiza 12Y engine, for which the Bolsheviks had bought a production licence from the French. Semyon Lavochkin, who was languishing from stupid bureaucratic work, gladly agreed with the proposal of his boss. By the end of the conversation, the partners, who had an ideal psychological compatibility, shared the responsibilities for implementing their idea. Experienced aircraft designer Semyon Lavochkin would design the fighter, and experienced aviation official Vladimir Gorbunov would promote it to receive state funding. However, the most difficult factor was the problem of the initial personnel and financial support for their start up. Both experienced aviation officials knew perfectly well how design bureaux worked in the USSR. To present the idea to the People's Commissariat of Aviation Industry of the USSR, an initial project was needed, which, in addition to a general description of the design, had to contain calculations of many characteristics of the future aircraft. To develop an aircraft project, it is necessary to have an equipped room where qualified engineers will work and appropriate funding to pay them. Naturally, in a country where private entrepreneurship and private property were completely destroyed, the only source of money for working on an aeroplane and hiring qualified engineers was the state. However, the head of the department, Gorbunov, and

Klimov M-105 aircraft engine.

his employee Lavochkin did not have a design bureau. Moreover, all their entourage and superiors knew them as middle-level aviation bureaucrats and did not suspect at all that they had the ambitions of chief aircraft designers. Since the decision to design a new fighter was their exclusively personal initiative, they could only rely on their own modest forces.

However, the straightforward Vladimir Gorbunov found the simplest solution to this complex problem. He took advantage of his official position and habitually violated all the bureaucratic rules and job descriptions. Gorbunov released his subordinate Lavochkin from all the work assigned to him by his position and allocated him a small office for designing a new fighter. Lavochkin's only assistant was a female secretary who typed texts on the project. Then Gorbunov committed another official crime and provided Lavochkin with secret drawings of the Hispano-Suiza 12Y engine, which was supposed to be installed on the future high-speed fighter. Work on the project began immediately and was carried out in secret, hidden from the management and other employees of Gorbunov.

To an outside observer, the idea of designing a fighter by one person looked completely delusional. Tens of thousands of man-hours are needed by a single aircraft designer to calculate all the parameters of the future aircraft. For example, in 1939, the Polikarpov Design Bureau employed more than 500 people. This large team of qualified specialists was divided into working groups. Each of these groups of engineers, in accordance with their specialization, was engaged in solving the problems of strength, aerodynamics and other key characteristics of the future aircraft. The more modest design bureaux of the less well-known Soviet aircraft designers numbered up to 100 engineers, and the principle of division into working groups was the same. However, as life has shown, Vladimir Gorbunov's bold decision to make a preliminary design of the aircraft by one person turned out to be correct. The indefatigable and experienced Semyon Lavochkin, who was used to sitting at calculations for sixteen hours a day, was able to implement the crazy idea of the two companions alone.

The main advantage of young adventurists is the innovative 'delta wood'

When determining the initial design of the new fighter, in addition to the Klimov M-105 (Hispano-Suiza 12Y) engine which, in its characteristics and design, was similar to the V-shaped engine of the German Bf 109, the

Workers at one of the Soviet Aviation Industry plants.

companions faced the problem of choosing a structural material for the airframe manufacture. Designing the most advanced all-metal fighter did not make sense, since in the Soviet Union in the 1930s there was a complete shortage of aluminium. Stalin, knowing about this problem, decided to build only multi-engine bombers out of metal. Single-engine compact fighters were to be made of wood with little use of aluminium, steel and other materials. Soviet engineers believed that, unlike bombers, the strength characteristics of wood, although at the limit, still allowed the building of fairly light fighters. Thus, the question of what material to build the future LaGG-3 from was not relevant for Gorbunov and Lavochkin. However, the companions were concerned about the problem of ensuring the strength of the main components of the wooden high-speed fighter. Until 1938 the only solution to this problem in the USSR, introduced by Nikolai Polikarpov, was the use of wing centre section and wing elements made of steel alloy. But even this version of ensuring the strength of the structure, mastered in the production of the I-16, had disadvantages. Welding of steel elements required skilled workers and sophisticated equipment.

An original solution to the problem of the strength of the most important nodes was proposed by Semyon Lavochkin. Working under the guidance of invited French aircraft designers, he gained extensive experience in creating solid-wood aircraft. After that, he became an ardent supporter of the manufacture of fighters from wood and materials based on it. Lavochkin believed that the advantages of this affordable material were underestimated to any proper extent. In addition, the future creator of the LaGG-3 was one of the first Soviet aircraft designers who participated in the design of objects using new composite materials based on wood. In 1935 Semyon Lavochkin had received a position in the Chief Directorate of the Northern Sea Route, where, together with the designer Oskar Kaplur, he engaged in the construction of high-speed gliders made of Kaplyurit, a composite material consisting of plywood reinforced with internal steel mesh.

In the same year, Soviet aircraft engineer Leonty Ryzhkov developed the 'delta wood' production technology at the Karbolit plant, a composite material originally intended for the manufacture of aircraft propellers. The production of 'delta wood' was similar to the production of plywood. The main difference was the impregnation of wood veneer with a thickness of 0.5mm with bakelite resins (thermosetting phenol formaldehyde resin, which had a dark brown cherry colour), and the pressing of the resulting package assembled from many layers at high pressure and high temperature. The material obtained in this way had a strength of 27kg/sq mm, twice exceeding pine in this indicator and approaching duralumin (45kg/sq mm). The heavy weight of 'delta wood' (twice as much as an ordinary tree) was compensated by high strength. Thus, this innovative material could be used for the manufacture of particularly important components of the aircraft structure: wing longerons, wing ribs, etc. At the same time, the high-quality manufactured 'delta wood' was distinguished by moisture resistance and fire resistance. Lavochkin, who was well acquainted with the properties of 'delta wood', chose it as the main material for the manufacture of the wing longerons of the future fighter.

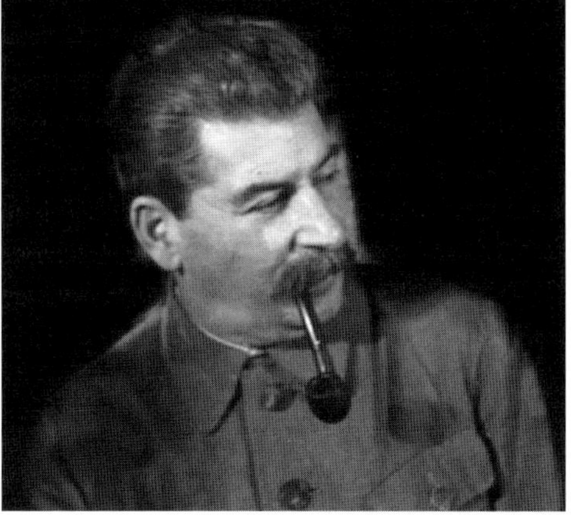
Stalin with his favourite smoking pipe.

By the end of 1938 the preliminary design of the aircraft was ready. The main competitive advantages of the Semyon Lavochkin all-wood fighter were the simplicity and manufacturability of the design, availability and cheapness of materials. High-speed indicators were supposed to be achieved due to the good aerodynamics of the carefully polished wooden surface of the aircraft. The main feature of the project was the use of a new composite material – 'delta wood'. It was these arguments, vigorously promoted by the partners at the highest level, that became the basis for a future victory in the competition for Stalin's attention.

How to become Stalin's 'Nazgul'?

The approval of People's Commissar of Aviation Industry Mikhail Kaganovich allowed the triumvirate to continue working on the aircraft officially. Vladimir Gorbunov, using his connections and official position, was able to include the project of the future fighter in the experimental work plan of the People's Commissariat of Aviation Industry of the USSR. Thus, the status of the Gorbunov, Lavochkin and Gudkov design group and the participation of their project in the competition for the creation of a new type of fighter was finally confirmed officially. However, only on 31 August 1939 were the young officials released from their main work in the People's Commissariat of Aviation Industry. From that moment, the difficult organizational work began to prepare the conditions for the creation of the triumvirate's own design bureau. It took a lot of time to find an aviation plant at which it was possible to produce an all-wood aircraft. This question for the inert Stalinist bureaucracy led by People's Commissar of Aviation Industry Mikhail Kaganovich turned out to be difficult for many reasons. After numerous senseless reforms and re-organizations, the situation in the Soviet aircraft industry resembled a medieval patrimonial system. Each aviation plant had a design bureau headed by some 'genius' aircraft designer, whose creativity completely depended on the wishes of the director of the plant. The director's interest was in the development of aircraft by the factory design bureau, which would be possible to produce on this aviation plant in series, and therefore receive praise and benefits from Stalin. Thus, the main indicator of the success of a particular aviation plant was the number of aircraft produced. The engineers of the factory design bureau, resigned to such a subordinate position, were forced to refuse to make any significant innovations in the design of fighters that could affect the number of aircraft produced. For that reason, in 1939 the already outdated I-16 monoplane and the even more archaic I-153

Fighter I-301 (LaGG-3).

biplane were produced at all Soviet aviation plants with minimal changes. Naturally, the *mafia* groups, formed from directors and aircraft designers, were not interested in the arrival of competitors in their warm places. Only the 'godfather' Stalin could singlehandedly regulate the attachment of a particular design bureau to a specific aviation plant. If the interaction of the chief aircraft designer and the director of aviation plant did not suit the 'Red Tsar', then the 'guilty' were demoted and sent to the periphery of a giant country. There, at the new aviation plants under construction in Siberia or the Far East, in the conditions of an acute personnel shortage, everyone was glad to see the arrival of valuable specialists. However, at the end of the 1930s, angry with the failure of the aviation industry, the 'Red Lord' increasingly sent the 'guilty' to prison or executed them. There were no other ways to effectively 'manage' the activities of the aviation industry in the Soviet totalitarian state.

Initially, Lavochkin, Gorbunov and Gudkov were assigned to the small Aviation Plant No. 167 (in 1938, this enterprise was called a furniture factory for the purposes of stupid Stalinist secrecy) in the town of Kuntsevo near Moscow. This small plant was engaged in the production of propellers and ski landing gear for aircraft. Finally, on 29 July 1939, a place was 'vacated' at Aviation Plant No. 301 in the village of Khimki near Moscow, which was also disguised as a furniture factory. Soon 'The Three Musketeers', Lavochkin, Gorbunov and Gudkov, simultaneously became chief aircraft designers of the design bureau of this aircraft factory.

After the appearance of its own design bureau and the allocation of state funding, work on the project of a new aircraft for Stalin accelerated noticeably. By 18 September 1939, a full-size mock-up of the future fighter was ready. However, six more difficult months passed before the end of the construction of the first prototype of the LaGG-3 fighter.

The Fall of a High Patron

On 10 January1940, a new serious obstacle appeared on the thorny path of creating the LaGG-3 fighter. The People's Commissar of Aviation Industry Mikhail Kaganovich, who had angered Stalin, was removed from his post and sent into exile to the city of Kazan, where he was appointed director of Aviation Plant No. 124. The further fate of Stalin's former favourite is typical for that time. Warned about the impending arrest by his own brother, who was part of Stalin's inner circle, Mikhail Kaganovich shot himself on 1 July 1941 in the toilet of the People's Commissariat of Aviation Industry of the USSR building.

Another of Stalin's favourites, a young party functionary Aleksey Shakhurin, was put in the place previously occupied by professional locksmith Kaganovich. In accordance with Stalin's criteria of professional selection, the son of a peasant, Shakhurin, had no significant relation either to aviation or to the management of the aviation industry. However, the new People's Comissar of Aviation Industry differed favourably from its predecessor Kaganovich by having a higher education and the ability to correctly use aviation terminology. In addition, Aleksey Shakhurin was an ardent fighter against 'enemies of the people', which earned Stalin's special attention and sympathy.

Stalin's speech.

The new People's Commissar of Aviation Industry, who took over affairs from the disgraced Kaganovich, began, on Stalin's

LaGG-3 1st Series fighter at a field airfield, 1940.

orders, to analyze the state of work on the creation of fighters of the 'New Type'. As expected, Shakhurin recognized the results as completely unsatisfactory. Among the many experimental works that were revised, there was also the project of the future LaGG-3. Meanwhile, the personal relationship of the frivolous spoiler of fate Vladimir Gorbunov and the strict Stalin's 'Jesuit' Aleksey Shakhurin, to put it mildly, did not work out. The project of a new fighter was again under threat and Gorbunov, the former leader in promoting the future LaGG-3, had to go into the shadows. The sociable and compromise-prone Semyon Lavochkin saved the situation. He always managed to establish communication even with the most aggressive interlocutors. Soon, Lavochkin and Shakhurin developed favourable business relations. However, the main threat to the implementation of the project of a new all-wood fighter came from Stalin himself.

Soviet fighter made of foreign parts

1 May 1940. Moscow. Military parade on Red Square.

An air armada of 634 planes flew over Stalin standing on the podium of the mausoleum. Among this huge number of fighters, bombers and other types of aircraft, the prototype of the future LaGG-3 stood out in particular. This first aircraft was made at the beginning of March 1940 at Aviation Plant No. 301, and in accordance with the plant number in the documents was designated as I-301.

'Red Lord' was already at the age when you can't rely on visual acuity. It is unlikely that Stalin could clearly see a small fighter among the hundreds of planes flying over him. However, he did not leave the Lavochkin fighter without his special attention. On Stalin's orders, samples of the latest German aircraft were purchased in friendly Germany, as well as a large number of innovative components and parts for them. They had become a pleasant addition to the samples of advanced aviation equipment previously purchased in France. Thus, the prototype LaGG-3 was a funny mixture of French and German devices. The engine, the landing gear and wing-flap release device, and some other important units were originals or licensed copies of products from the French companies Hispano-Suiza and Caudron. Propeller spinner, oil cooler, aircraft hydraulics and some other units were original parts of the German company Heinkel Flugzeugwerke, originally intended for the non-serial fighter No. 100. The power frame of the aircraft was assembled from Soviet materials (wood). Some particularly important components of the structure were made of 'delta wood'.

The Klimov M-105 engine (Hispano-Suiza 12Y) was attached to a motor frame welded from steel pipes and closed with duralumin hood flaps. All the external wooden surfaces of the aircraft were covered in several layers of the same resin that gave strength and fire resistance to delta wood. The resin (which was designated thermosetting phenol formaldehyde resin VIAM-B3 in the USSR although invented in the USA) painted the tree and, consequently, the entire aircraft in a bright cherry colour. To create a perfect aerodynamic surface, the aircraft was polished carefully. For the colour and shine, the workers who assembled the prototype LaGG-3 at the 'furniture factory' dubbed it the funny name 'Royal' (piano). During tests, the fighter showed a maximum speed of 605km/h.

Personal test of 'delta wood' by Stalin

8 October 1940. Moscow. The Kremlin. Stalin's reception room.

People's Commissar of Aviation Industry Aleksey Shakhurin and chief aircraft designer of the new fighter Semyon Lavochkin timidly entered the huge office. Stalin, a short man dressed in a military uniform without insignia, greeted them and in a low voice invited the visitors to tell him about the new fighter. Lavochkin took out drawings from his briefcase, as well as samples of aircraft parts made from delta wood, and spread them out on a huge meeting table. Then the young aircraft designer began his typical story about the design and characteristics of the new aircraft, which he had repeated before the heads of different levels.

Chief Designer Lavochkin in his office at Gorky Aviation Plant No. 21.

However, Lavochkin probably did not realize that this time not only the fate of the new fighter, but also his own life, depended on the listener's reaction. During the report, Stalin began to walk up and down his office as usual, puffing on his pipe. The 'Red Emperor' was in a bad mood, and the voice of an intellectual demonstrating something on the drawings spread out on the table irritated him. He decided to expose the 'fraudster' aircraft designer, who promised him another 'wonder fighter', which always turned out to be a failure in the end. When it came to the main advantage of the aircraft, the almost complete absence of scarce aluminium and the replacement of difficult-to-process steel in the most important nodes with a new material, 'delta wood', the 'Red Lord' frowned and asked Lavochkin incredulously: 'Comrade aircraft designer, why do the Germans make their planes from expensive aluminium, and not from cheap wood soaked in some kind of resin? Are they fools?'

Lavochkin in response began to patiently tell the narrow-minded Stalin about the physical properties of the new material: about its strength, water resistance and, most importantly, fire resistance. After these words of the young aircraft designer the 'wisest of the wise' resolutely walked up to the table where there were samples of parts from 'delta wood' and poured burning tobacco from his pipe on one of them. After waiting for some time, he brushed away the remnants of smouldering tobacco and began carefully to examine the effects produced by the fire. To his surprise, the part was not only not charred but there were practically no traces of high temperature exposure left on it. Next, the incredulous son of a shoemaker grabbed a penknife and began to scratch the surface of the delta wood with a sharp blade with an effort. Despite all his efforts, Stalin could not cause any

Test pilot Aleksey Nikashin.

noticeable damage to the parts. 'Delta wood' proved to be as solid as a stone. Semyon Lavochkin's life was saved.

The trick with the invulnerable 'delta wood' was very much liked by the intellectually limited 'Great Leader' and had an effect greater than thousands of boring and incomprehensible lectures by the intellectual Lavochkin. Turning in his hands a part of the plane that he himself had tested, Stalin shone like a small child with a new toy. Then, overwhelmed with emotions, he ordered officials to reward the inventor of 'wonder material', praised the Lavochkin project and approved the continuation of work on the creation of an all-wood fighter.

So, the failed village priest Stalin 'blessed' the creation of a new 'wonder fighter' from a 'wonder material'. The childishly emotional and intellectually limited 'wisest of the wise' was very easy to deceive. And, this feature of Stalin's 'Great' was not only used by the intellectually gifted Lavochkin.

'I'm standing alone!'

7 November 1940. Moscow. Kuntsevo Dacha (Stalin's country residence). The annual festive dinner in honour of the anniversary of the seizure of power by the Bolsheviks.

The event brought together the closest servants of 'Red Lord':

- Chairman of the Council of People's Commissars of the Soviet Union (Head of government of the Soviet Union), People's Commissariat for Foreign Affairs (Minister) Vyacheslav Molotov
- Chairman of the Presidium of the Supreme Soviet of the Soviet Union (formally, the Soviet President) Mikhail Kalinin
- Deputy Chairman of the Council of People's Commissars of the Soviet Union, Marshal of the Soviet Union Kliment Voroshilov
- Marshal of the Soviet Union Semyon Budyonny

- Chairman of the Party Control Commission of the Central Committee Communist Party of the Soviet Union (Stalin's chief 'Jesuit in the party') Andrey Andreyev
- People's Commissar of Railways of the Soviet Union (Minister) Lazar Kaganovich
- People's Commissar of Internal Affairs (Minister) Lavrentiy Beria
- People's Commissar of Foreign Trade (Minister) Anastas Mikoyan
- Chairman of the Soviet of Nationalities (Chairman of the upper house of the Soviet 'Parliament') Nikolai Shvernik
- Deputy Chairman of the Council of People's Commissars of the Soviet Union Nikolai Bulganin
- Secretary of the Communist Party of the Soviet Union (Stalin's deputy in the party), Head of the Communist Party's Cadres Directorate Georgy Malenkov
- First Secretary of the Moscow Regional Committee of the Communist Party Aleksandr Shcherbakov
- Commander Moscow Military District General of the Army Ivan Tyulenev
- General Secretary of the Executive Committee of the Communist International Georgi Dimitrov
- People's Commissar for Defence of the Soviet Union (Minister of War) Semyon Timoshenko.

Stalin sat at the head of the festive table, gloomy and thoughtful. The servants, as they could, tried to distract the 'Red Tsar' from disturbing thoughts. The 'Leader of Progressive Humanity' reacted sluggishly to several toasts praising the socialist revolution carried out under the leadership of Lenin and Stalin. The servants, trembling with fear, felt that another 'storm' would soon break out. Finally, after the first glasses of wine, Stalin got up from his seat. Everyone present hurriedly jumped up and prepared, as usual, to listen to the speech of the 'wisest of the wise'. Stalin, in his characteristic manner, began his diatribe in a low voice:

> It is necessary to constantly study and retrain every two to three years. But in our country we don't like to study. We do not study the lessons of the war with Finland, the lessons of the war in Europe.
>
> We defeated the Japanese at Khalkhin Gol. But our planes were lower than the Japanese ones in terms of speed and

> altitude. We are not ready for such a war, which is going on between Germany and England.
>
> It turned out that our planes can only stay up to thirty-five minutes in the air, and German and English planes can stay for several hours!
>
> If our air forces, transport, and so on are not at the equal height of our enemies (and all the capitalist states and those that disguise themselves as our friends are against us!), they will eat us.
>
> Only with equal material forces can we win, because we rely on the people, the people are with us.
>
> But for this you need to learn, you need to know, you need to be able to.
>
> Meanwhile, no one from the military department signalled about the planes. None of you have thought about it.
>
> I talked to our aircraft designers and asked them: is it possible to make our planes stay in the air longer? They answered: You can, but no one gave us such a task! And now this flaw is being corrected.
>
> Now our infantry is being rebuilt, the cavalry has always been good, we need to seriously engage in aviation and air defence.
>
> I deal with this every day now, I receive aircraft designers and other specialists.
>
> But I am the only one dealing with all these issues. None of you even think about it. I'm standing alone.
>
> After all, I can study, read, follow every day: why can't you do this? You do not like to study, you live complacently for yourself. You are squandering the legacy of Lenin.[2]

Then there was a painful pause. Mikhail Kalinin, who unofficially played the role of Stalin's buffoon, tried to relieve tension with a neutral phrase: 'We need to think about the distribution of time, somehow there is not enough time!'

'No, that's not the point!' Stalin retorted sharply.

2 Nevezhin, V.A. *Stalin's table speeches: Documents and materials*, Moscow, AIRO-XX, 2003, pp.234–5.

LaGG-3 1st Series Cabin.

There was a dead silence in the hall. In the eyes of Marshal of the Soviet Union Kliment Voroshilov, recently removed by the 'Red Tsar' from the position of People's Commissar for Defence of the Soviet Union (Minister of War) for the failure of the lightning invasion of Finland, tears appeared. Stalin cast a hard look at the cowering servants and continued:

> People are careless, they do not want to learn and retrain. They will listen to me and leave everything as it was before. But I'll show you if I get out of patience. (You know how I can do this). I'll hit the fat guys so hard that everything will crack![3]

Despite the severe nervous shock, the 'fat guys' surrounding Stalin did not suffer from his anger. The main blow fell on the young aircraft designers, who were in a hurry to create a new generation of fighters for the 'Red Lord'.

3 Nevezhin, V.A., op. cit. pp.234-5.

Stalin's order about to transform 'Royal' (piano) into 'Flying log'

On 2 October 1940 a resolution was issued by the People's Commissariat of Aviation Industry of the USSR and the air force leadership, prescribing an increase in the range of new types of fighters to 1,000 kilometres at a value of 0.9 of the maximum speed without the use of external fuel tanks. None of the aircraft designers, including Semyon Lavochkin, paid much attention to this requirement. The prototypes of the new fighters, in accordance with the old requirements, were designed for a range of 600 kilometres. However, soon a categorical order was received from the leadership demanding the immediate execution of the resolution to increase the range of fighters.

Almost until the end of the twentieth century, Russian aviation historians argued about the reasons and, most importantly, about the initiator of such a significant change in the requirements for the range of new fighters. Only thanks to the detailed notes of the General Secretary of the Executive Committee of the Communist International, Georgi Dimitrov, who was present at the festive dinner, was it possible to establish accurately the authorship of this disastrous decree. Stalin, who was frightened by the first conclusions of the results of the 'Air Battle for England', was behind the decision. The battles took place at a great distance from the Luftwaffe bases in France. The German fighters, engaged in escorting their bombers on flights across the English Channel, did not have enough fuel for long air battles over British territory. The 'Red Lord', who himself had long dreamed of conquering the hated England, realized with horror that his own fighters, including the promised fighters of the 'New Type', suffered from the same disadvantage. At the same time, complete incompetence in the aircraft industry did not allow the 'wise' leader of the USSR to realize that changing the range from 600 to 1,000 kilometres would require aircraft designers to abandon the almost finished design or, at least, make significant changes to the design of the new aircraft. Stalin's best friend, the know-it-all Adolf Hitler, was also inclined to the same 'brilliant' solutions to all problems. The Führer also liked to give advice to his 'lazy' designers on improving all kinds of weapons and insisted on the strict implementation of his various idiotic technical 'ideas'.

A new misfortune fell on the head of the talented Semyon Lavochkin at the moment when he was painfully finalizing the second prototype of his fighter. The young aircraft designer was forced to dutifully fulfill the order of the 'chief aviation specialist' of the USSR. Having discarded dreams of high-flight characteristics of his fighter, he installed two additional fuel tanks on the plane. Thus, taking into account the two additional tanks placed in the wing consoles, the total number of internal fuel tanks had increased to five. Such violence against himself and over the flight qualities of the future fighter allowed Lavochkin to report formally on the 'successful' execution of Stalin's order. On 9 December 1940, in accordance with the decree of the Soviet government and the order of the NKAP, the first prototype of the Semyon Lavochkin fighter was renamed from the I-301 to the LaGG-1. Its 'improved version' with five fuel tanks and, accordingly, with a range of 1,000 kilometres became known as the LaGG-3.

However, the consequences of such a 'modernization' turned out to be catastrophic. The weight of the empty aircraft increased from 2,478 to 2,680kg, the take-off weight from 2,968 to 3,346kg. Accordingly, the heavier fighter at low altitude showed a speed below 500km/h. At an altitude of 5,000 metres, 'Stalin's Falcon' Aleksey Nikashin was able to achieve only a speed of 575km/h. The climb time had also increased significantly. Such a result obtained on the prototype LaGG-3 without weapons in ideal conditions (windless and clear weather) was very far from the requirements of the Soviet Air Force for fighters of the 'New Type'. In the case of mass production, it was possible to expect a further significant decrease in the flight characteristics of the new fighter. Thus, as a result of the 'refinement' of the design, the elegant and high-speed 'Royal', built from original imported parts, turned into a clumsy and slow 'Flying log', hastily assembled from disgusting copies of French and German aircraft.

LaGG-3 1st Series Fighter, front view.

The triumph of young aircraft designers and the failure of serial production of the fighter

At the end of December 1940 'The Three Musketeers', Lavochkin, Gorbunov and Gudkov, were awarded the State Stalin Prize for Outstanding Inventions for developing a new aircraft design. Each was given 100,000 rubles. At that time, with the average monthly salary of a qualified worker or engineer at 1,000 rubles, this was a fantastic amount of money. Despite the formal awarding of the entire group, chief aircraft designers LaGG-3 had not worked together for a long time.

Life has shown that both Lavochkin's partners ended up at the position of chief aircraft designer by accident. Having left their talented colleague, they were imprinted in the history of the Soviet aircraft industry in the image of chronic losers with great ambitions. Vladimir Gorbunov became entangled in his own passions and divided his life between alcohol and women. In 1945, while riding a motor boat under the influence of alcohol, he drowned, accidentally falling overboard. Mikhail Gudkov, on the contrary, lived a long life, but was not marked by anything significant, except for participation in the 'development' of the LaGG-3 fighter. His own ambitious project to create a Soviet replica of the American Airacobra Gu-1 ended in a crushing failure. On 12 June 1943, in the first flight, an experimental Gu-1 aircraft crashed; the pilot, Aleksey Nikashin was killed.

LaGG-3 8th Series Fighter.

Meanwhile, despite the 'triumph' of the new aircraft design, the difficult work of launching serial production of the LaGG-3 aircraft was just beginning. Frightened by the possibility of the failure of plans to wage an aggressive war against the entire Western world, Stalin personally allocated five aviation plants at once for the organization of serial production of the Semyon Lavochkin fighter: Aviation Plant No. 21 (Gorky), Aviation Plant No. 23 (Leningrad), Aviation Plant No. 31 (Taganrog), Aviation Plant No. 165 (Rostov-on-Don) and Aviation Plant No. 153 (Novosibirsk). At the same time, the posts of chief aircraft designers in the design bureau were 'released' for Lavochkin and his colleagues and the corresponding plant directors were replaced. Stalin was in such a hurry that the new aircraft was put into mass production without actually passing state and military tests, even without formal adoption into service.

The first serial LaGG-3, factory number 31211-1 (according to other sources 31211-0), assembled in Gorky, was lifted into the air on 23 January 1941 by an experienced test pilot, Aleksey Nikashin. On 1 February People's Commissar of Aviation Industry Aleksey Shakhurin appointed Semyon Lavochkin as the sole chief aircraft designer of the LaGG-3. At the same time, Gorky Aviation Plant No. 21 became the main enterprise for the serial production of LaGG-3. As a result, Semyon Lavochkin had to travel with his family from Moscow to the city of Gorky, a remote province located 400 kilometres from the capital.

The development of serial production of the LaGG-3 at Gorky Aviation Plant No. 21 was very difficult. This plant, which previously specialized in the production of the I-16, was not ready for the production of all-wood fighters. There was little in common between I-16 and LaGG-3. In the annual report on the work of Aviation Plant No. 21 for 1941, it was reported:

> The main task of the plant was the transition to the LaGG-3, that is, to new aircraft, more advanced and technically sharply different from previous models of fighters. This required the plant to solve a number of large and complex problems and, first of all, to radically restructure the workshops of the main production .... A special feature of the LaGG-3 is the wooden construction. At I-16, the volume of woodworking work was 10%, now it has increased to 36%, duralumin work has decreased from 32% to 12% .... The plant faced the problem of creating a cadre of carpenters and mastering by them the complex technique of manufacturing the main structural

> elements on the new VIAM-B3 glue using a little-studied material – 'delta wood' (wing, wing centre section) ... . The production of LaGG-3 is a complex combination of various processes: mechanical, locksmith-welding, woodworking, metalworking, carpentry-assembly, sewing and others.[4]

The second significant problem that hindered the production of the new fighter turned out to be the usual design change in the production process for the Soviet aviation industry. Despite the pretentious State Stalin Prize, the LaGG-3 was not ready for mass production. In fact, it was still being designed, making numerous changes and improvements to the drawings in the process. At the end of January 1941, the number of changes in the drawings was 2,228, and in February 1941, 777. In total, during the year, about 6,000 various changes and additions were made to the design of the aircraft. This situation could not but affect the implementation of ambitious plans for the production of Stalin's fighters of the 'New Type'. According to the plan, during 1941, Gorky Aviation Plant No. 21 was to produce 2,000 LaGG-3s with an M-105P (motor cannon) engine. In reality, until the end of 1941, 1,445 LaGG-3s were produced there. Thus, neither the initial annual production plan of 2,000 aircraft, nor the reduced one – 1,838 – could be fulfilled.

The haste caused by Stalin's fears was reflected in the armament of the LaGG-3. Plans to create an experimental 'wonder cannon' 23mm MP-6 by Yakov Taubin failed, and the designer himself was arrested on charges of sabotage and shot on 28 October 1941. Serial production of another aircraft gun, the 20mm ShVAK, unfolded very slowly. There was an utter shortage of this type of weapon for Semyon Lavochkin fighters. Thus, neither on the first, nor on the second, nor most of the third Series LaGG-3, were motor cannon installed. Its place in the 'V' between cylinder banks was taken by the third large-calibre 12.7mm BS machine gun.

The Pillar of Shame

The first production LaGG-3s began to arrive at the military airfield in the city of Lyubertsy near Moscow in early 1941. The operation of the new

4 GU TSANO. Foundation 2066, Inventory 6, Case 570, Sheet 12.

LaGG-3 on takeoff, winter 1941.

fighter in military units brought new surprises unknown to experienced military mechanics. The LaGG-3 was the only fighter of the 'New Type' equipped with a hydraulic landing gear cleaning and release device, developed in France and produced under licence in the USSR. However, the quality of manufacturing and installation of these very important parts during mass production, was extremely low. Planes often had spontaneous 'folding' and 'unfolding' of landing gear ('legs', as they were often called then), both in flight and on the ground. The most unpleasant surprise for the pilots was the situation when one landing gear leg could come out, and the other could not. Moreover, such cases occurred at the most unexpected moment and often led to accidents and catastrophes.

Vladimir Slugin, Deputy Head of the Maintenance and Repair Service of Gorky Aviation Plant No. 21, recalled:

> The planes were driven to the airfield by the pilots of the plant. For their acceptance and subsequent transfer to military units, a large factory team consisting of specialists of various profiles was sent. During the inspection of the arriving aircraft, massive leaks of all systems were detected on each: hydraulic fluid, gasoline, water and air. Probably, during the flight, the connections were depressurized. When eliminating the leak by tightening the nut, 'biting' along the thread inevitably

> occurred and it entailed the mandatory replacement of both the duralumin fittings and the pipeline. I had to organize a pipe workshop. Pipes and fittings were brought from the factory literally by carts, like firewood.
>
> LaGG-3 had a retractable landing gear in flight, but the hydraulic lifts were without hydraulic locks for the released position. During prolonged parking, the pressure from the system, due to the lack of tightness, decreased to zero. It was enough for a slight effort – a gust of wind or leaning against the plane – for one of the landing gear struts to slowly fold, and the wing lay down on the ground. In the morning, entering the hangar, we observed the usual picture: several planes were lying, collapsed on one wing.
>
> Every day we did the same work. We crawled under the wing, and used our backs to raise the wing, at the same time we created pressure with a manual pump in the cabin. To solve the problem, the Yezerov gear pump was invented. Its resource was enough for three to five flight hours. In general, the hydraulics worked poorly, and before each flight day it was necessary to check its operability with the help of a remote pump powered by an electric drive. For this purpose, a pillar was installed near the Division's command post and electricity was supplied. In the morning, a queue of 10-15 aircraft formed near the pillar to test the hydraulics. All the rolling of the fighters was done manually. We called this place the 'pillar of shame'. And in reality, this was not far from the truth. We carried out this work under the windows of the Division command, but there was no confidence that the aircraft would work a full flight day. The effect of this tedious procedure was enough for a maximum of two or three flights.[5]

In addition to the above technical problems, the LaGG-3 unexpectedly revealed several dangerous design defects at once. First of all, it was spontaneous spinning of the propeller when diving and a stall into spin.

5 Slugin, V.E., 'We started with difficulties', *Working Life*, 1997, No. 18, 20. p.23.

223 defects

Based on the results of military tests conducted from 18 to 31 March 1941, the Red Army Air Force Research Institute prepared a detailed report for People's Commissar of Aviation Industry Aleksey Shakhurin. It noted the following main disadvantages of the LaGG-3 fighter:

- the plane turns to the right when taking off and turning
- rudder's deviation to the left is less than to the right, which makes takeoff dangerous
- spontaneous folding of the landing gear
- frequent need for undercarriage activation of landing gear in an emergency way
- spontaneous folding of the tail wheel
- strong vibration of the aircraft at a speed of over 575km/h
- unsatisfactory mode (overheating) of water and oil at an altitude of 5,000m and above
- insufficient strength of the wing centre section, which led to the deflection of the structure
- frequent cases of failure of duralumin forks on control handle rods.

Forced landing as a result of landing gear failure. LaGG-3 5th Series № 3121565, 26 June 1941.

LaGG-3 shot down by Luftwaffe fighters.

In total, during the military tests, 223 defects were revealed, of which 186 required correcting drawings and changing the design. At the same time, it was not about an experimental plane or a test prototype, for which such a list of shortcomings was a common thing, but about a serial fighter that had already begun to enter service with Aviation Regiments.

As for the volume of output, it grew very slowly and did not fit into the stated plans in any way, despite all the measures taken and haste. If for the entire first quarter of 1941 Gorky Aviation Plant No. 21 handed over only thirty-seven aircraft instead of the 200 planned, then in April with great difficulty it was possible to produce forty-seven and the same number in May 1941.

All the 'extra' overboard!

The main test for the LaGG-3 was participation in combat operations against Luftwaffe aircraft. 'Stalin's Falcons' complained about the low speed and poor manoeuvrability of the 'Flying log' ('it was too heavy for its airframe', 'it was inferior to the Bf 109 E on a turn', 'it accelerated for a very long time', etc.) in comparison with German fighters. The 'improvement' of the LaGG-3 design in the course of combat operations was mainly by lightening the aircraft. The only way to get rid of the excess weight of the aircraft was to remove weapons and other equipment from it. Starting with aircraft No. 31213-76 (seventy-sixth plane of the third series), a 20mm ShVAK gun was installed on the fighter, and the right 12.7mm BS machine gun was dismantled. The capacity of the fuel tanks was reduced to 340 litres, as a result of which the nominal range was reduced to 400km (800km range). In combat conditions, the range was even less. In fact, all fighters of the 'New Type' could be in the air for no more than an hour.

Endless improvements to the LaGG-3 led to a significant deterioration in the characteristics of the fighter. In August 1941, starting with the sixth and seventh series, the aircraft was equipped with landing-gear wheels of a larger diameter (650 by 200mm), which were supposed to provide better taxiing and take-off on unpaved airfields. However, it was not possible to increase the undercarriage bays, so the landing gear was not completely covered in them. In addition, in order to improve the temperature regime of the engine (to reduce overheating), it was necessary to increase the radiator air intake. The tail wheel was still placed in the jammed position. All this significantly worsened the aerodynamics of the aircraft. With a take-off weight of 3,280 kg, the 'lightweight' LaGG-3 barely reached a speed of up to 550km/h. The actions of the pilots also made a significant contribution to reducing the maximum speed of the fighter. As the reviews of Red Army Air Force showed, 'Stalin's Falcons' preferred to fly with an open cockpit, as on fighters of the 'Old Type'. The pilots had objective reasons for such a violation of the rules. Firstly, the windows were constantly splashed with oil and, secondly, the view from the cabin was otherwise unsatisfactory.

As part of the further struggle for weight relief, they continued to remove everything 'superfluous' from the LaGG-3. In the autumn of 1941, starting with seventy-one aircraft of the tenth series (according to other sources, already with the eighth series), 7.62mm ShKAS machine guns were abandoned. So there was a modification of the LaGG-3, the armament of which consisted of only one 20mm ShVAK gun and one 12.7mm BS machine gun. At the end of 1941, starting with the eleventh series, units for mounting external fuel tanks were no longer installed on the fighter. This decision was justified by the fact that the suspended external fuel tanks on the LaGG-3 were not used. Firstly, there were not enough external fuel tanks, secondly, external fuel tanks made it difficult for the fighter to take off (the LaGG-3 was very unstable during take-off), and thirdly, it was not possible to ensure the correctness of their work. However, the rejection of the attachment points of the external fuel tanks did not affect the weight of the aircraft, since devices for suspending bombs and rockets were soon installed in their place. The shortage of ground-attack aircraft forced the Red Army Air Force command to use fighters of the 'New Type' for strikes against ground targets. Therefore, the LaGG-3 received six rails for RS-82 rockets and mounts for hanging two 50-kg bombs.

However, the 'modernization' of aircraft was carried out not only at the factory, but also directly in military units. 'Stalin's Falcon' Yemelyan Kondrat, who commanded 274th Fighter Aviation Regiment from September 1941, recalled:

> There were already radio stations on the LaGG-3, but we removed them to lighten the aircraft. Everything that could be removed was removed. And radio stations, and oxygen equipment, in short, everything that is possible ... .[6]

'Flying log' turns into a 'flying coffin'

In total, during the period of serial production (1941-1944), about 6,500 LaGG-3 fighters were produced, including 3,583 at Gorky Aviation Plant No. 21. The cost of production of one LaGG-3 was approximately 310,000 rubles, while the latest modification of the I-16 Type 29 cost 115,690 rubles to the poor and half-starved people. Thus, the new aircraft, whose flight characteristics increased very slightly, cost about three times more than the fighter of the 'Old Type'. The reason for such a significant increase in the cost of production was an excessively large share of manual labour in the manufacture of LaGG-3. Endless design changes, new components and assemblies that were absent on the simpler I-16, led to a very slow development of mass production of Stalin's new fighter by unskilled personnel. In order to at least get closer to the planned indicators of fighter production, the staff at Gorky Aviation Plant No. 21 had to be almost doubled.

Were such investments justified? 'Stalin's Falcons' on LaGG-3 performed a huge amount of combat work – they conducted tactical reconnaissance (due to the lack of specialized units), weather reconnaissance, engaged in attacking a variety of ground targets, disrupting the work of the enemy rear and 'exhausting' the enemy. LaGG-3 pilots spent a lot of effort and resources on aimless patrolling and 'covering' troops and important military facilities.

6 Kondrat, E.F., *We got a restless century: A documentary story*, Moscow, DOSAAF, 1978. p.54.

LaGG-3 No. 322123-2 with external tanks, March 1942.

However, in reality, the only result of sending large numbers of fighters over the front line and rear cities was to raise the morale of the ground troops and the population. Stalin demanded that Soviet people 'should see stars in the sky, not crosses'.

The failure of the LaGG-3 fighter was obvious to everyone. As early as December 1941 the 'Red Lord' proposed to stop the production of the aircraft at Gorky Aviation Plant No. 21. Instead of building the 'Flying log' in Gorky, it was supposed to produce the Yak-7. However, People's Commissar of Aviation Industry Aleksey Shakhurin and his deputy, Peter Dementiev, objected that Alexander Yakovlev would not be able to launch the production of his Yak-7 quickly at two leading aviation plants in Novosibirsk and Gorky. Therefore, a compromise decision was made – production of the LaGG-3 at Novosibirsk Aviation Plant No. 153 to stop, with production in Gorky to continue for the time being, simultaneously improving flight characteristics. In mid-August 1942 the production of the LaGG-3 in Gorky at Aviation Plant No. 21 was discontinued, and all further improvements were carried out at Aviation Plant No. 31 (Tbilisi, Georgia). However, as the further development of events showed, in 1942 the history of the Semyon Lavochkin fighter did not end.

Chapter 5

Yak-1 – 'best' Russian fighter

'Triumph of the Will' and the adoption of a young aircraft designer

12 July 1935, Tushino airfield (north-west of Moscow, fourteen kilometres from the city centre). The official event was an aviation holiday, a display of the achievements of air sportsmen of the Central Aero Club of the USSR, designed specifically for Stalin and his closest servants.

The Central Aero Club of the USSR was established on 11 March 1935 with the joint participation of two Bolshevik political organizations, Osoaviakhim (The Society for the Assistance of Defence, Aircraft and Chemical Construction) and Komsomol (All-Union Leninist Young Communist League). Sports achievements were proclaimed as the formal goals of the Aero Club. However, the real activity was aimed at promoting military aviation among young people and training future pilots, technicians and designers of military aircraft. Similar organizations with the same militaristic goals were created in Nazi Germany. Stalin and Hitler competed with each other for the number of young people fooled. To realize their pathological desire for death, they needed millions of young fanatics with as yet unformed critical thinking. The upcoming battle for world domination between the red and brown 'Evil Empires' was supposed to be a battle of engines on land, water and air. All male teenagers of the USSR and Germany had to get as many skills as possible in handling modern military equipment.

Hundreds of young aircraft designers, pilots, gliders, parachutists and aircraft modellers were gathered on the huge airfield. Fanatical Soviet teenagers and young men arrived from different cities of the huge 'Red Empire'. The audience was waiting with excitement for the arrival of the main Soviet 'deity' – Joseph Stalin! To see, even from afar, the wisest 'Father of Nations' was the greatest honour for every teenager or male youth. For long months, inspired by Stalin's propaganda, without sleep or rest, they prepared their products for showing to Stalin.

Aviation holiday in Tushino airfield.

In the western sector of the Tushino airfield in the bend of the Moscow River, an impressive exhibition of aircraft, gliders and aircraft models designed and built by the hands of young Soviet men was organized. A strict commission carefully selected products worthy of demonstration to Stalin. Only the best of the best got access to the aviation holiday. Each lucky person who passed the selection wanted to attract the attention of the Soviet 'deity' to his work. The excitement of the young enthusiasts was increasing by the minute. Many anxiously looked at the gloomy sky and low clouds, which could interfere with such a grand event.

The selected representatives of the Soviet youth did not suspect that each of them was only an extra, and their hard-assembled products were only elements of the scenery at a grandiose performance staged by Stalin's servants. But the most important surprise of the aviation holiday was prepared for the evil and suspicious Soviet 'deity', who considered himself the only person to manage and control everything that happened in the red empire. The 'Red Lord' did not realize that he was going to play the role of 'Stalin', who descended from a typical Soviet propaganda poster. For many years, the 'Great Leader' created this vulgar image with the help of servants and the enslaved Soviet people, and eventually became a hostage of this role himself.

Finally, three heavy black Rolls Royce cars appeared in the distance. They drove up and stopped not far from an excited group of Stalinist youth. Numerous guests of the aviation holiday got out of the cars. The company of Soviet bosses, mostly dressed in military uniforms, was headed by a short, moustachioed man dressed in a military overcoat, a cap and soft leather boots. Every Soviet person knew that this was the much-loved 'Father of Nations', Joseph Stalin. The choice and location of the people surrounding the Soviet 'deity' corresponded strictly to the idea of the holiday. On the right, just behind the 'Red Lord', there was a devoted servant, the People's

Glider and balloons for Stalin's entertainment.

Commissar for Military and Navy Affairs (Minister of War) Kliment Voroshilov. With his presence, he emphasized the military orientation of the event. On the left, also somewhat behind, was the leader of all the Stalinist youth, 31-year-old Aleksander Kosarev, emphasizing with his presence the age of the main participants of the holiday. Stalin, accompanied by his entourage, approached the young sportsmen, who were trembling with excitement. Habitually playing the role of a kind father and mentor, he warmly welcomed them. The same ritual with smiles, handshakes and pats on the shoulder was performed by Stalin's servants accompanying him.

Then the leader had a traditional conversation with 'random', but in fact selected, representatives of the Stalinist youth. Stalin, being in a good mood, shone with his 'knowledge' in the field of aviation and, smiling paternally, had high hopes for the younger generation of builders of communism. Young air athletes, who surrounded the 'Father of Nations' in a dense mass, listened with bated breath to Stalin's primitive speeches. When, finally, a quiet voice with a strong Georgian accent praising the Soviet youth fell silent, the young air athletes gave the Soviet 'deity' a whole storm of applause. It was clear from their enthusiastic faces that they were ready to give all their strength and, if ordered, their very lives for Comrade Stalin and the prosperity of the communist motherland.

Finally, after completing a short ritual, satisfied with the fanaticism of his young people, the 'Red Lord' ordered the celebrations to begin. The event organizers had prepared an extensive programme, taking into account the preferences of the 'Great Leader'. The glider pilots were the first to demonstrate their skills. The 'Father of Nations' looked with interest at the individual and group flights of gliders. The best masters of this sport showed very effectively examples of virtuoso control techniques of non-motorized aircraft. However, soon the silent gliders in the sky tired the elderly leader. The organizers, who sensitively read his mood, immediately moved on to another feature of the festive programme.

Then, as in any circus performance designed for a narrow-minded, poorly educated audience, it was time for the clown to perform. In accordance with the format of the event, the clowning was performed with the help of an aeroplane. Pilot Alekseyev on a U-2 biplane trainer, designed by Polikarpov, demonstrated 'the first independent flight of a student on an aeroplane'. It was an aviation caricature. Alekseyev deliberately made gross mistakes, forcing the plane into unnatural positions in the air, such as an inexperienced student could have done. In the hands of a skilled pilot, the aircraft performed obediently the most ridiculous aerial tricks and finally landed with such big bounces that watchers could think that it was going to

Stalin and Voroshilov talk to pilots at Tushino airfield.

fall apart. The primitive Stalin liked the circus in the air very much. Like a bloody Roman emperor at a performance in the Colosseum, he laughed loudly and applauded. The retinue, subtly feeling the emotional state of its 'Master', repeated all his reactions. Loud applause did not subside for a long time.

The pilot Alekseyev, pleased with Stalin's reaction, continued the spectacular circus performance. It was time to show the so-called 'deadly number' in the air. The role of an angry wild animal, into the mouth of which the trainer had to stick his defenceless head, was performed by the same U-2. According to the plan for the airshow, Alekseyev was supposed to show Stalin the deliberate dropping of the aircraft into a deadly spin. In this state, the aircraft loses lift and begins to fall, rotating. Then it was planned to exit the spin at the very ground with a simultaneous spectacular landing in front of the audience. The trick was repeatedly rehearsed, and the skill of the pilot and the reliability of the aircraft guaranteed the safety of its execution. However, the presence of such a high-ranking spectator played a role, and the trick did not end according to plan at all. The pilot, wanting to surprise Stalin, violated the usual technique for exiting a spin, and the plane crashed into the Moscow River beside the airfield. A huge fountain of spray marked the scene of the accident. Fortunately, the speed was not very

Meeting between Joseph Stalin and Alexander Yakovlev. The faces of the 'enemies of the people' who were shot later were deliberately erased.

high, and the water softened the fall. The plane was completely destroyed, but the unharmed Alekseyev was taken directly to Stalin in an ambulance. The pilot accepted his guilt for a gross mistake. He explained his wrong actions to Stalin at length and hoped for leniency. The leader had a great opportunity to demonstrate to his loyal subjects his royal kindness and readiness to forgive. The 'Red Lord' took full advantage of this opportunity. Stalin approached Alekseyev, shook his hand and gave him a fatherly hug. This meant that the violator of aviation discipline was mercifully, and fully royally, forgiven. A tribunal and punishment of the pilot for the crash was cancelled! The unfortunate aviation incident, to the universal delight of all those present, was over.

Meanwhile, the aviation show, organized exclusively for the entertainment of Stalin and his entourage, continued. It was time to demonstrate racing in training aircraft. Several trainers were lined up in the air at an altitude of 150-200 metres. Against the background of archaic biplanes, such as the Polikarpov U-2, an unusual UT-2 monoplane trainer stood out. This aircraft had been created by a representative of the Soviet youth, 29-year-old aircraft designer Alexander Yakovlev. The signal given, the race started. This time, everything developed according to a pre-approved scenario. The Polikarpov plane, as a representative of the 'dark' past, designed by a former tsarist engineer and son of a priest, immediately began to fall behind and came to the finish line last. The leader of the competition was the UT-2, Alexander Yakovlev's monoplane. The plane, completing the race, roared past in front of Stalin's nose. This event caused the 'Red Tsar' a storm of children's delight and loud applause. The emotions of the leader were supported by a large retinue and numerous elite Stalin youth.

Then 'Stalin's Falcon' Julian Piontkovsky, who piloted the UT-2, brilliantly performed a repeatedly rehearsed manoeuvre, spectacularly landing next to Stalin. The next act of the play began, in which the intellectually limited 'Red Tsar', in exact accordance with the script, played the role prepared for him.

Alexander Yakovlev in his memoirs described in detail the carefully prepared and orchestrated meeting with Stalin:

> Stalin came closer to the plane, tapped his finger on the wing.
>
> 'A tree?' he asked.
>
> 'Mostly pine and birch plywood,' I replied.
>
> 'What is the highest speed?'
>
> '200km/h.'

'And what is the maximum speed of the U-2 aircraft?'

'150.'

'And on which aircraft is it better to train pilots for I-16 fighters? On U-2 or on this one?' Stalin asked the pilots who were crowding around.

'Of course, on this plane,' everyone shouted with one voice.

'And why?'

'But this one has a higher speed and it is a monoplane, just like the I-16, and the U-2 is a biplane.'

'It turns out that it is necessary to switch to these more modern aircraft?'

'That's right,' the pilots answered in one voice.[1]

Thus the 'wisest of the wise' once again fell into a primitive trap set by his loyal entourage. The task of the 60-year-old leader's retinue was to distort reality and turn it into a bright propaganda poster that was pleasant for Stalin. This false picture symbolized the indissoluble connection of an elderly psychopath and Stalin's youth, who were ready to give their lives for the sake of their leader to build a bright future. In the centre of the propaganda cliché, as if by chance, there was a bright representative of the younger generation of Stalin's aircraft designers, Komsomol member Alexander Yakovlev. The symbol of a bright communist future easily defeated the representative of the old, still tsarist school of aircraft construction, non-party Nikolai Polikarpov. The holiday was recognized by Stalin as a successful one. Thus, the 'director' of this 'performance', the main youth chief (Führer) Alexander Kosarev had achieved all his goals. His companion, Alexander Yakovlev, who brilliantly played the role of a representative of Stalin's youth, aroused Stalin's undoubted sympathy.

However, it was not only Komsomol chief Aleksander Kosarev who had the capabilities and talents to influence the pathologically suspicious Stalin. Four years after the events described another 'talented director', People's Commissar (Minister) of Internal Affairs and main executioner Lavrentiy Beria, played another performance on the theme 'there are only enemies around' in front of Stalin. After a brilliant 'premiere', the chief (Führer) of

1 Yakovlev, A. S., *The purpose of life: Notes of an aircraft designer*, Moscow, Politizdat, 1987, p.126.

Aircraft designer Nikolai Polikarpov (third from left) among the cadets of the Aviation Plant No. 39 Flying Club (Moscow) against the background of the U-2 biplane.

Stalin's youth, Aleksander Kosarev, was declared an 'enemy of the people' and on 23 February1939 was shot in Lefortovo prison in Moscow.

For the main character of this story, the young Alexander Yakovlev, the meeting and subsequent close relations with Stalin ended exceptionally well. The 'Great Leader' really liked the fanatical, bold and talented aircraft designer. Yakovlev became his favourite for a long time. In fact, at the end of the aviation holiday an informal adoption of aircraft designer Yakovlev by Stalin took place. The future creator of the Yak-1 describes the details of this event in this way:

> Our guests, participants and organizers of the festival were very satisfied and decided to take a picture in memory of this show, which played a big role in the development of mass aviation sports in our country. A large group was formed on which photographers and cameramen aimed their lenses. I remember lingering near my plane and when I came up, I was

> confused, because the whole group for photographing had already been completed. Stalin beckoned me with his finger, inviting me to sit next to him, and put his hand on my shoulder. This is how the photographer captured us at this significant moment in my life.
>
> At this review, for the first time, I had the opportunity to talk with the leaders of the party and the government and get acquainted with Stalin.[2]

Alexander Yakovlev kept the photo taken at the aviation festival as his greatest souvenir. It always hung in the office of the creator of the Yak-1, reminding him of the event that changed his life radically.

The Stalin's fanatic of aircraft construction

On 1 April 1906 the first child was born in Moscow in the family of Sergei Yakovlev, an accountant of the petroleum production company Nobel Brothers Limited, whose parents named him Alexander. For the Yakovlevs this was a very important and long-awaited event and so the first-born male was surrounded by love and care from the first minutes of his life. The happy childhood of Alexander Yakovlev was also promoted by the prosperous financial situation of the family. Despite the peasant origins of his great-grandfather, the father of the future aircraft designer was a well-educated third-generation city dweller. For the Russian Empire, where the majority of the population were illiterate peasants teetering on the verge of hunger and poverty, such excellent social opportunities were extremely favourable for the formation of a child who showed extraordinary abilities from an early age.

His mother played a key role in the upbringing and primary education of Alexander Yakovlev. Despite the appearance of two younger children, she gave all her attention and care to her eldest son. The future engineer had a huge number of toys as a child: wind-up steam locomotives, trams and cars. Young Alexander ruthlessly broke all this expensive splendour, trying to satisfy his childish curiosity and see what was inside. As he grew up, the main toys of the young lover of technology became screwdrivers,

2 Yakovlev, A.S., op. cit, pp.126-7.

pliers, wire cutters and a hand drill. His mother strongly encouraged her son's natural inclinations and was firmly convinced that Alexander would certainly become a famous engineer.

As already noted, the future aircraft designer received his primary education under the guidance of his mother, who had outstanding pedagogical abilities and prepared her son perfectly for admission to the preparatory class of the elite Moscow gymnasium.

Unlike the state gymnasiums, there was no official rigour in this private educational institution, and the teachers paid the greatest attention not to senseless cramming but to the comprehensive development of a student's personality. Alexander studied with great pleasure, and his favourite subjects were humanities (history, geography and literature). The lessons that taught the basics of natural sciences (physics and chemistry) were not among his favourites. However, in general, the results of the future creator of the Yak-1 were very high. A favourite teacher for young Alexander was a mathematics teacher who contributed to the development of the future aircraft designer's innate tendency to mathematical order, to the accuracy of all records and calculations when solving problems.

In addition to the brilliantly organized training, the gymnasium had great opportunities for developing the diverse creative abilities of its students in their free time. So Alexander was for some time the editor of the student literary and historical magazine and a member of the gymnasium theatre. The student's interest in technology was also fully satisfied. The future aircraft designer was consistently engaged in the young radio amateurs club,

Trainer aircraft UT-2 in flight.

aircraft modelling, and then in the glider club. Another hobby that later became an important professional skill of an aircraft designer was drawing. Alexander's mother strongly encouraged her son's artistic development and gave him expensive drawing notebooks, paints and pencils.

An integral attribute of the life of a young gymnasium student was reading. The number of books Alexander read was huge; this was facilitated by an excellent library, which is part of the educational atmosphere of an elite gymnasium. However, in addition to the fascinating, and full of technical devices, works of Jules Verne, Alexander encountered and became interested in reading a special kind of book. Their authors promoted Russian militarism and imperial greatness. It was this false 'patriotic' literature, full of obscurantism and primitive self-assertion due to the seizure of the territories of neighbouring countries that contributed to the development of Yakovlev's primitive totalitarian worldview. Due to this, and a number of other reasons, until the end of his long life Alexander Yakovlev could not refuse religious worship before the 'Red Emperor' Joseph Stalin.

In 1917, under the burden of total failures in the First World War and the blows of the revolution, the Russian Empire, rotten to the foundation, fell. The short period of democratic Russia, governed by the Provisional Government, was replaced by the bloody dictatorship of Vladimir Lenin.

Aleksandr Kosarev (centre in the first row) among parachutists and pilots, 1935.

Stalin puts his hand on Alexander Yakovlev's shoulder, 12 July 1935.

Like the vast majority of Moscow residents, the Yakovlev family experienced great domestic difficulties due to the complete economic chaos created by the Bolsheviks who came to power. Money was cancelled and a half-starved existence became the norm. The only source of physical existence for the Yakovlev family of five, including three children, was a meagre food set given to the head of the family as 'payment' for his work. The parents were faced with a difficult choice of the death of their younger children from starvation or the employment of their 11-year-old eldest son Alexander, the hope and future support of the family. Contrary to everyday misconceptions, Alexander, the student of the elite gymnasium, who grew up in love and care, turned out to be a surprisingly independent and responsible teenager. He not only accepted the difficult decision of the family council without objections but felt completely confident in the new status of the breadwinner of a large family. Soon, his father arranged for the future aircraft designer to work as a courier in the bulky and monstrously inefficient state department of the Bolsheviks, engaged in the administrative distribution of energy resources.

Thanks to his early business qualities and skilful communication with various minor Soviet officials, Stalin's future aircraft designer was promoted quickly enough and was appointed secretary to the head of the department. However, the most pleasant consequences of working life were the early self-affirmation of Alexander and receiving the informal status of 'head of the family' from his mother. The food packages that the young secretary received to pay for his work turned out to be much more significant than his father's contribution to providing for the family! So a 12-year-old had his first successful experience of independence. These qualities of character became a key factor in his unusually early and surprisingly successful career as an aircraft designer, and then as Deputy for Experimental Development People's Commissar of Aviation Industry.

Beyond his age, the pragmatic Alexander left his job a year before the end of the gymnasium. He decided not to risk passing the exams at the end of the gymnasium course. However, this does not mean that he devoted all his time exclusively to studying. Skilfully distributing his time and energy, Alexander participated actively in the public life of the gymnasium and, most importantly, he clearly determined the goal of his future life – aviation. It must be admitted that, at that turbulent time, it was by no means a trivial decision. Alexander was determined to become an aircraft designer in a poor and hungry country where aeroplanes were an exceptional rarity.

Alexander Yakovlev (in the centre) among the circle members of the Society of Friends of the Air Fleet, 1923.

But, on this direct path to the future, aircraft designer was waiting for new and, from the outside, seemingly insurmountable difficulties. The paradox of the change of power in the 'Evil Empire' was that the Bolsheviks, having given rights to some social groups, completely deprived other strata of society of their rights. For Alexander Yakovlev, son of a wealthy family, the path to the red university was closed. However, the strong-willed young man independently found the only possible way to realize his goal – gliding. The Bolsheviks stimulated the development of gliding sports in Russia, intending to use the specialists trained in this way for their militaristic goals. Alexander designed and built gliders with his own hands, which was even more surprising for his age. The key to the success of Yakovlev on this difficult path was the co-operation with people who were passionate about aviation. He was not a lone genius but, on the contrary, he saw the advantages of joining forces with other people who were equally capable but without such pronounced leadership qualities as he had. Early on Yakovlev also realized all the advantages of partnership with people with a high social status. It should be noted that all the successes of the young aircraft designer were accompanied by the patronage of older men of power, experience and resources – in fact, fatherly figures. For backward Russia, where there was traditionally a cult of worship before superiors, such an approach was inevitable. However, unlike most typical sycophants, Yakovlev did not show blind slavish worship in front of any boss. He chose his high patrons not only by position but by the degree of their usefulness for the realization of the goal of his life – aviation. Despite the sincere feeling of gratitude that Yakovlev felt for such figures, it must be admitted that they were only a means to an end for him. The first impressive and 'powerful' figure, for whom a recent teenager, who had just graduated from the Alexander Yakovlev gymnasium, felt great respect, and even awe, was the young aircraft designer Sergey Ilyushin. The future creator of Stalin's beloved Il-2 ground-attack aircraft was ten years older than Alexander and began to play the role of a caring older brother in his life. For the peasant's son Sergey Ilyushin, who served in the Red Army for a long time and proved his loyalty to the Bolsheviks, there were no obstacles to entering the Zhukovsky Air Force Engineering Academy. Thus, the student Sergey Ilyushin became the first mentor of his young colleague Alexander Yakovlev. He not only provided him with lecture notes on special disciplines for studying but also helped him calculate the glider design. Under the guidance of his favourite teacher, Yakovlev received the necessary initial knowledge for designing gliders. The first glider he built became a prize winner at the competition, and Alexander received an award of 200 rubles for his debut.

How to build a professional career in Bolshevik Russia?

Alexander's dreams of further professional growth in Bolshevik Russia encountered an insurmountable obstacle. Despite his success in the design and construction of gliders, the path for admission to the Zhukovsky Air Force Engineering Academy was still closed for him. After the nationalization, the Bolsheviks took control of the entire aviation industry and, consequently, aviation education. The criminal Bolshevik group dreamed of world domination and considered aviation solely as an important type of modern weaponry. Everything related to aircraft and the training of aviation specialists was concentrated in the hands of the Soviet military. We have noted that Semyon Lavochkin, to whom, under the tsar, the path to university was closed, was sent by the new Bolshevik government to Moscow Higher Technical School after three years in the Red Army. Exactly the same path to aviation was taken by Soviet aircraft designers Sergey Ilyushin, Vladimir Gorbunov and Mikhail Gudkov. All of them, despite their formal civil status, had military ranks, and Sergey Ilyushin preferred to wear a military uniform. The only exception to this rule was Nikolai Polikarpov. Not only had he never served in the army but, what was quite surprising for his 'King of Fighters' status, he was not a member of the Communist Party.

Relying on the estates (workers and peasants) oppressed under the tsarist regime, the Bolsheviks literally considered all people from the well-off strata as potential enemies of the Soviet government. Forced by necessity to attract former nobles, children of priests and tsarist employees to work in the most responsible positions, they treated them with great suspicion. In the end, this pathological intolerance to intelligence, competence and, most importantly, critical thinking resulted in the almost universal extermination of the majority of representatives of the tsarist intelligentsia and their descendants. The arrests and executions of the most educated and intellectually developed citizens of the USSR continued from the middle of the 1930s until Stalin's death in 1953. However, this does not mean that the millions of victims of the Stalinist regime were exclusively former nobles or priests. Ninety per cent of Gulag prisoners were just workers and peasants so 'beloved' by Stalin, who, on farfetched pretexts, and sometimes just by chance, ended up in the bloody hands of Stalin's executioners.

Thanks to the patronage of Sergey Ilyushin, in March 1924 Alexander Yakovlev was taken into military service in the training workshops of the Zhukovsky Air Force Engineering Academy. Now he had to prove his loyalty to the Bolsheviks with hard work. It was the dirtiest, hardest and most unattractive military service. A representative of the 'hostile' class of the tsarist intelligentsia could only count on the status of a second-class serviceman. Daily maintenance of aircraft, including towing from hangars, cleaning and repair became the main content of Alexander Yakovlev's life. Three years of heavy military service was brightened up only by the fact that he was near the planes he loved. However, Alexander not only passed all the tests with honour, but also found time and energy for further professional development. With the support of several patrons, primarily Ilyushin, Yakovlev managed to organize a group of young enthusiasts who, under his leadership, built a light aircraft in eight months. The beginning of construction was preceded by a busy year of designing the aircraft and calculating its structures.

Aircraft Engine Repair Specialist Workers' and Peasants' Red Air Fleet, Alexander Yakovlev. Moscow, mid-1920s.

Talent for Finding Powerful High Patrons

Soon Alexander Yakovlev had a new high patron – Chairman of the Council of People's Commissars of the Soviet Union (head of government of the Soviet Union) Aleksey Rykov. In those years he formally had more power than the General Secretary of the Communist Party of the Soviet Union, Joseph Stalin. With the patronage of Aleksey Rykov, Osoaviakhim (The Society for the Assistance of Defense, Aircraft and Chemical Construction) immediately allocated money for the construction of the aircraft. As a sign of gratitude for the assistance provided, Alexander Yakovlev called all his aircraft AIR (Aleksey Ivanovich Rykov). This tradition was involuntarily interrupted by Yakovlev in 1937. On 27 February 1937 Aleksey Rykov was arrested, and later, on 15 March 1938, he was shot at the Kommunarka NKVD shooting ground near Moscow.

By 1 May 1927, the AIR-1 biplane was ready and turned out to be so successful that the designer himself and pilot Julian Piontkovsky made a record 1,500-kilometre sports flight from Moscow to Kharkiv to Sevastopol and back to Moscow. As a reward for the good design of the aircraft, Alexander Yakovlev was finally accepted into the Zhukovsky Air Force Engineering Academy. In April 1931 he graduated with honours from the Academy and received a diploma of higher professional education.

Continuing to create sports aircraft under the auspices of Osoaviakhim, the ambitious Alexander Yakovlev set himself a new goal – the design of military aircraft. However, in this prestigious and generously-funded area of the Soviet aircraft industry, there were already established design bureaux headed by former tsarist engineers such as Andrei Tupolev and Nikolai Polikarpov. Not one of them was interested in the emergence of young competitors, nor was the leadership of the Soviet aviation industry. Yakovlev repeatedly had to hear a categorical statement from the authorities of the aircraft industry that he would never design fighters. He was explicitly told that he should be content with a niche of not serious sports planes, suitable only for the entertainment of the crowd.

However, such categorical judgements did not stop the young aircraft enthusiast. With the support of his high patron, Yakovlev secured funding for his new project of an AIR-7 fighter with an M-22 engine, a licensed copy of the British Bristol Jupiter aero engine. With this aircraft, according to others, the daring upstart Yakovlev challenged the newest biplane fighter, the I-5, designed by the future Stalinist 'King of Fighters' Nikolai

Aleksey Rykov and Joseph Stalin.

Polikarpov. The fact is that the Yakovlev project assumed that the aircraft would reach a speed of 320km/h. That was 40km/h higher than the speed of Polikarpov's fighter with analogous weight characteristics and similar engine. Yakovlev intended to achieve such an increase in speed by switching to a new monoplane design with more advanced aerodynamics. In addition, another important advantage of the Yakovlev fighter project was the two-seat cockpit.

At the end of the summer of 1932 the AIR-7 was built. Its appearance at the airfield caused a sensation. The fact is that the construction of the aircraft was carried out unknown to the management of the aviation plant where a small team under Alexander Yakovlev was based. Once again, the young aircraft designer realized his dreams against the active opposition of the aviation bosses. The only hope of Yakovlev's numerous detractors was an accident or catastrophe of an experimental aircraft built as a single example. However, on the first flight, the plane proved itself brilliantly. On the second flight on 20 November 1932, on an AIR-7 aircraft, pilot Julian Piontkovsky with 'passenger' Alexander Yakovlev reached a Soviet Union record speed of 325km/h.

However, despite the unexpected success, the Soviet aviation authorities did not find any worthy application for the AIR-7. The only suggestion was to use the record-breaking Yakovlev aircraft for fast delivery of newspaper matrices to major cities. Such a 'wise' decision, of course, could not satisfy an ambitious young aircraft designer. Yakovlev continued to experiment with the AIR-7, trying to show that his plane was able to show even greater speed. But, in 1934, an accident occurred on one of the AIR-7 test flights when, because of flutter, then a completely unexplored phenomenon, an aileron broke away. An experienced pilot, Julian Piontkovsky managed to avoid a disaster and skilfully landed the experimental aircraft on a tiny platform located between numerous wooden buildings. It was what Yakovlev's numerous detractors had hoped for. The young designer was immediately accused of incompetence, flights of his plane were strictly prohibited, and Yakovlev and his associates were ignominiously expelled from the aviation plant.

There should be only one High Patron of Soviet aircraft designers left!

However, the enemies of the young aircraft designer underestimated Yakovlev's ability to mobilize his forces after each failure. He not only overcame the crisis again but was also able to climb another step on the way to realizing his dream. Using his talent in the presentation of his aircraft, he found a new high patron in Deputy Chairman of the Council of People's Commissars of the Soviet Union (deputy head of government of the Soviet Union) Jānis Rudzutaks. The high chief was so impressed with the Alexander Yakovlev aircraft that he immediately ordered that all the young designer's requests be granted. The Head of the Main Department of Aviation Industry People's Commissariat of the Defence Industry of the Soviet Union, George Korolev, who had a personal dislike for Yakovlev, was forced not only to officially recognize the Yakovlev Design Bureau, but also to allocate him his own aviation plant as a production base although the small factory for the production of beds could only conditionally be termed an aviation plant. However, a few years later, thanks to the efforts of Yakovlev and his team, several dirty hangars had been turned into the small high-tech Aviation Plant No. 115. The plant was distinguished by exemplary German order and cleanliness and, completely unprecedented for technologically backward Russia, competent staff dressed in white coats. It was there that all the prototypes of Yakovlev aircraft were designed and built, including the Yak-1 fighter. At the same time, Yakovlev's main detractor George Korolev was shot on Stalin's orders in 1938 for the 'disintegration' of the Soviet aviation industry.

During the second half of the 1930s, the 'competition' between Yakovlev's high patrons reached its climax. Following Aleksey Rykov, another defender of the young aircraft designer, Jānis Rudzutaks, was removed from all positions. The same sad fate awaited him. Rudzutaks was executed by firing squad on 29 July 1938. Now Alexander Yakovlev, like all residents of the Soviet Union, could have only one high patron – serial killer Joseph Stalin. However, several years had passed since Yakovlev's spectacular meeting with the 'Great Leader'. To get the coveted status of Stalin's favourite, the young aircraft designer needed a brighter military aircraft in all respects than the trainer aircraft UT-2.

Stalin's Table Talk

27 April 1939. Moscow. The Kremlin. Stalin's reception room.

Thirty-two-year-old aircraft designer Alexander Yakovlev was looking forward to the reception with excitement. That excitement did not come from the unknown or from fear. Rather, the young aircraft designer was experiencing an emotional uplift in anticipation of the proximity of the realization of a long-set goal. Yakovlev had studied closely the peculiarities of the relationship between Stalin and key representatives of the Soviet aviation industry and knew why he was invited. Not only was he able to design and build a new military aircraft, his entrance ticket to the highest league of Soviet aircraft designers, Yakovlev was able to present skilfully the flight characteristics of his aircraft, albeit, as it transpired, greatly inflated so that the information was guaranteed to reach the cherished addressee in the Kremlin. The numerous talents of the young aircraft designer included

Yakovlev at the AIR-4 plane.

not only engineering abilities but also the ability to understand clearly the relationships in the strict hierarchy of Soviet power and to adapt quickly to changing conditions without changing their own goals. In 1939 the time came in the USSR for which Yakovlev had been waiting so long. The ageing leader was in a hurry to see the long-awaited fruits of the industrialization he had started ten years before. Angered by the constant failures of his beloved aviation, Stalin was looking maniacally for scapegoats. The older generation of Stalin's aircraft designers, still recent favourites of 'Red Tsar', was subjected to cruel purge ('Chistka'). It began to seem to Stalin that everyone wanted to deceive him and slip him bad planes. Once, distressed by another failure of Soviet aircraft, the psychopath Stalin told Alexander Yakovlev that 'the aircraft designer sees no flaws in his offspring, just as the mother – even though the child is crooked – thinks that he is the most beautiful'. Yakovlev's senior competitors irrevocably lost the trust of the suspicious Soviet 'deity', and some of them were in prison. As the time of the planned conquest of Europe approached, the 'Red Lord's' alarm grew. To correct the catastrophic situation of permanent failures of Soviet aviation, Stalin searched feverishly for new people with whom to replace the exposed 'deceivers' and 'enemies of the people'.

At exactly 18.00, Alexander Yakovlev was invited to Stalin's office. In addition to Stalin, the closest servants of the 'Father of Nations' were in the office: the formal head of the Soviet government Vyacheslav Molotov and

AIR-7 aircraft.

the People's Commissar for Defence of the Soviet Union (Minister of War) Kliment Voroshilov. The young aircraft designer sat down modestly next to a huge conference table. On the other side of the table, opposite Yakovlev, sat Molotov and Voroshilov. Stalin, as usual, smoking a pipe, walked along the huge table behind the backs of his servants. The 'Red Lord', demonstrating his friendly attitude to the young aircraft designer and sincere interest in his new aircraft, began to ask Yakovlev about his work. Gradually, from the small details of everyday life of the Yakovlev Design Bureau and modern trends in aircraft construction, the conversation turned to the main question – Soviet high-speed bombers. Soon Stalin's servants joined the conversation. All three of them were interested in the characteristics and, first of all, the speed of the new Alexander Yakovlev short-range BB-22 bomber in comparison with the mass-produced high speed bomber SB, designed by 'enemy of the people' Andrey Tupolev. In his memoirs Yakovlev thus conveys a conversation with Stalin and his entourage:

> 'How did you manage to get a speed exceeding the speed of the SB with the same engines and the same bomb load as the SB?' Stalin asked.
>
> 'It's all about aerodynamics, Comrade Stalin. SB was designed six years ago, and science has moved far ahead during this time. In addition, our Design Bureau managed to make its bomber much lighter than the SB.'
>
> Stalin kept walking around the office, was surprised and said, 'Miracles, just miracles, this is a revolution in aviation. It is necessary to immediately launch the BB-22 into mass production!'
>
> Stalin looked in the direction of the People's Commissar for Defence of the Soviet Union (Minister of War) Voroshilov and he quickly wrote something on paper and handed it to the leader. Stalin read it and nodded his head in agreement and returned the document to Voroshilov.
>
> Then Voroshilov read the text of the petition to the Presidium of the Supreme Soviet about awarding me the Order of Lenin, a ZIS-101 car and a prize of 100,000 rubles. The petition was immediately signed by all three of them.[3]

3 Yakovlev, A.S., op. cit., p.188.

Despite the expectation of success, Alexander Yakovlev was stunned by such a generous award. Out of surprise, he could only ask for an award to the members of his design bureau. To this, Stalin replied that he should immediately submit a list of employees who worked on the new aircraft in order to reward them as well. Then Stalin said a friendly goodbye to the new favourite and wished the young aircraft designer further success in his work.

Only the next morning, when Yakovlev was woken up by a call from Stalin's personal secretary, did he realize that getting into the top league of Soviet aircraft designers had come to him 'at a high price'. In fact, after the conversation with Stalin, he began to play the role of a personal informant of the 'Red Lord' and would have to report to him regularly about the most intimate secrets of the aviation industry. However, Alexander Yakovlev, whose goal in life was aeroplanes, was not at all against such a mutually beneficial 'co-operation'.

An offer that cannot be refused

Already on 11 May 1939, at a meeting on the topic 'On measures to introduce new and modified aircraft into production', an informal meeting of Yakovlev with Stalin took place. The 'Red Lord', tired of boring reports of venerable Soviet aircraft designers and lengthy arguments between the military and representatives of the aviation industry, ordered his staff to urgently call his young favourite. The chief's order was carried out immediately. Yakovlev did not know where he was being taken, because the meeting was secret and the young aircraft designer did not yet know that he was among the invited.

Stalin greeted his new favourite affably. In a casual conversation, the 'Red Lord', with the air of a connoisseur, discussed with Yakovlev the state and level of German, English and French aviation. Stalin clearly enjoyed communicating with a young aircraft designer, who was ideally suited for the role of a son by age. However, the paternal feelings of the 'Great Leader' were only a mask hiding the desire to use the talents of the young aircraft designer to realize his base goals. The fact is that the plan for creating new fighters presented at the People's Commissar of Aviation Industry meeting frankly did not please Stalin. The very appearance and manner of communication of Mikhail Kaganovich had recently become increasingly annoying to the 'Red Tsar'. This displeasure of the 'Master' was a sure sign that soon the loyal People's Commissar of the Aviation

Alexander Yakovlev, Zinovy Raivichier (Head of Frunze Central Aerodrome) and Julian Piontkovsky, 1935.

Industry would go into oblivion. Disappointed with how things were going in his beloved aviation, Stalin decided to intervene in the process and show the stupid Kaganovich how to find 'brilliant' aircraft designers and how to give them a task to develop a fundamentally new aircraft. At the end of the conversation, without dropping the image of a kind and wise 'father', he half-jokingly, half-seriously suggested that Alexander Yakovlev create a new fighter. Accepting Stalin's game, the young aircraft designer, showing his humility, promised to think about the proposal by the 'wisest of the wise'. Yakovlev understood that Stalin was not joking with him, and took the words correctly, that is, as an order from a cruel head of state. He was well aware of how quickly the careers and lives of former Stalin favourites, who dared to object to the 'Red Lord' or in some way did not justify his trust, ended.

After returning from a conversation with Stalin, Yakovlev immediately gathered all the members of his Design Bureau at Aviation Plant No. 115.

A brainstorming session began to find ideas for fulfilling Stalin's urgent task. Fortunately, the Yakovlev team already had all the prerequisites for determining quickly the overall appearance of the future Yak-1 fighter. Aircraft designer Evgeny Adler, one of the members of the Yakovlev team, recalled the details of these events in his memoirs:

> Pointing to one of the BB-22 engine nacelles, 'Leon Schechter,'[4] said Yakovlev, 'Take this nacelle together with the engine in the place where the landing gear is removed, put the pilot, attach the wings and tail – that's a ready-made fighter for you. You also need to push the barrel of the cannon through the screw shaft. It will turn out quite modern.'
>
> Standing next to Kirill Vigant, the first deputy of Yakovlev, noticed, 'Everything is simple for Leon. Even such a luminary as Polikarpov has not been able to solve this problem for some year.'
>
> Yakovlev replied, 'Well, perhaps Kirill, Leon Schechter is not inferior to Nikolai Polikarpov.'
>
> This fleeting, half-joking conversation turned out to be historical. I inadvertently stood at the cradle of the famous Yak-1 fighter.
>
> The short-sighted Schechter, almost touching the paper with his nose, quickly sketched a draft of a single-seat cannon fighter with an M-105P (motor cannon) engine.[5]

'And you, that unless an American?'

20-21 June 1939, Moscow. The Kremlin. Stalin's reception room.

Alexander Yakovlev had already managed to get used to constant invitations to Stalin. However, this time he was surprised to find that almost all Soviet aircraft designers known to him had gathered in the large reception room and were waiting for an invitation from the occupant of the office. There were representatives of both the older generation, such as

---

4 Aircraft designer Leon Schechter was one of the designers of the Yakovlev Design Bureau

5 Adler, E.G., *Earth and sky. Notes of an aircraft designer*, Moscow, 'Russian Aviation Society' (RUSAVIA), 2004, p.39.

High Patron of Soviet aircraft designers.

Ilyushin, and those recently accepted into the top league of Soviet aircraft designers, Lavochkin, Gorbunov and Gudkov. In addition, Yakovlev noticed two aircraft engine designers, Vladimir Klimov and Alexander Mikulin. Their presence clearly indicated a change of priorities in the development of Soviet military aviation. Radial engines, so popular throughout almost all of the 1930s, had faded into the background. They were replaced by almost complete domination of the 'Soviet' liquid-cooled V aircraft engines: the M-105 from Vladimir Klimov and AM-35 from Alexander Mikulin.

Despite the warm welcome of fellow aircraft designers, Yakovlev clearly felt his special status at this event. All those present were invited by the official organizer of the event, People's Comissar of Aviation Industry Mikhail Kaganovich. Only Yakovlev had been invited personally by the real head of the Soviet aviation industry.

The meeting at Stalin's office was held in a special format. Aircraft designers were called in one by one to an appointment with the Soviet 'deity'. Finally, it was Alexander Yakovlev's turn, and he entered Stalin's familiar office. In his memoirs, this meeting is described as follows:

> In the office, in addition to Stalin and People's Commissar of Aviation Industry Mikhail Kaganovich, there were Voroshilov, Molotov and someone else from Politburo[6] members, I don't remember who, as well as Deputy Chief of the Air Force of the Red Army Philip Agaltsov.
>
> Stalin asked me, 'Well, did you decide to make a fighter with the Klimov engine?'
>
> 'Yes, I contacted Klimov and got all the data about his engine. We have worked out the issue in detail, and our design bureau can come up with a proposal to build a fighter.'
>
> I named the flight data of the future fighter: speed, ceiling and flight range.
>
> 'How will you arming it? Will there be a cannon on it?'
>
> 'But of course! Our fighter will be equipped with a 20-millimeter cannon and two rapid-firing machine guns.'
>
> 'It's good,' Stalin replied, pacing around the office in thought.
>
> 'Do you know,' he asked, 'that we are ordering the same fighters from some other aircraft designers and the winner will be the one who not only creates the best fighter in terms of flight and combat qualities, but also makes it earlier so that it can be put into mass production faster?'
>
> 'I understand, Comrade Stalin.'

6 The Political Bureau of the Central Committee of the Communist Party of the Soviet Union was a collective authority consisting of Stalin's closest servants. The actual function of the Politburo was, on the one hand, a cover for Stalin's total autocracy under the mask of a group of rulers, and, on the other, the extension of responsibility for Stalin's bloody crimes to a group of closest servants.

> 'Understanding is not enough. We need to make the fighter faster.'
>
> 'How much time do I have?'
>
> 'The sooner, the better. Will you make a fighter for the New Year?'
>
> 'I have not been engaged in the construction of such aircraft, I have no experience … . But the Americans are making a new fighter in two years … .'
>
> 'And you, that unless an American?' Stalin interrupted me. 'Show what a young Russian engineer is capable of … . Then you will be a good fellow, and I will have to invite you for a cup of tea.'
>
> 'Thank you, if necessary, we will definitely do it. But let me ask you one question? Here we have invited about two dozen aircraft designers, and everyone is given a task. Does the country need so many fighters and bombers? Is it possible to launch all of them into mass production?'
>
> 'We ourselves know perfectly well,' Stalin replied, 'that we do not need so many planes. But out of all the planes, with God's blessing, there will be five or six of them that will be suitable for mass production. And such a number of new aircraft does not bother us.'
>
> So Stalin talked with all the invited guests. Everyone got a task. We left for the design bureaux excited, charged with the spirit of creative competition, with a firm intention to defeat our 'rivals'.[7]

For the first time in the history of Soviet aviation such a large number of aviation specialists were attracted to participate in the competition for the creation of a new fighter. Moreover, most of them represented the younger generation and did not have much experience in creating aircraft. The primitive idea of the leader was to increase competition between Soviet aircraft designers. Everyone gathered understood that only the best projects fighters of the 'New Type' would receive Stalin's approval and would be put into mass production as soon as possible. However, this time the innovation in the 'clever' policy of manipulating Soviet aircraft designers was the

7 Yakovlev, A.S., op. cit., p.194.

Stalin's giant office in the Kremlin, Moscow, 1935.

unprecedented generosity of the promised huge monetary rewards and other benefits for the winners of the competition to create the best fighter for the conquest of Europe. Such conditions of the competition especially motivated young aircraft designers who received very modest salaries and lived in terrible conditions.

'Triumph' for young Russian engineer

Further events developed rapidly. Alexander Yakovlev was one of the last to join the race to create a fighter of the 'New Type'. The young Russian engineer had less than six months to complete the Stalinist task. However, the prudent Yakovlev had important advantages over competitors, primarily over the creator of the LaGG-3, Semyon Lavochkin. Stalin's favourite had a small but very effective design bureau, consisting of talented aircraft designers, for whom Alexander Yakovlev was an indisputable leader and authority. In addition, another important advantage was the presence of its own production base (Aviation Plant No. 115), which Yakovlev and his team had created almost from scratch. But the main accelerator for creating the future Yak-1 was high patron and the main customer of fighters of the

'New Type' Joseph Stalin. Thanks to the 'Great Leader', Yakovlev solved two major problems in creating his fighter: financial and engine. Stalin immediately found money for the construction of two prototypes, verbally allowing the use of funds allocated for the construction of prototypes of the previous Yakovlev aircraft – the twin-engine short-range bomber BB-22. Lavochkin's competitor had to wait more than six months for the monstrously inert Soviet bureaucratic system to make a decision to allocate state funding for the construction of the LaGG-3 prototype in 1939.

The situation with the new M-106 aircraft engine (a development of the Klimov M-105) was also very difficult. It was based on the declared characteristics of this aircraft engine that Yakovlev and Lavochkin designed the flight characteristics of their fighter prototypes. However, it is necessary to state that, in the middle of 1939, this engine simply did not exist. An attempt by aircraft engine designer Vladimir Klimov to create another modification of the licensed French Hispano-Suiza 12Y aircraft engine ended in complete failure. The situation typical of the implementation of the idiotic Stalinist planning was repeated. The 'Architect of Communism' in his usual manner provoked designers to assume unrealistic obligations on the terms of creation and characteristics of a new engineering object. Under the widely advertised capabilities of the new device, aviation designers designed new aircraft, spending time and material resources. This was followed by failure and a search for the guilty.

To solve the engine problem, aircraft designers from the Yakovlev team had to make changes to the design of the new fighter and provide, instead of the M-106 aircraft engine, for the installation of its predecessor M-105P (motor cannon) with a capacity of 1,050/1,100 horsepower with a 20mm ShVAK gun. Although the dimensions of this aircraft engine were exactly the same as of the M-106, its claimed power was less, which should have affected the speed of the future fighter. However, the M-105P also existed only conditionally, or rather in the form of several experimental samples. Despite titanic efforts to finalize the engine, which lasted for more than two years, the designer Vladimir Klimov again violated his obligations to Stalin. The first version, with the possibility of installing a cannon in the 'V' between cylinder banks (M-105P motor cannon), which was scheduled to appear in the second quarter of 1939, was assembled only in August. In October 1939 the M-105P engine passed the factory tests with great difficulty. Only in the second half of December 1939 on Aircraft Engine Plant No. 26 (Rybinsk, Yaroslavl Region), was serial production launched, and the first assembled M-105 engines only appeared on 23 December 1939.

Thus, in order to meet Stalin's deadline for creating the fighter of the 'New Type', Alexander Yakovlev needed to get several prototypes of the M-105P engine made by autumn 1939. A real bureaucratic battle had begun between the Lavochkin and Yakovlev teams for scarce aircraft engines. Stalin's note to aircraft engine designer Vladimir Klimov about speeding up the process of sending two M-105P engines to the Yakovlev Design Bureau is known. After the intervention of the 'Red Emperor', the first aircraft engines naturally reached Yakovlev.

Finally, on 1 October 1939, feverish work began on creating the first prototype of the future Yak-1. Engineers and workers worked almost around the clock. With a major lack of time, the degree of complexity of the engineering problems that the Alexander Yakovlev team had to solve was extremely high. They needed to design and test fundamentally new fighter systems in flight for the first time, namely a water and oil cooling system for the engine, a variable-pitch propeller, retractable landing gear and much more. Many components of these complex systems existed only in the form of experimental prototypes and required further development in the testing process. Given the lack of time, this meant a real design nightmare for the Yakovlev team. In some cases, to preserve the flight characteristics of the fighter promised to Stalin, engineers had to take an unjustified risk, ignoring the problem of the strength of the main power structures of the aircraft. However, most often, the problems identified during construction of the prototype were solved only partially for the sake of saving time, in the hope of subsequent final elimination during flight tests. One compromise that worsened the characteristics, and especially the safety, of the future aircraft followed another. On 30 December the 'ready' prototype of the Yak-1 (official name I-26-1) was transported from Aviation Plant No. 115 to the Frunze Central Aerodrome for the first stage of testing. Formally, Yakovlev had fulfilled Stalin's task to create a fighter in record time! However, the reality was very far from a pompous report to the 'Red Lord'.

Sending the next 'Terminator'

The bloody tyrant Stalin, who was responsible for terrible crimes, never committed them with his own hands. Being a coward and a nonentity, the 'Red Lord' was afraid of direct reprisals against competitors. He always acted with someone else's hands, pushing opposing groups, consistently destroying competitors and replacing them with incompetent, but

High speed bomber SB.

personally loyal, servants. The period of real struggle for power ended in 1929 when Stalin became the sole master of the USSR. By this time, all the associates of Vladimir Lenin, who represented at least a hypothetical threat to the dominance of the 'Leader of Progressive Humanity', were defeated. At the beginning of the 1930s the psychopath Stalin no longer had any real enemies, but his paranoid character traits continued to intensify. In this regard, an even fiercer period of searching and fighting with already imaginary enemies began. Stalin was obsessed with a persecution mania, which intensified as he interfered in all spheres of domestic and foreign state policy. He was concerned about any informal relations between his servants, which he considered all Soviet officials and high-ranking commanders to be. As a rule, Soviet civilian and military leaders appointed by Stalin to responsible positions, copying his management style, very quickly began to acquire their own personally devoted servants. In the middle of the 1930s, against the background of large-scale industrialization, the importance of the new Soviet bosses grew enormously. In the gigantic Soviet bureaucratic apparatus, competing structures were spontaneously formed, fighting for Stalin's influence and forming medieval feudal relations in the style of Eastern despots. Stalin, himself selecting people on the basis of personal loyalty, had a negative attitude to similar actions by his subordinates. In these informal clans, the suspicious 'Red Tsar' saw the reason for the constant failures of unrealistic plans for the production of modern weapons, and sometimes a direct threat to his unlimited power. However, the processes of the degeneration of the Soviet feudal system were so global that the 'Red Emperor' himself was involved in the interdepartmental intrigues of the opposing clans. When, finally, the information reached the intellectually limited, but monstrously cruel, Stalin that his servants were playing dangerous games, it was time for another bloody massacre carried out by someone else's hands. A lover of manipulating people preferred to use fanatically loyal servants as a tool for punishing 'enemies'. By the end of the 1930s the ageing 'Father of Nations' increasingly selected aggressive and fanatical young people for this role.

The failure of the I-16 and the difficulties in creating a fighter of the 'New Type' clearly showed the real archaic state of the Soviet aviation industry. According to Stalin, it was time for another purge of the entire leadership of the People's Commissariat of Aviation Industry of the USSR and, accordingly, the clan of directors of the largest aviation plants inextricably linked with it. Fanatical Alexander Yakovlev, who for many years was disparaged by Soviet aviation bosses, like no one else, was suitable for the role of a battering ram, hacking into the Soviet quasi-mafia structures that had developed in the aviation industry under the 'wise' leadership of Stalin. In December 1939, the young aircraft designer with the support of the 'Architect of Communism' attacked the leadership of the People's Commissariat of Aviation Industry of the USSR with devastating criticism. The first to collapse, unable to withstand the aggressive pressure of youth, was the recent undivided owner of the Soviet aviation industry, Mikhail Kaganovich. Further events clearly showed that the change of the leadership of the People's Commissariat of Aviation Industry of the USSR was only the beginning of the process of radical changes in the industry. Moreover, Stalin's favourite, Alexander Yakovlev, would play one of the key roles in these upcoming events.

Stalin's Iron aircraft designer

On 8 January 1940 the young Russian engineer received from Stalin the influential position of Deputy for Experimental Development to the new People's Commissar of Aviation Industry, Aleksey Shakhurin, and complete freedom of action. Yakovlev, who had pronounced authoritarian traits of character, began to destroy the structures created by his predecessors with extraordinary enthusiasm and determination. The aviation fanatic sought to capture the most valuable resource for the production of his aircraft – aviation plants. It was about those that Alexander Yakovlev dreamed of throughout his short life. The instrument of capturing aviation plants was the organization of mass production of the future Yak-1 in them. The former People's Commissar of Aviation Industry, Mikhail Kaganovich, until the last day of his stay in power, did everything possible to prevent the promotion of the Yakovlev fighter. He made a bet on an alternative LaGG-3. For that reason, the Yak-1 was not included in the fighter production plan for 1940. The fall of Kaganovich cancelled all plans and created a favourable opportunity for the monopoly of Yak-1 (I-26-1) production at all Soviet aviation plants.

In his new administrative position, Deputy People's Commissar Alexander Yakovlev, as usual, acted quickly and soon won his first small victory. Within a few days after the start of factory tests of the Yak-1 (I-26-1), preparations for its mass production began. On 9 February1941, Yakovlev achieved a decision on the serial production of twenty-five Yak-1 (I-26-1) fighters at Aviation Plant No. 301. Although it was not the largest aviation

Short-range bomber BB-22.

plant, Stalin's favourite for the first time vividly demonstrated his claims to the vacant 'position' of 'King of Fighters'. In addition, the takeover of Aviation Plant No. 301 was beneficial to Yakovlev for another reason. It was on this plant that the Lavochkin Design Bureau was located and the LaGG-3 prototype was built. Thus, the main competitor of the Yak-1 (I-26-1), the future LaGG-3, was under the threat of 'Chistka'. As readers know from the previous chapter, the Semyon Lavochkin fighter was saved from going into oblivion only by Stalin's suspicions; he was afraid of a repeat of the situation with the I-16 monopoly.

As in the classic Blitzkrieg, time worked against Alexander Yakovlev. The continuation of the LaGG-3 development was the first serious defeat for Yakovlev not only in the struggle for dominance in the aviation industry of the USSR, but also in the struggle for influence on Stalin. Despite the fall of Kaganovich, a number of powerful directors of aviation plants retained their positions. However, they could not directly oppose Yakovlev with Stalin standing behind him. The further development of events in the 'war' of Yakovlev against the clan of directors depended on two important factors over which he no longer had power.

First, according to the results of the tests of the two prototypes of the Yak-1 (I-26-1 and I-26-2), the applicant for the regalia of the 'King of Fighters' realized that the characteristics of the fighter created in a feverish hurry were very far from those promised to 'Father of Nations'. Yakovlev had a very good idea of what happens to those who deceived the great Stalin. Although the latter's trust in Yakovlev was still at a high level, the situation could very quickly change to the opposite.

Fighter I-26-1 (Yak-1).

Secondly, the clan of aviation bosses, who realized the deadly danger of the 'Terminator' sent by Stalin, feverishly put together a resistance to the total domination of the Yakovlev fighter. The essence of their counter-action strategy was to prepare a new powerful competitor for the Yak-1. Only if this hypothetical fighter was successful would it be possible to discredit Yakovlev in the eyes of Stalin and maintain or even strengthen their own position in the leadership of the aviation industry. The history of the implementation of this insidious plan will be described in the next chapter.

The first victim

27 April 1940. Moscow. Frunze Central Airfield.

The living mascot of Alexander Yakovlev, the permanent test pilot of all his aircraft, Julian Piontkovsky, was preparing to perform his forty-third flight in the prototype Yak-1 (I-26-1). The famous 'Stalin's Falcon' was 44 years old, but no one doubted the experience and skill, as well as his excellent physical form.

The fourth month of testing of the Yak-1 (I-26-1) was underway, accompanied by endless modifications and alterations of the experimental aircraft. The deadline for submitting a new fighter to state tests had passed. Factory tests of the Yak-1 (I-26-1) were to be completed by 18 January 18 and state tests on 28 January 1940. By the end of January, only six 'flights' had been completed. However, Julian Piontkovsky continued the test programme at constant risk to his life, gradually increasing the number of flights performed. Fifteen take-offs ended with forced landings due to dangerous engine overheating and malfunctions of the controls of the variable-pitch propeller. Since February 1940 the new People's Commissar of Aviation Industry, Shakhurin, concerned about the lack of progress in the tests, began to demand daily reports. However, Yakovlev, who became deputy to Shakhurin at the desire of the almighty Stalin, easily found acceptable reasons to explain the failure of the tests of his aircraft. Designed and built in an incredible hurry, the fighter turned out to be a very difficult 'child'. During the tests on the Yak-1 prototype, the oil piping system was repeatedly redesigned, oil radiators of various designs were installed, the engine was changed three times due to bearings that collapsed from overheating, the VISH-52 propeller (variable-pitch propeller) was replaced with a new VISH-61P propeller (also variable-pitch) from the first experimental series. However, progress in flights came only after the

Yakovlev team received a new radiator installed on the LaGG-3 prototype from its competitor Lavochkin. After that, the engine overheating decreased and 'normal' flights became possible.

However, the most terrible disappointment of the Yakovlev team was the speed of the prototype. The first measurements showed that it was much lower than promised to Stalin. Flights continued, and there was a faint hope that, after endless improvements, the plane would approach the cherished milestone of 650km/h. It was assumed that the second significantly modified prototype of the Yak-1 (I-26-2), which began flying on 14 March 1940, would show better speed characteristics.

In parallel, flights of the first prototype of the Yak-1 (I-26-1) continued. Aircraft designers in practice identified those problems that they could not take into account due to the crazy rush when designing. The main role in this painful and extremely dangerous work was played by the chief pilot of the Yakovlev team, Julian Piontkovsky. On 27 April Piontkovsky started and warmed up the engine, checked full throttle, and taxied to the start. The take-off was performed flawlessly. Experienced employees on the airfield, who watched thousands of flights, could clearly see that the plane was controlled by a real master. At an altitude of about 1,000 metres, Piontkovsky began to perform a complex barrel roll. In front of the mechanics who serviced the plane, he successfully completed two elements. However, when performing the third barrel roll, the plane lost speed and broke into a spin. Observers saw that the pilot controlled the fighter until the last second and tried to take the plane out of the spin. But, to perform a life-saving manoeuvre, there was not enough altitude and, at high speed, the plane crashed into the ground. The pilot had no chance of escape. A few days later, Julian Piontkovsky was buried with military honours at the Novodevichy Cemetery in Moscow.

A special commission was created to investigate the Yakovlev plane crash. Investigators, having studied the wreckage and the testimony of eyewitnesses, checked two possible causes of the aviation tragedy: pilot error and a defect in the design of the aircraft.

The strength of the wing of the first prototype of the Yak-1 caused great doubts among many aviation specialists not included in the Yakovlev team. There were objective grounds for such an unfavourable opinion in relation to the Stalinist favourite. It was precisely because of the insufficient strength of the wing that the Yak-1 (I-26-1), assembled in a feverish hurry, could not withstand ground tests and was sent for modification on 20 December 1939. The weak point was the cutouts in the wing for the undercarriage bay, which significantly reduced the strength of the leading edge. Unlike the prototype

Klimov M-105P engine (motor cannon) on the experimental fighter I-26-2 (YAK-1).

LaGG-3, the power elements of the wing (wing longerons) which were made of the innovative 'delta wood', the Yak-1 wing was manufactured using the technology of the 1920s. All elements of the wing, including the longerons, were made of wood, and the skin was plywood. The strength of such a structure was achieved by carefully glueing all the elements of the wing. Contrary to the requirements of the military, the wing was made as a single structure with no detachable wing consoles. It would seem that such an archaic approach, which made it difficult to repair and transport a fighter by ground transport, should have increased the strength of the wing. However, in reality, the limited strength characteristics of the wood forced the Yakovlev designers to make a dangerous compromise between the strength and weight of the wooden wing. Before the tragic flight on 27 April, aerobatics had been performed on the plane, and there were no visible signs of wing destruction. But on that ill-fated day, luck turned away from Julian Piontkovsky.

A continuation of the theme of insufficient wing strength was the explanation for the disaster: the undercarriage leg lock had failed under the action of overloads when performing the barrel roll which led to the separation of the plywood skin of the wing. Ground tests on 20 December showed that the skin was not held firmly enough by animal glue and nails. Such a failure of the wing's leading-edge skin could easily cause a breakdown into a spin and the destruction of the aircraft. However, the commission did not show much zeal in searching for direct evidence of defects in the design of the fighter. Such restraint by the investigators may be explained by possible pressure from Alexander Yakovlev, who by that time had become one of the most influential people in the aviation industry of the USSR.

The theory of human error also had only indirect evidence. An opinion was expressed that Julian Piontkovsky died because of immoderate vanity and excessive self-confidence. Many believed that the crash of the prototype Yak-1 (I-26-1) largely repeated the crash of Polikarpov's prototype 'Super Rat'(I-180). Based on this version, Piontkovsky's performance of potentially dangerous aerobatics on an experimental aircraft was a gross violation of the flight task and almost aviation hooliganism. The motive that prompted this famous 'Stalin's Falcon' to take such a reckless step was

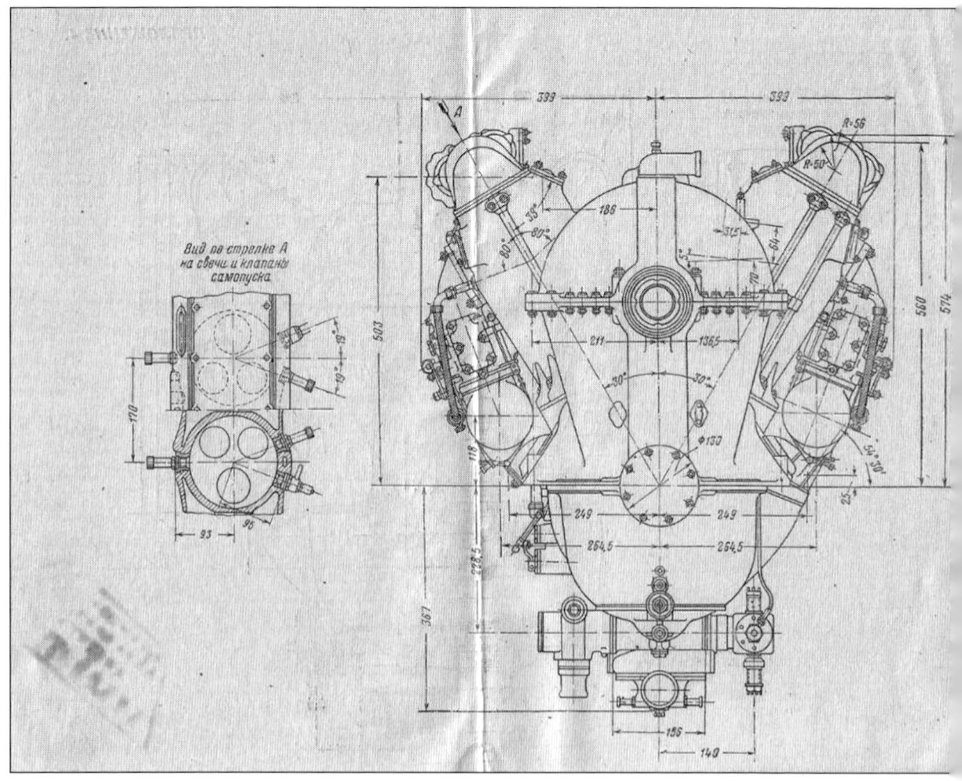

Drawing of the M-105P engine, front view.

Fighter I-26-1 (Yak-1) on a ski landing gear.

a banal resentment against Alexander Yakovlev. People who knew Julian Piontkovsky well noted that his character traits were similar in many ways to those of Valery Chkalov, who died while trying to attract Stalin's attention to the new Polikarpov fighter.

In his memoirs, a member of the Yakovlev aircraft designer team, Evgeny Adler, gives his version of the reason for the inadequate mental state of Julian Piontkovsky, which led him to the crash:

> Even before the second prototype was built, the Yak-1 (I-26-2), Yakovlev invited a second test pilot, Sergei Korzinschikov, anticipating the possibility of delaying flight tests with one pilot. This caused a strong dissatisfaction with Julian Piontkovsky. Trying to mitigate the situation, Yakovlev appointed Piontkovsky as the chief pilot of Aviation Plant No. 115 and also offered him to choose in advance which of the two planes he wanted to fly. Piontkovsky chose the I-26-1, not thinking that the second one would be better finished. While Piontkovsky carefully and methodically practised flight after flight of the engine-propeller combination, Korzinschikov, after several introductory flights, began measuring flight characteristics, including the maximum speed value at different altitudes, and even began performing aerobatics.
>
> As it turned out later, before the next flight of Piontkovsky, one of the pilots in the flight room made fun of his lagging behind Korzinschikov. This affected the proud Piontkovsky

> like red on a bull. On the flight on 27 April 1940, with the task of fine-tuning the characteristics of the same ill-fated engine-propeller combination, Piontkovsky was in a state of extreme emotional excitement, and instead of a given flight in a circle, he began to perform aerobatics. When performing one of them at low altitude in the area of Petrovsky Park, the plane did not come out of the dive and crashed into the ground.[8]

However, all the above-mentioned versions of the causes of the disaster remained unproven. The Commission noted in its conclusion that it was not possible to establish the true cause of the disaster. Thus, perhaps not without pressure from Alexander Yakovlev, the case was closed. All doubts about possible defects in the design of the aircraft of the Stalinist favourite were rejected by a strong-willed decision. Everyone tried to forget about the disaster as soon as possible, explaining it as a ridiculous accident.

Meanwhile, factory tests continued on the second prototype of the Yak-1 (I-26-2). On the fateful day for Julian Piontkovsky, test pilot Sergei Korzinschikov managed to accelerate the second prototype only to a speed of 590km/h. It was a real failure for Yakovlev who explained such a poor result by the problems of the M-105P engine. This statement by Yakovlev would be absolutely true if it were not for the results of the prototype LaGG-3 which, with the same engine, but with a larger mass, reached a speed of 605km/h.

Stop testing!

In early May 1940 Stalin, concerned about the delay in the deployment of mass production of new fighters, ordered People's Commissar of Aviation Industry Aleksey Shakhurin to finish testing prototypes of new fighters. Such a blatant violation of the test regulations did not cause any protest from People's Comissar Shakhurin who was completely loyal to Stalin.

Despite the fact that two months had passed since the beginning of factory tests (14 March) of the second prototype of the Yak-1 (I-26-2), and the first prototype of the Yak-1 (I-26-1) flew for almost four months before its crash, the programme of factory tests of the aircraft was only 80 per cent

8 Adler, E.G., op. cit., p.49.

complete. On 9 May 1940, by a strong-willed decision of Shakhurin, the factory tests of the Yakovlev fighter were stopped and preparations for its serial production began. However, the decision on the admission of the future Yak-1 to state tests could only be made by the official customer – the leadership of the Red Army Air Force. The military department did not obey the People's Commissar of Aviation Industry and was very sceptical about the new fighters. This meant that Alexander Yakovlev had to face another powerful force – the military.

The results of factory tests of the Yak-1 prototype were sent for study to a special body that performed state tests of all Soviet aircraft – the Red Army Air Force Research Institute. The head of the Institute, Major General Alexander Filin, was an experienced test pilot who was very strict about his duties. He rightly believed that it was necessary to avoid by all means the repetition of the problems of the I-16, the catastrophes of

The crash site of the I-26-1 (Yak-1) fighter, in which test pilot Julian Piontkovsky was killed.

which claimed hundreds of lives of Soviet military pilots. In this regard, Yakovlev's attempt to submit an unfinished prototype for state tests, before factory tests were complete, ended in a complete collapse. Knowing about the 'features' of the new Yakovlev fighter, the specialists of the Red Army Air Force Research Institute approached the study of previously conducted factory tests of the Yak-1 with truly German accuracy. In the voluminous conclusion of the military engineers, a large list of the most important elements of the prototype test programme that were not implemented was indicated. In addition, they demanded a thorough study of the results of the wing reinforcement carried out on all Yak-1s after the crash of the first prototype. Based on those arguments, the engineers of the Red Army Air Force Research Institute refused categorically to accept the Yakovlev fighter for state tests until the problems they identified were eliminated.

The Institute's position of the military caused Yakovlev deep indignation and he turned to Stalin for help. In a conversation with the 'Father of Nations', Alexander Yakovlev accused the leadership of the Red Army Air Force Research Institute of deliberately sabotaging state tests of a high-speed fighter that was so necessary for Soviet military aviation.

The complaint to Stalin miraculously changed the opinion of the military regarding the readiness of the Yak-1 for state tests. No one in the USSR could say 'no' to Comrade Stalin. On 29 May 1940, by order of the Head of the Main Directorate of Aviation Supply of the Red Army Komdiv (approximately Major General) Pavel Alekseev,[9] the Red Army Air Force Research Institute accepted the Yak-1 (I-26-2) for state tests. At the same time, the air force command ordered that the state tests of the future Yak-1 should be the first and main task. Two leading pilots were appointed to conduct them: 'Stalin's Falcons' Alexander Nikolayev and Pyotr Stefanovsky. They were supposed to carry out continuous flights on a prototype fighter, relieving each other. This solution made it possible to reduce significantly the duration of the state testing procedure for the aircraft. However, despite significant concessions, Alexander Filin made it clear that he considered Yakovlev another upstart who was trying to impose a fighter that did not meet their requirements in any way.

9 Komdiv Pavel Alekseev, a zealous executor of Stalin's will, was arrested on 19 June 1941 and accused of 'wrecking the Red Army Air Force, accepting defective and incomplete aircraft from the industry, delaying the re-armament of aviation units with fighters of the 'New Type'.' The Special Council of the USSR NKVD sentenced him to death. He was shot on 23 February 1942.

The Yak-1 fighter did not pass the state tests!

State tests of the prototype Yak-1 (I-26-2) were carried out in record time (1 to 15 June 1940). In two weeks, test pilots Nikolayev and Stefanovsky carried out fifty-two very unusual flights. The fact is that Stalin's orders could not eliminate the defects inherent in the design of the aircraft and engine. Despite the months-long struggle of the Yakovlev team with the cooling system, the engine stubbornly continued to overheat. According to the memoirs of test engineer Israel Rabkin, take-off, for example, was carried out in two steps: first taxiing to the start, then cooling the engine for ten to fifteen minutes, after which the engine was started again and the fighter took off at full engine speed. Flights to determine the rate of climb were carried out with 'platforms' (horizontal flight without climbing) to cool the engine. Such 'innovations' in the methodology of conducting state tests cast serious doubts on their results.[10]

Other shortcomings of the Yakovlev prototype were also identified, which directly affected the combat capabilities of the future Yak-1. The retraction-extension system landing gear did not meet the Red Army Air Force requirement for the possibility of retracting landing gear when climbing. The weapons test, which consisted of one 20mm ShVAK motor cannon and two 7.62mm ShKAS machine guns, could not be carried out. During the first attempts of shooting, a dangerous hit of spent cartridges and links on the horizontal stabilizer was noted, as well as great efforts (27kg) on the triggers of the machine guns.

As a result of various modifications, the flight weight of the Yak-1 (I-26-2) increased to 2,700kg. Such a significant excess of the fighter, compared to the estimated weight of 2,300kg, called into question the strength of the wing. This circumstance forced the specialists of the Red Army Air Force Research Institute to change the test programme, excluding spin and dive from it.

The indicators of the maximum speed of the fighter also greatly disappointed the military. During the state tests in horizontal flight at an altitude of 5,000 metres, a maximum speed of 585.5km/h was achieved, and the climb to that altitude was completed in six minutes.

Summing up, the engineers of the Red Army Air Force Research Institute issued a conclusion that stated that the Yak-1 (I-26-2) fighter did not pass

10 Rabkin, I.G., *Time, people, planes*, Moscow, Moskovsky rabochy, 1985, p.28.

Yak-1, Winter 1941.

state tests. The chief designer, Alexander Yakovlev, was to eliminate the detected shortcomings as soon as possible and submit the aircraft for repeated state tests.

At the Technical Council of the Red Army Air Force Research Institute held on 19 June 1940, dedicated to discussing the results of state tests of the Yak-1 (I-26-2), a heated discussion developed between the Head of the Research Institute, Filin, and aircraft designer Yakovlev. Stalin's favourite, feeling the constant strengthening of his position, disputed the claims of the military and with difficulty agreed to satisfy only some of them. As a result, an agreement was reached between the Yakovlev Design Bureau and the Red Army Air Force Research Institute that the third prototype of the Yak-1 (I-26-3) would be presented for repeated state tests. During the construction of this prototype, some shortcomings claimed by the military would be eliminated.

The collapse of competitors and the modest success of Alexander Yakovlev

Despite the failed state tests of the second prototype of the Yak-1 (I-26-2), Yakovlev soon had some reasons for optimism. Two dangerous competitors who developed fighters with the M-88[11] star-shaped engine suffered a

11 'Modified' by Russian engineers, the star-shaped 14-cylinder French Gnome-Rhône 14K Mistral Major engine.

complete and final collapse at once: the 'Super Rat' (I-180) from Nikolai Polikarpov and the I-28 from Vladimir Yatsenko. Their prototypes, which showed many defects during the tests, were not better or worse than the Yakovlev fighter. However, the main difference was the lack of informal support from Stalin or other influential forces. In particular, Nikolai Polikarpov turned from a favourite of the 'Red Lord' into a disillusioned outcast who found himself on the margins of the Soviet aircraft industry. His peer Vladimir Yatsenko, for whom the I-28 fighter was the last chance in the career of an aircraft designer, was never able to achieve success.

The departure of competitors meant the liberation of aviation plants, where the production of their fighters was planned. Gorky Aviation Plant No. 21, the second most powerful fighter manufacturer in the USSR, where it was planned to launch mass production of the 'Super Rat' (I-180) from Nikolai Polikarpov, was not yet available to Alexander Yakovlev. However, the Saratov Aviation Plant No. 292, the former 'ancestral land' of Vladimir Yatsenko, was at the full disposal of the energetic and aggressive Yakovlev. On 29 May 1940 it was decided to deploy the serial production of the future Yak-1 at the aviation plant, which was average in terms of production capacity.

Tests of the Yak-1 fighter of the first series at the Red Army Air Force Research Institute for the possibility of manual engine start.

In addition, in May 1940, Stalin issued another order on the distribution of aviation plants for the serial production of fighters of the 'New Type'. According to this order, Aviation Plant No. 301 and the under-construction Aviation Plant No. 126 were officially assigned to Alexander Yakovlev. However, it should be noted that plant No. 126 located in the Far East in the city of Komsomolsk-on-Amur never started production of the Yak-1. The capacity of the small plant did not allow it to master serial production of the Yak-1 in parallel with the Ilyushin DB-3 long-range bomber already in production there. Based on the full support of Stalin, it was a rather modest success for Yakovlev in the battle for aviation plants. The resistance of the opposing clan of directors of Soviet aviation industry enterprises to the expansion of Yakovlev was growing and his chances of obtaining the largest aviation plants producing fighters (State Aviation Plant No. 1 (Moscow) and Aviation Plant No. 21 in Gorky) were diminishing.

The absurd decision to mass-produce a semi-finished aircraft

Meanwhile, Stalin was in a hurry. He was annoyed by the 'slowness' of his aircraft designers, testers and aviation plants. It had been a year since the 'Red Lord' wished for a new 'wonder fighter', but his 'Stalin's Falcons' were still flying the I-16. Incompetent and stupid Stalin, who loved empty chatter about his beloved aviation, could not understand why things were going so badly. Endless meetings, sleepless nights, direct bribery, threats, reprimands and, finally, prisons, torture and shootings did not lead to anything. Again, nothing was ready. Everything was only half done. What to do? After a night of drinking with his most loyal servants, a solution was found. Having habitually convinced himself that without his intervention there would have been nothing at all, the 'Father of Nations' continued his usual rape of aircraft designers, testers and the beloved aviation industry.

Stalin gave two months to the management of Aviation Plant No. 301 to organize serial production of the Yak-1, and three months to the management of Saratov Aviation Plant No. 292. The absurdity of the decision to start serial production of the aircraft before the completion of the full test cycle did not surprise anyone. This was a common practice in the Stalinist economy. Just like the latest fighters, and with about the same disastrous result, tanks, guns, destroyers and submarines were built. Stalin generously spent the resources taken from the half-starved population of the USSR to satisfy his base vanity.

After receiving Stalin's order, another production fever began at Aviation Plants No. 301 and No. 292. No one cared about the colossal losses of material resources and time for the endless reworking and refinement of fighters already in serial production. The main task of the directors of aviation plants was to have time to fulfill Stalin's order. Not only their careers, but also their lives depended on this result. The Soviet people simply did not believe in the possibility that the serial production of a fighter that had not passed the tests would fail. Soviet 'deity' can't be wrong.

Aviation Plant No. 301. Aircraft designers made 3,950 changes to the drawings of the Yak-1

Aviation Plant No. 301 was the first to start the serial construction of Yak-1 fighters. In March 1940 the first plane was collected. However, what happened at the aviation plant during the first year of the organization of serial production of the Yakovlev fighter can be called an endless production hell. To understand the scale of the senseless time and resources spent, it is necessary to turn to the figures. In total, from 1 February to 1 October 1940, engineers from the Yakovlev Design Bureau made 3,950 changes to the drawings of the Yak-1. The reason for such a huge number of changes lay in the desire of the Yakovlev team to continue testing the Yak-1 prototype at any cost although time was short. This forced them to look for temporary solutions to eliminate the identified shortcomings. Such a vicious practice led to repetition of the same mistakes. As a result, many parts and even systems of the aircraft were redesigned several times. Accordingly, each time changes were made to the working drawings for Aviation Plant No. 301. This meant another alteration of the components and assemblies

'Stalin's Falcons', Aleksandr Nikolaev

of ready-made 'serial' aircraft. For example, after the crash of the first prototype, the design of the Yak-1 wing was changed. After that, on all examples of the fighter made at Aviation Plant No. 301, including those that were 100 per cent ready, a complex operation had to be performed to replace the wing. Thereafter, endless changes and alterations continued. From the beginning of the tests until 1 August 1940, the Yak-1 oil system was changed seven times, the air system four times, the armament and engine covers twice. In addition to the constant alterations, which caused engineers and workers complete despair, the supply of important components from other factories was constantly disrupted. There were many days of production downtime due to the lack of engines and other important parts of the aircraft.

The results of such a 'mass production' of Yak-1 fighters at Aviation Plant No. 301 turned out to be deplorable. Instead of hundreds of planned planes, the plant produced only forty-eight aircraft in 1940. Moreover, the military recognized only thirty-six of them as suitable, and only twelve fighters left the plant (eleven of them were sent for military tests).

The quality of the 'serial' aircraft produced at Aviation Plant No. 301 was depressing. Moreover, the main reason for the low quality was not low qualifications, but the deliberate sabotage by workers. A reasonable question may arise: how could the workers, despite many years of propaganda of the advantages of socialism and total state ownership, deliberately disrupt Stalin's order? The answer is banal: the employees of the aviation plant needed money to support their families. No one in the USSR distributed

Yak-1 of the first series, Spring 1941.

Yatsenko I-28 fighter.

bread and other products for free. Every Soviet worker and engineer was interested in getting the highest possible salary and bonus for overtime work. However, the money for the aviation plant to pay salaries and bonuses did not appear out of thin air; it was transferred only after the delivery of finished aircraft to the customer – the official representative of the customer (Red Army Air Force). Since, due to repeated alterations, the final assembly of the Yak-1 could not be completed for several months, the workers received only 6-8 rubles as a reward for their work during all this time. At the same time, in a country where workers and peasants were in power, the company's personnel had no opportunities to protect their rights. The employees of Aviation Plant No. 301 literally had to pay for the mistakes of the Yakovlev team caused by the mad rush in the design process. Thus, for the staff of Aviation Plant No. 301, Alexander Yakovlev and his plane became a symbol of all their troubles and failures. However, a high-ranking Deputy People's Commissar of Aviation Industry was unavailable for their criticism. The only object on which the workers could vent their indignation was the long-suffering Yak-1 fighter under construction at the plant. We must admit that the workers achieved brilliant results in this direction. The manufacturing quality of the Yak-1 fell so low that the Red Army Air Force leadership had the prevailing opinion that aircraft produced by Aviation Plant No. 301 should not be sent to military units too far from the plant. Therefore, the vast majority of Yak-1s assembled at the aviation plant in the city of Khimki (Moscow Region) entered the regiments of the Moscow Military District. After that, the repair crews of Aviation Plant No. 301 were almost constantly in military units, performing improvements and eliminating production defects according to complaints under the guarantees in the contract with the Main Directorate Red Army Air Force[12].

A bright contrast against the background of the terrible situation with the production of the Yak-1 was the situation with the development and construction of the LaGG-3 prototype. Lavochkin Design Bureau was also based in the Aviation Plant No. 301 and involved the same workers and engineers to work on its fighter. The work on the LaGG-3 prototype was not only generously paid, but also stimulated by additional bonuses in large volumes.

Thus, an unfavourable psychological atmosphere had developed at the plant. Despite the formal subordination of plant employees to the decree to manufacture the Yak-1, the attitude of Aviation Plant No. 301 to this order was purely negative. Embittered and exhausted management, engineers and the most qualified workers secretly hoped for the collapse of Yakovlev and his damned fighter. No commissions, persuasions and even punishments could change the situation with the 'mass production' of the Yak-1 at the plant. In the first quarter of 1941, under the formal pretext of the lack of interchangeability of parts and assemblies of aircraft produced by Plants No. 292 and No. 301, the production of Yak-1 fighters at No. 301 was discontinued. Thus, for more than a year of 'production', Aviation Plant No. 301, contrary to the 'iron' will of Stalin, produced only 114 Yak-1 fighters.

Aviation Plant No. 292. Aircraft designers made 7,460 changes to the drawings of the Yak-1

When preparing for the serial production of the Yak-1 at Saratov Aviation Plant No. 292, Alexander Yakovlev took into account the negative experience of Aviation Plant No. 301. All sources of potential resistance to the introduction of the Yak-1 were eliminated in advance by force measures. The entire management of the plant was replaced by people loyal to the Stalinist favourite, and Design Bureau Saratov Aviation Plant No. 292 was re-organized. The head of the design bureau, a competitor of Yakovlev, aircraft designer Yatsenko, was removed from the factory. His project of an alternative fighter, I-28, was officially recognized as unpromising and work on it was discontinued.

12 TSAMO RF, Foundation 35, Inventory 11287, Case 24, Sheet 15.

Serial production of Yakovlev fighters.

However, even such harsh measures could not protect Saratov Aviation Plant No. 292 from the failure of the Yak-1 production plan. The history of the production hell that had occurred earlier at Aviation Plant No. 301 was repeated. From 9 June 1940 and the beginning of receipt of drawings to 1 January 1941, 7,460 changes were made to the drawings of the Yak-1. Moreover, errors in the drawings already corrected at Aviation Plant No. 301, due to bureaucratic delays and idiotic secrecy, were repeated persistently at Saratov Aviation Plant No. 292. The reason was that the correct sets of Yak-1 drawings took more than a month to reach Saratov from Moscow.

In addition to the problems common with Aviation Plant No. 301, Saratov Aviation Plant No. 292 had its own specific difficulties. Rejoicing in the abundance of aviation plants marked on the map of the USSR and, their paper successes, the narrow-minded Stalin did not understand that most of his numerous plants were fully or partially impotent. For several months, fruitless attempts to weld the Yak-1 fuselage frame from steel pipes continued at Saratov Aviation Plant No. 292. The results remained depressing for a long time. The fuselage frames were either completely curved or fell apart at the first touch. Alexander Yakovlev's beautiful thesis about the

Rolling out Yak-1 fighters from the assembly workshop Saratov Aviation Plant No. 292.

simplicity of production of his Yak-1 fighter, presented to the 'Father of Nations', was completely refuted by the harsh reality of the technological backwardness of the new aviation plants. Similar difficulties that appeared earlier on Aviation Plant No. 301 were caused by the production of an all-in-one all-wooden wing for the Yak-1. Its production required the creation of an extremely complex technological process at Saratov Aviation Plant No. 292. A lot of time was spent on the development of special devices to ensure the strength of this critical structural element of the fighter.

The results of the development of the Saratov Aviation Plant No. 292 'mass production' of the Yakovlev aircraft turned out to be very deplorable. In 1940 the company produced only sixteen Yak-1 fighters (five of them were accepted by the military in November and eleven in December 1940), and not a single aircraft from this number was sent to the military units of the Red Army Air Force.

From March 1941 Saratov Aviation Plant No. 292 was the only manufacturer of the Yak-1 fighter. Improvements and alterations of the 'serial' aircraft continued. During 1941, 7,023 changes were made to the drawings and introduced into production. In total, approximately 8,500 Yak-1 fighters were produced at Plant No. 292 during the period from 1939 to 1944.

Lavochkin Unexpected victory

Despite the problems with the introduction of the Yak-1 into production at Aviation Plants No. 301 and No. 292, Alexander Yakovlev continued attempts to obtain other aviation plants. However, even Stalin's support was not a guarantee of the realization of Yakovlev's ambitions for total domination in the production of fighters. He lost the first fierce battle for the best piece. The largest and best-equipped State Aviation Plant No. 1 (Moscow), the former 'ancestral land' of Nikolai Polikarpov, remained in the hands of implacable enemies of Yakovlev. The next battle unfolded for the second most important Aviation Plant, No. 21, located in the city of Gorky. Yakovlev prepared better for this 'battle', and the 'enemies' were much weaker. The former 'King of Fighters', Nikolai Polikarpov, weakened to a shadow state, did not resist the termination of the 'serial' production of the 'Super Rat' (I-180) at this plant. Incidentally, in ten months, only four 'serial' examples of the fighter were produced at Gorky Aviation Plant No. 21. With its own Gorky Aviation Plant No. 21 project, the I-21 fighter, designed by Mikhail Pashinin, the influential Alexander Yakovlev dealt gently but effectively. Although the project was not formally closed, it did not receive any further development and, at the beginning of 1941, everyone forgot about the experimental I-21 fighter and its creator.

In the early autumn of 1940 Alexander Yakovlev created all the conditions for the Yak-1 to become the only mass-produced fighter with the M-105 engine. By this time, the Yakovlev fighter had only one competitor left – the LaGG-3. Stalin's favourite estimated the chances of success of the Lavochkin fighter as extremely low. However, Yakovlev's ambitious plans were destroyed by his high patron. On 2 October 1940, Stalin ordered a sharp increase in the range of new fighters to 1,000 kilometres, and at the expense of fuel in the internal tanks. This decision dealt a crushing blow to Yakovlev's plans. The open-work design of the Yak-1, which had the pronounced roots of a sports aircraft, was overloaded to the limit with numerous modifications. The weight of the aircraft had already exceeded the design by more than 500kg. Further significant increase in the mass of the fighter, which was inevitable when carrying out Stalin's order, was simply impossible.

The design of the LaGG-3 fighter, despite similar problems with increasing excess weight, had large reserves for modernization. In the shortest possible time, without significant alterations of the aircraft, Semyon Lavochkin managed to dramatically increase the range of the LaGG-3 by placing additional fuel tanks in the wing consoles. When the suspicious Stalin learned about the success of the Lavochkin fighter modernization, he abruptly changed his mind about the transfer of the second-largest aircraft factory to Yakovlev. In November 1940 the 'Red Lord' decided to produce LaGG-3 fighters at Gorky Aviation Plant No. 21. Thus, the peaceful and calm Semyon Lavochkin, who never built intrigue against competitors, turned out unexpectedly to be the winner in the fight with the aggressive and ambitious Alexander Yakovlev.

Pashinin I-21 fighter.

Chapter 6

MiG-3 – 'heavy in piloting 'Ivan'
We can't give our Aviation Plant to an alien!

7 December 1939. Assembly hall of State Aviation Plant No. 1. Meeting on the results of the work of the special commission 'On the prospects of mass production of new aircraft at State Aviation Plant No. 1'.

The assembly hall was quite crowded. In addition to the members of the factory commission, there were all the management of State Aviation Plant No. 1, a number of bosses from the People's Commissariat of Aviation Industry of the USSR and representatives of the command Red Army Air Force. Most of the Soviet managers sitting in the hall considered this meeting a waste of time and had prepared in advance to participate in a boring bureaucratic procedure. Only a few initiates knew that this seemingly

Designers and top managers of the Soviet Military Industry in the editorial office of the *Pravda* newspaper.

routine meeting would become an event that would radically change the situation in Soviet fighter aviation.

The beginning of the meeting did not portend anything revolutionary. The chairman of the commission, the Head of production of State Aviation Plant No. 1 Yuri Karpov came to the podium. He began to read out a boring report on the results of the commission's activities. Karpov told about the 'great' work on the 'selection' of the most promising fighter model for the organization of mass production at Plant No. 1. To this end, the members of the commission visited the Yakovlev Design Bureau and became acquainted with the characteristics of the new Yak-1 fighter. In conclusion, Karpov concluded that the Alexander Yakovlev prototype made a good impression on the commission, and by its design was optimally suited for mass production at the largest aviation plant in the USSR specializing in the production of fighters.

After these words, the listeners, yawning from boredom, felt that the event was nearing its end. Then, in accordance with the procedure of such events, a formal vote was to be held. Few of those present doubted that the decision to confirm serial production of the Yak-1 fighter at State Aviation Plant No. 1 would be adopted unanimously. No one expected any surprises from this meeting. Those present knew about Stalin's special attitude to Yakovlev and had already come to terms with the idea that the largest factory for the production of fighters would be placed at the full disposal

Mikulin AM-37 engine before state tests, June 1941.

of Stalin's favourite. There were simply no other alternatives. However, before the vote, in accordance with the bureaucratic procedure of such meetings, it was necessary to perform one small formality. Strictly fulfilling his function, the head of the commission, Karpov, invited the members of the commission to speak. Usually in such situations, there were no people willing to speak. However, this time the meeting clearly did not go according to Karpov's plan. Suddenly, a member of the commission, aircraft designer of State Aviation Plant No. 1, Aleksey Karev, asked for the floor. Surprised by such an unexpected act, the head of the commission was forced to give up his place on the podium to a young aircraft designer. Those present, anticipating an unusual development of events, immediately came out of a half-dream and began to look at each other in bewilderment. Something extraordinary was planned clearly.

From the first words, a handsome young aircraft designer, who was not yet 30 years old, attracted everyone's attention. Aleksey Karev unexpectedly emotionally accused the commission of serious shortcomings. Such a statement was a hint of deliberate sabotage which, in the conditions of Stalin's terror, threatened death. The members of the commission tensed internally and stared at the young aircraft designer with surprise and fear. Karpov was speechless with horror, and in response to the terrible accusation he could only helplessly spread his hands. Further, Aleksey Karev pathetically informed those present at the meeting that the Polikarpov Design Bureau, located on the territory of the aviation plant, had an almost ready draft design of a fighter with the Mikulin AM-35 engine. In his opinion, this aircraft had better flight characteristics than the Yakovlev fighter. Karev's performance had the effect of an exploding bomb. There was a noise in the hall, shouts were heard: 'That's right!', 'We need to figure out whose plane is better!'

Based on the resulting effect, it was obvious that Karev coped perfectly with the role that the management of State Aviation Plant No. 1 had prepared for him. It was Director Pavel Voronin and Chief Engineer Peter Dementiev, in collusion with People's Commissar of Aviation Industry Mikhail Kaganovich, who were the main organizers of this brilliantly played performance. The plan of the conspirators was completely successful for a very simple reason. There were too many detractors of the upstart Yakovlev in the hall, who, in addition to his engineering competencies, had a brilliant 'talent' in creating enemies for himself.

The meeting was disrupted. A spontaneous and very emotional discussion of the project of the new 'wonder fighter' 'suddenly' discovered in its own Design Bureau State Aviation Plant No. 1 began. Despite the calls for calm and the ringing of the bell, the noise in the hall continued. A big scandal was brewing. There was a threat that such a clearly manifested dissatisfaction with Yakovlev could break out of the meeting hall. It was necessary to act immediately. To stop the outpouring of hatred towards the Stalinist favourite, the Director of Plant No. 1, Pavel Voronin, had to intervene. The director's authority was so great that, as soon as he rose to the podium, the noise immediately subsided and the ability to listen returned to the audience. In a calm voice, Pavel Voronin promised the outraged listeners that he would deal with the situation as soon as possible and, together with the plant commission, would present detailed information about the new fighter to the People's Commissariat of Aviation Industry of the USSR. After such an exhaustive statement by the director, the passions subsided somewhat. Voronin took advantage of the situation and offered to vote for this proposal. All those present unanimously supported the proposal of the director and the fateful meeting ended.

It was a complete victory for the conspirators. The possibility of serial production of the Yakovlev fighter at State Aviation Plant No. 1 was now out of the question.

Useless aircraft 'wonder engine'

The Achilles' heel of the Soviet aviation industry was aircraft engines. If there were already dozens of design bureaux engaged in the creation of aircraft by the end of the 1930s, there were only a few design teams specializing in aircraft engines. Soviet aircraft designers could offer Stalin dozens of new aircraft, but only one or two types of engines could be installed in them and, as a rule, of very questionable quality. According to Nikolai Polikarpov, the success of the new fighter was 60 per cent dependent on the engine. Consequently, it was on its characteristics that the fulfilment of Stalin's task of achieving a speed of 650km/h by fighters depended. To cope with this task, aircraft designers needed an engine with a capacity of more than 1,000 horsepower, mass-produced by Soviet industry.

The USSR had never developed aircraft engines of their own design. At best, there was a modernization of licensed copies of foreign aircraft engines, and at worst, pirated copying. During the 1930s, almost the only type of engine installed on Soviet fighters was the one-row star-shaped air-cooled engine. The possibilities for increasing the power of such an engine were limited and, by the middle of the 1930s, its characteristics

M-88 aircraft engine.

reached their physical limit. At the end of the decade a more promising twin-row radial engine appeared. Such a star-shaped 14-cylinder French Gnome-Rhône 14K Mistral Major engine was installed on the failed 'Super Rat' (I-180) fighter designed by Nikolai Polikarpov. However, the Soviet 'modernized' replica of this engine (M-88) not only did not show the promised power characteristics, but also turned out to be completely unusable. Thus, the work on the powerful twin-row radial engine and, accordingly, on fighters with that type of engine had reached a dead end. After a trip to Germany and getting acquainted with the latest German fighters, the fashion for the star-shaped engine finally passed. There was an authoritative opinion, generally supported by Stalin, that the star-shaped engine was an anachronism that should be replaced by a new generation of V-shaped engines. Accordingly, the interest in this type of engine on the part of Stalin and the aviation specialists who carried out his will increased dramatically. The designers of V-shaped aircraft engines immediately felt both an increase in funding for their work, and a huge responsibility for fulfilling the order of the 'Red Tsar'.

By the end of the 1930s there were only two design bureaux in the USSR that were engaged in refining foreign V-shaped aircraft engines with water cooling: Vladimir Klimov and Alexander Mikulin. The main activity of the Mikulin Design Bureau was the licensed German engine BMW VI, which, after a number of adjustments, received the name Mikulin M-17 in its Soviet version. The engine was a real breakthrough not only for Soviet aviation, but also for Soviet armoured troops. The M-17 was installed on the first mass-produced Soviet medium T-28 and heavy multi-turret T-35 tanks. Moreover, the M-17 conquered not only the air and land, but also the water element. Its numerous copies powered light sea and river boats and minesweepers.

In 1932, based on the M-17, Alexander Mikulin developed the AM-34 engine, with a take-off power of 850 horsepower. This engine was installed on almost all Soviet bombers during the 1930s. However, soon Alexander Mikulin's almost monopoly of the V-shaped engine segment with water cooling was shaken. A new competitor in the form of Klimov Design Bureau with a promising M-100 engine (a copy of the licensed French Hispano-Suiza 12Y engine), quickly moved forward among the Stalinist favourites. Stalin's aggressive plans to conquer Europe proclaimed the priority of the production of fighters over other types of aircraft. This 'Red Lord' solution made the lightweight and compact Klimov M-105 engine with a capacity of 1,000 horsepower the undisputed leader in the production of aircraft engines in the USSR.

Aircraft engine designer, Alexander Mikulin.

The only chance of his competitor Alexander Mikulin winning a share in the fat fighter 'pie' was the new AM-37 engine. According to his calculations, this 'wonder' of Soviet technology could produce power of 1,400 horsepower, phenomenal for the end of the 1930s. The key to the success of the new engine, a further development of the AM-34, was the supercharger and a number of other technical improvements. According to the optimistic plans of aircraft engine designer Alexander Mikulin, the new 'wonder engine' was supposed to be ready by the end of 1939. Therefore, it was necessary to start an 'advertising campaign' to promote the AM-37 in the Soviet aircraft design bureaux as early as possible. However, there were no willing Soviet aircraft designers who wanted to implement the vaunted 'wonder engine'. Moreover, it is necessary to recognize the existence of objective reasons for such a sceptical attitude to the 'brilliant' Soviet aircraft engine designer Alexander Mikulin. Fighter aircraft designers were confused by the huge weight (850 kg) and large dimensions of the AM-37. It seemed to many of them that it was simply impossible to fit such a monster into the fuselage of a small high-speed aircraft, which was a typical fighter in those years.

'Shadow' aircraft designer, Nikolai Polikarpov.

However, the Soviet aircraft engine designer, experienced in cabinet intrigues, did not accept failure and found a more effective way to 'advertise' the AM-37. Numerous complaints to Stalin, which Alexander Mikulin transmitted through a devoted servant of the People's Commissar for Defence of the Soviet Union (Minister of War) Kliment Voroshilov finally produced the desired effect. A way out of the impasse was found. The designer of the useless aircraft engine, People's Commissar of Aviation Industry Mikhail Kaganovich sent for negotiations to the Polikarpov design bureau.

In February 1939 a large team of 'King of Fighters' relocated to the territory of State Aviation Plant No. 1 (Moscow). The chief designer of the largest fighter production plant in the USSR, Nikolai Polikarpov, had extensive experience in developing fighters with different types of engines. Only his design bureau had the objective capabilities and resources to develop a new fighter with the AM-37 engine. However, after the tragic death of Chkalov and the subsequent fall from grace in Stalin's eyes, Polikarpov was in a deep depression and actually lost interest in design work. Deep and irreversible changes had taken place in the personality of the talented

Mikulin AM-35A engine on the test bench.

aircraft designer, turning him into a pathetic shadow of the former powerful 'King of Fighters'. In connection with this mental breakdown, Polikarpov reacted to the proposal of aircraft engine designer Alexander Mikulin rather coldly. The idea of installing the AM-37 'wonder engine' on a fighter did not cause him the expected design enthusiasm. However, anticipating possible troubles, the former 'King of Fighters' did not categorically refuse the aircraft engine designer. He vaguely promised Mikulin to try to create a fighter project with his engine.

The birth of the fighter 'X'

In the summer of 1939, the Polikarpov Design Bureau began unhurried work on the preliminary design of a fighter with the AM-37 engine. Despite initial doubts, experienced engineers managed to marry the engine and the airframe. The first theoretical calculations showed that the future fighter, thanks to the presence of a supercharger, could fly at altitudes up to 6,000 metres without losing engine power. Thus, at a high altitude, where the air density is lower, it would not only reach the cherished speed target of 650 km/h, but also exceed it by 20 km/h. With such promising characteristics, the fighter project had every chance of winning the Stalinist competition. However, the former 'King of Fighters', after the failures that befell him, continued to be in a gloomy mood and was in no hurry to announce information about a promising fighter. Soon Polikarpov's pessimism about the project had new grounds. The weak point of the prototype fighter was expected to be its engine, or rather its absence. Soviet aircraft engine designers had traditionally been very generous with promises. In the presentation of plans, they offered aircraft designers a huge number of modifications of engines with revolutionary characteristics. However, the Soviet aircraft engine designers almost never fulfilled their promises. Due to numerous problems, the deliveries of the promised 'wonder engines' were shifted at best by one or two years. Many of the promising engines had never been created. Aircraft designers often had to put on their planes what they were given. The projected characteristics of the 'wonder fighters' with such compromises with engines naturally fell and, in reality, approached those of the notorious 'outdated' I-16.

To solve the problem, the helpful Alexander Mikulin offered Nikolai Polikarpov another 'almost ready' engine, the AM-35A. The designer assured him that it was as good as the hypothetical AM-37 and, most importantly, was already implemented in metal. However, by the middle of 1939, the AM-35A engine existed only as an experimental prototype. The first bench tests of the new engine, as expected, revealed numerous defects, which took a very long time to eliminate. There were quite objective reasons for such an expected outcome. The reserves of modernization of the reliable, but already outdated, German BMW IV engine were exhausted. The increase in its power was achieved by very risky design decisions, sometimes turning into outright adventures.

In accordance with the AM-35A engine proposed by Alexander Mikulin, minor changes were made to the 'X'[1] fighter project. This decision turned out to be very farsighted, since the creation of the AM-37 engine ended in complete failure. In 1941, after the release of twenty-nine units,

1 In accordance with the traditions of idiotic Stalinist secrecy, each prototype fighter of the 'New Type' was assigned a code designation at the paper design stage. For example, the future LaGG-3 was designated in secret documents as 'Object K'.

the production of the AM-37 was discontinued under the pretext of the evacuation of the aircraft engine plant and was never resumed.

Further work on the fighter project was going on in secret. Polikarpov, burdened with numerous projects, was mortally tired of the constant race and dreamed of a quiet job without constant night calls from Stalin. In November 1939 the preliminary design of the fighter, which received the designation I-200, was in a high degree of readiness. The team of engineers made a fundamental decision to choose a traditional mixed airframe and wing design with a predominance of wood for Polikarpov aircraft. The approximate composition of the new aircraft's armament was determined (two 7.62mm ShKAS machine guns and one 12.7mm BS machine gun). For the organization of mass production, Gorky Aviation Plant No. 21 was chosen, which was most suitable for the production of the next heir of the I-16. However, according to Nikolai Polikarpov, the preliminary design of the I-200 fighter could not be considered complete in any way. Entangled in emotional experiences and constant doubts, the former 'King of Fighters' had lost the ability to make risky decisions. He painfully sorted through the possible variants of the fighter's design, afraid of making another fatal mistake. In particular, Polikarpov intended to redesign the wing, reducing the bearing area, which, according to the aircraft designer, should have improved the aircraft's flight qualities. On the part of his team, such a position by the chief designer was perceived as a loss of leadership and a voluntary surrender in the fierce competition in the competition for the best Stalin's fighter of the 'New Type'. The psychological estrangement between Nikolai Polikarpov and the most talented and ambitious members of his design bureau was growing and threatened to develop into the expected split in the near future.

The conspiracy of the Directors

In the autumn of 1939 Nikolai Polikarpov had new reasons for alarm. From the management of State Aviation Plant No. 1 it was impossible to hide information about a new promising aircraft being developed at Polikarpov's design bureau. Director Pavel Voronin and Chief Engineer Peter Dementiev began persistently to ask Polikarpov officially to join the competition for the development of a fighter of the 'New Type'. They tried to convince Stalin's beloved aircraft designer that he needed to send the draft design of the I-200 fighter with the AM-37 engine to the People's Commissariat of

Above left: Pavel Voronin.

Above right: Peter Dementiev.

Aviation Industry of the USSR for approval as soon as possible. Voronin and Dementiev motivated their requests with a completely logical argument that there was no decent model of the latest aircraft for mass production at the largest plant in the USSR specializing in the production of fighters in 1940. Produced at State Aviation Plant No. 1 in 1939, the I-153 biplane fighter, also designed by Nikolai Polikarpov, lost its relevance and had rather illusory prospects for further serial production. Thus, the official reason for their persistence was explained by the complete uncertainty with the choice of types of fighters for further production. However, the real reason for the appeal of Voronin and Dementiev to Polikarpov had nothing to do with aeroplanes but was due to the banal struggle for influence on Stalin and, consequently, for power and control over the entire aviation industry of the Soviet Union.

At the end of 1939 everyone connected with aviation felt the approach of radical changes in the People's Commissariat of Aviation Industry of the USSR. People's Commissar Mikhail Kaganovich increasingly became the object of Stalin's public verbal bullying. The 'Red Lord' no longer hid his negative attitude towards him. The fact that Stalin was looking for a replacement for Kaganovich among the representatives of the new generation of Soviet managers could not escape the eyes of an attentive observer. Pavel Voronin, a 36-year-old former locksmith, and Peter Dementiev, a 32-year-old young engineer, were among the most likely candidates for the high positions that were being vacated. However, the struggle for Stalin's attention was complicated by the appearance of a new dangerous competitor in the person of Alexander Yakovlev. The first experience of interaction between Voronin and Dementiev with Stalin's new favourite turned out to be sharply negative. Organization of serial production of the twin-engine short-range BB-22 bomber at State Aviation Plant No. 1 resulted in an acute confrontation between them. Relations between the new potential leaders of the Stalinist aviation industry clearly did not develop well.

Yakovlev did not hide his huge administrative ambitions and clearly did not want to share future power with someone else. Gaining strength every day, Stalin's favourite sought to establish total control over the entire Soviet aviation industry through the mass production of his aircraft at most aviation factories. Thus, the interests of Yakovlev entered into a clear contradiction with the interests of Voronin and Dementiev. The fight between Stalin's young 'tigers' was inevitable. This option of intensifying the competitive struggle was quite acceptable to Stalin, who liked to pit his 'sons' against each other and always watched the outcome of this often deadly battle with interest.

As a tool for the struggle for power, competitors chose the victory in the competition for the best fighters of the 'New Type'. The referee in this confrontation was supposed to be the 'Red Lord' himself.

While Yakovlev and his team of engineers were working feverishly on the prototype of the Yak-1, Voronin and Dementiev made their desperate bet on the I-200 project from Nikolai Polikarpov. State Aviation Plant No. 1 hoped that, during the tests, the I-200 'wonder fighter' would surpass the Yak-1 in all respects. They had every reason to trust fully the talent and experience of the 'King of Fighters'. In addition, the 'old man' Polikarpov, unlike the promising manager Yakovlev, was never considered by the management of State Aviation Plant No. 1 as a competitor in the struggle for power. If the I-200 fighter won the competition, Voronin and Dementiev would not only retain control of the aviation plant, but also get the prospect of taking the main positions in the leadership of the Soviet aviation industry. In the event of an unlikely failure, they, knowing the peculiarities of Yakovlev's character, could not count on the mercy of the merciless Stalinist favourite. Thus, the stakes in the fight against Yakovlev were very high. The future career, and possibly the lives of Voronin and Dementiev, depended on the possibility of

Brothers Anastas and Artyom Mikoyan.

launching mass production of a fighter as soon as possible, an alternative to the Yakovlev aircraft. However, an unexpected obstacle appeared on the way to the implementation of the brilliant plan of the young managers. Polikarpov, referring to the objective unavailability of the project, gently refused to provide the I-200 drawings to the aviation plant management. Voronin and Dementiev had to retreat temporarily from the implementation of their ambitious plans. Although the former 'King of Fighters' had lost most of his 'strength', he still remained a favourite of Stalin. No one other than the 'Great Leader' could directly order him. Having failed to find support from Polikarpov, Voronin and Dementiev showed reasonable flexibility in this difficult situation. They began to look for supporters of their position within the team of the former 'King of Fighters'. In this direction, the conspirators were accompanied by a natural success.

Hundreds of engineers worked in Polikarpov Design Bureau, the largest in the USSR. Not all of them shared the views of the pardoned 'enemy of

Artyom Mikoyan, 'The Headless Horseman'.

the people', Nikolai Polikarpov, who was not a member of the Communist Party and did not hide his positive attitude to religion. After the crash of the 'Super Rat' (I-180), in which the beloved 'Stalin's Falcon' Chkalov died, Polikarpov's life hung in the balance. Many of his 'employees' remembered the recent months-long disfavour that the 'King of Fighters' got into. And although the danger of immediate reprisals receded, many aircraft designers from the Polikarpov team considered the career of the 'King of Fighters' hopelessly ruined and were afraid of possible accusations of co-operation with the next 'enemy of the people'.

Purposeful conversations about the accelerated implementation of the I-200 project, conducted by Voronin and Dementiev with employees of the design bureau of State Aviation Plant No. 1 gave brilliant results. As known, the hearts of men are easily corrupted. Most of the aircraft designers from the Polikarpov team were ready to leave the defeated 'King of Fighters'. However, there were no people willing to openly oppose their boss and teacher. Hesitating engineers needed certain conditions to make a decision. If Polikarpov had suddenly disappeared from view for a long time, then it would have become much easier to commit betrayal. Voronin and Dementiev had only to wait anxiously for a favourable moment to implement their plan, and soon such a moment presented itself. Fortunately for Polikarpov, on 25 October 1939, he disappeared not because of expected arrest by the NKVD, but on a long business trip at the will of Stalin. As part of the Soviet delegation, which also included Alexander Yakovlev and Peter Dementiev, the former 'King of Fighters' left for Germany. The purpose of the trip of the large Soviet delegation was to study the experience of developing new types of aircraft and analyze the organization of the German aviation industry.

We need to act immediately!

After Nikolai Polikarpov left for Germany, the main obstacle was removed and the conspirators began to implement their plan into reality. Fortunately, there were quite favourable conditions for this. The I-200 fighter project was ready, which meant that the leadership of State Aviation Plant No. 1 no longer needed the talent of Polikarpov. Moreover, by the beginning of November 1939, a group of about eighty of the best aircraft designers was finally formed, ready to leave the former 'King of Fighters'. And, most importantly, Voronin and Dementiev had their candidate for the position of chief designer ready. He was supposed to replace the intractable and capricious 'old man' Polikarpov in this post. This candidate turned out to be an unknown young military engineer, Artyom Mikoyan, completely controlled by the leadership of State Aviation Plant No. 1. The main advantage of this modest young man was his older brother and Stalin's closest servant, People's Commissar of Foreign Trade (Minister) Anastas Mikoyan.

The only obstacle to the implementation of the I-200 project was Mikhail Tetivkin, acting chief designer of State Aviation Plant No. 1. Guessing about the plans of the plant's management, Nikolai Polikarpov, shortly before his business trip to Germany, appointed his deputy Tetivkin to this position. So, childishly naively, the 'King of Fighters' tried to protect his design bureau from a raider takeover by the leadership of State Aviation Plant No. 1. Tetivkin was a man devoted to his boss, but he could not resist the administrative resource of the experienced Pavel Voronin. On 14 November 1939, the Head of the 1st Main Department of the People's Commissariat of Aviation Industry of the USSR, Makar Lukin, appointed Artyom Mikoyan to the post of chief designer. Nikolai Polikarpov's appointment of Tetivkin to the position was cancelled. Thus, important prerequisites were created for the transfer of control over the Polikarpov Design Bureau and the I-200 fighter project into the hands of Director of State Aviation Plant No. 1 Voronin.

Despite the first victory in the protracted war with Yakovlev, the situation of the conspirators remained critical due to lack of time. The assembly of the Yak-1 prototype was going ahead at a rapid pace, and the Stalinist favourite persistently offered to choose State Aviation Plant No. 1 (Moscow) to master the serial production of his fighter. However, Voronin and Dementiev were lucky again. As already mentioned, Yakovlev, after Polikarpov, was also sent to Germany on a long business trip. Although he returned to the Soviet Union a month earlier than Polikarpov, the urgent fulfilment of Stalin's task to complete the Yak-1 for a long time deprived him of the opportunity to resist Voronin and Dementiev.

Thus, Voronin only needed to effectively use his advantage over the competitor. Having staged the performance described above at the failed meeting on the results of the work of the special commission, he not only masterfully repelled Alexander Yakovlev's encroachments on the seizure of State Aviation Plant No. 1, but also made a public presentation of a new promising I-200 fighter.

Experimental Design Department

On 8 December 1939, fulfilling the promise made to the excited participants of the meeting, Voronin launched a powerful psychological attack on Polikarpov's deputies. He demanded that the confused aircraft designers submit a draft design of the I-200 fighter, allegedly for study by a special commission. After a short hesitation, the documents were provided, and the engineers who worked on the project answered all the questions asked by the members of the commission. After a short meeting on the results of familiarization with the project, the commission, as expected, considered the I-200 project the best.

Further, a lengthy bureaucratic procedure for approving the fighter project by numerous increments was expected. However, in the case of the I-200, the entire complex procedure took a few days. The commission's decision was immediately reported to the People's Commissariat of Aviation Industry of the USSR, and all the documentation on the draft project was sent there. The People's Commissariat of Aviation Industry, in turn, informed the Red Army Air Force Command and the Central Committee of the Communist Party of the Soviet Union about the I-200 project. Soon Stalin's approval was received for the immediate organization of work on the construction of a prototype and preparation for mass production of a new fighter. The author does not know at what stage Voronin and Dementiev, through the People's Commissar of Aviation Industry Kaganovich, who was in collusion with them, informed Stalin about the I-200. However, such a fantastic speed of approval of the project by the Soviet bureaucracy could be achieved only in the case of personal intervention of the 'wisest of the wise'.

Artyom Mikoyan at the beginning of his career, 1925.

On the same day, 8 December 1939, after receiving Stalin's approval, Voronin began the long-planned takeover of the Polikarpov Design Bureau. To give his actions a civilized look, the Director of State Aviation Plant No. 1 performed a number of bureaucratic tricks. The Polikarpov Design Bureau was re-organized by separating several separate structures from it. The main result of the manipulations was the concentration of all the best Polikarpov engineers in a separate structure, which was called the Experimental Design Department. Thirty-four-year-old Artyom Mikoyan was appointed head of this department, intended exclusively for the implementation of the I-200 project. This appointment was also approved by Stalin.

'The Headless Horseman'

The end of the 1930s was a turning point for the Soviet aviation industry. Stalin's pathological dream of a new generation of Soviet aircraft designers who were completely loyal and controlled by him was fulfilled. However, even in this environment, the elevation of Artyom Mikoyan to the position of the successor of Nikolai Polikarpov was perceived with undisguised surprise. The former turner, who had recently graduated from the Zhukovsky Air Force Engineering Academy and had practically no experience in designing aircraft, was absolutely not suitable for the role of chief designer of the largest design bureau of the Soviet Union.

Despite the fact that, among the young Soviet engineers, there were many immigrants from workers and peasants, the path to the top league of Soviet aircraft designers was extremely difficult. Even the presence of a young specialist, a specialized education, and pronounced design abilities was not enough. The long-term work of the applicant under the guidance of representatives of the older generation, such as Polikarpov, Tupolev or Ilyushin, also did not guarantee success. It was necessary to have successful experience of independent design, as well as the ability to create a team of likeminded engineers. And, finally, the applicants for getting into the top league of Soviet aircraft designers needed a huge success, expressed in the conditions of the USSR in personal sympathy from the almighty Stalin. It was such a difficult path that Semyon Lavochkin and Alexander Yakovlev went through.

However, Artyom Mikoyan received huge power from Stalin, as if in advance. He had nothing but the sympathy of the 'Father of Nations'. Now, only the result of the implementation of the I-200 fighter project could show how this young engineer would cope with such a huge responsibility.

Shortly after his appointment, the young Artyom Mikoyan received from his young colleagues the offensive nickname 'The Headless Horseman',[2] which rudely hinted at his incompetence and lack of special abilities. The answer to the question of how serious a competitor he appeared to Yakovlev and Lavochkin have appeared as lies in the analysis of the biography of the future famous Soviet aircraft designer.

On 5 August 1905, on the far outskirts of the huge Russian Empire in the mountain village of Sanahin (Armenia), a third son was born to a worker, Ovanes Mikoyan. He became the fifth and youngest child in the family. At baptism the boy was named Anushavan. It cannot be said that the third son was a long-awaited child for his already elderly parents. To ensure the future of five children, the strength and means of the Mikoyan family were clearly not enough. Extreme poverty and the lack of any educational infrastructure, other than primary school, limited the educational opportunities for the residents of Sanahin village. Ninety per cent of the population of the Russian Empire were illiterate; the situation was even worse on the outskirts.

Ovanes Mikoyan understood that only the most capable of the three sons had a chance to break out of the vicious circle of poverty. All the hopes of the family were connected with the second son Anastas who, in 1906, became a student of the Tiflis Armenian Theological Seminary. After this important event, the modest resources of the Mikoyan family were exhausted. Burdened with numerous household worries, the parents could no longer pay enough attention to their youngest son.

Only two primary school classes at the monastery located next to the village were available to receive the basics of Anushavan education. However, the future Soviet aircraft designer started working earlier than studying. For this and many other reasons, his childhood and youth cannot be called prosperous. When Anushavan turned 10 years old, the First World War began. The front of the confrontation between the Russian Empire and the Ottoman Empire took place near the village of Sanahin. The war proved fatal for the two opposing empires. The Russian Empire was the first to collapse in 1917, and in 1918 the Ottoman Empire began to disintegrate. Against the background of all these grandiose events, the family lost its leader. Ovanes Mikoyan died when Anushavan was only 13 years old. The death of his father was a turning point in the fate of a teenager who grew up in a small village deep in the mountains. Further, Anushavan's life would

2 *The Headless Horseman*, a novel by Mayne Reid, was very popular in the USSR.

Polikarpov I-153 fighter.

be inextricably linked with big cities and a huge country that became his new homeland. Soon the mother sent her son to live with relatives in the city of Tiflis (now Tbilisi, Georgia), where he was able to continue his education in an Armenian school. It was quite difficult for a resident of a small mountain village to adapt to life in a big city. The trials experienced by Anushavan set him apart from his urban peers. A half-starved childhood left an indelible imprint on the appearance and health of Anushavan. His height was less than most of his peers. The teenager looked very thin and sickly. Physical weakness was compensated by pronounced strong-willed character traits, thanks to which Anushavan demonstrated incredible resistance to life's difficulties. An early manifested desire for independence, combined with an acute sense of social justice, created the ground for the emergence of sympathies in the teenager in relation to the revolutionary struggle waged by the communists in the Caucasus. A certain influence on the political outlook of Anushavan was also exerted by his older brother, Anastas Mikoyan, who by 1919 was already a well-known Bolshevik leader. Anushavan, who perceived his brother's activities as a model, also became a staunch supporter of the Caucasian communists.

In the early 1920s, the young 'Red Empire' began methodically restoring control over the lands lost after the collapse of tsarist Russia. In 1922 the Bolsheviks formed the Transcaucasian Soviet Federal Socialist Republic, which became part of the USSR. Young Anushavan, and especially his older brother, a well-known Bolshevik and close friend of Stalin, had huge opportunities. Their life plans were no longer limited to the territory of

Student of the Kharkov Technological Institute, Mikhail Gurevich.

little Armenia and even the entire Caucasus. In 1923 Anushavan moved to his brother in Rostov-on-Don where, after graduating from the professional technical school, the future aircraft designer qualified as a turner. In 1925, on the recommendation of his brother, Anushavan Mikoyan became a member of the Communist Party. His whole future life was inextricably linked with Bolshevik ideology, which he served faithfully until the last day of his life.

At the end of 1925, on the advice of his brother, Anushavan Mikoyan moved to Moscow. In a huge metropolitan city, he found himself without housing and work. For some time Anushavan lived with friends. Then, the future aircraft designer found a job as a turner at the electric machine-building plant 'Dynamo'. For better adaptation in the Russian-speaking environment, Anushavan changed his difficult-to-pronounce Armenian name to the name Artyom, which is common in Russia. Despite his hard work and responsible attitude to work, the turner's salary was not enough to meet the modest needs of the future aircraft designer. For a long time, Artyom Mikoyan lived in a dirty janitor's room, which he rented for a modest fee. The proud and independent young worker categorically refused the help of his influential older brother, who also moved to Moscow.

Hard work and poor living conditions seriously undermined the poor health of Artyom Mikoyan. Soon he fell ill with an acute form of tuberculosis, a common disease of the poor urban population. The epidemic of this potentially deadly disease had engulfed many residents of the Soviet Union weakened by years of famine and civil war. Thanks to timely treatment organized by the powerful elder brother, the dangerous disease was cured. However, later relapses of insidious tuberculosis remained the main factor in the poor health of the Soviet aircraft designer.

At the age of 22, a young worker, in addition to a lack of education, began to feel acutely the lack of military service experience. Artyom Mikoyan understood that in a totally militarized country, where all men had military ranks, no further career was possible without a document of service in the Red Army. Unlike Yakovlev, the son of a worker, Mikoyan had no problems with passing a strict selection in the Red Army. In 1928, the recruit Artyom Mikoyan was enlisted in the infantry and sent to the city of Livny Orel Region. Service in the infantry turned out to be a serious test for his poor health. Marches with heavy military gear over long distances turned out to be clearly too much for Artyom Mikoyan. He fainted several times – this was how the consequences of the tuberculosis he suffered shortly before the army were manifested, the fact of which he apparently hid during the medical examination.

In August 1929 Mikoyan was transferred to the newly-created Soviet tank school in the city of Ivanovo-Voznesensk. Perhaps it was during the study of the first Soviet tanks, which were primitive copies of a French tank from the First World War, that Mikoyan first thought about the profession of an engineer.

In 1930, after returning from military service, the career of a fanatical communist practically did not receive any development. Artyom Mikoyan had consistently held several positions at the very bottom of the party hierarchy. Apparently, he still categorically refused the help of his influential brother and decided to build his career independently in the Communist Party. Soon he had a chance to demonstrate his loyalty to Stalin.

In 1931, the 'Red Lord', seized by a persecution mania, was concerned about the state of affairs with the creation and production of new military aircraft. He was firmly convinced that the former tsarist engineers and designers who agreed to work for the Bolsheviks were potential enemies of the Soviet government. Since Stalin did not have his own dedicated engineering personnel, he was forced to put up with such an unpleasant situation for a while. This forced compromise bothered the 'Great Leader' and required a solution in the near future. Stalin's 'plan' was equally insidious and primitive. According to the 'wisest of the wise', only the organization of total control over the work of potential 'enemies of the people' could save the young Soviet Red Army Air Force

Aircraft designer, Mikhail Gurevich.

from sabotage and 'wrecking'. Stalin could entrust such responsible work only to young communists, whose loyalty he did not doubt. In addition, the 'Red Lord' hoped that during the implementation of proletarian control, young Stalin's agents would be able to gain valuable experience from tsarist engineers in designing and organizing mass production of aircraft. Thus, the narrowminded 'Red Tsar' expected that by the time all the 'enemies of the people' were shot or sent to rot in a Gulag, he would have a new generation of undividedly devoted aircraft designers and managers.

Yakov Alksnis was chosen to be responsible for the selection and introduction of young communists in design bureaux and aviation plants. He was appointed by Stalin to the post of Chief of the Red Army Air Force and enthusiastically began to fulfill the important assignment of 'Master'. However, fanaticism alone was clearly not enough to identify and eradicate 'enemies of the people' in the Soviet aircraft industry. Stalin's 'agents' needed specialized education. So Artyom Mikoyan found himself in a group of communists selected for admission to the Zhukovsky Air Force Engineering Academy. For the son of a worker who did not receive a systematic school education, preparing for exams to an elite military university became a real test. However, attending special courses and individual work with tutors allowed Artyom Mikoyan to fill in huge gaps in his education. After passing the exams, the future aircraft designer became a cadet of the Zhukovsky Air Force Engineering Academy.

Mikoyan studied with great passion, compensating with hard work and diligence for the limited knowledge he received in childhood and youth. On 22 October 1937 Artyom Mikoyan successfully defended his thesis project. After completing a long study at the academy, he was awarded the title of military technician of the second rank Red Army Air Force. Thus, it can be argued that Mikoyan got into aviation not by the call of his heart, but by order of Stalin. However, the successful professional career of this famous Soviet aircraft designer showed the correctness of this forced choice.

The Eye of Stalin in the Polikarpov Design Bureau

In the second half of the 1930s, Stalin's primitive dreams began to come true. Young engineers, personally devoted to him, began to be distributed among design bureaux and plants, which were part of a Soviet aviation industry that had grown to a huge scale. Military technician Artyom Mikoyan was appointed military controller at the largest State Aviation Plant No. 1.

Lisunov Li-2 (Douglas DC-3) in the parking lot.

Soon, the promising Stalin's engineer had an 'object' of control. However, they were not fighters produced at the factory, the quality of which Mikoyan, as an official representative of the military, had to control, but the 'King of Fighters' himself. In February 1939 the Polikarpov Design Bureau was transferred to this plant to organize the production of the I-153 fighter. By that time, the former 'King of Fighters', who had already lost most of Stalin's trust, had the informal status of a lame duck in the elite of Soviet aircraft designers.

Fanatical Artyom Mikoyan took Stalin's task very seriously. He devoted all his time to scrupulous study of a huge number of drawings and careful supervision of the work of the engineers of the Polikarpov Design Bureau. Mikoyan's inherent modesty and tact, combined with a genuine interest in design work, aroused the sympathy of the compromise-prone Polikarpov. In a short time, the young engineer established contact and friendly relations with almost all members of the Polikarpov Design Bureau. Very soon Nikolai Polikarpov accepted the inevitability that Artyom Mikoyan become an integral part of his Design Bureau. The former 'King of Fighters' did not suspect that in a few months this young military engineer would take his place.

However, at the end of 1939, Artyom Mikoyan was only a pawn in the big game of ambitious managers Voronin and Dementiev. Even then he showed enviable foresight, demanding to appoint an experienced and talented aircraft designer, Mikhail Gurevich, to be his deputy. Only after this condition was met did he agree to take the position of Chief Designer of the Experimental Design Department.

Nikolai Polikarpov, who returned from a long business trip to Germany, was forced to move from the excellent premises of the former Polikarpov Design Bureau to a cold and empty hangar. There, with a small group of devoted followers, he continued working on projects that were no longer needed by anyone.

The older 'brother' of Artyom Mikoyan

In contrast to the completely non-standard elevation of Artyom Mikoyan, the biography of Mikhail Gurevich repeats the general features of the life path peculiar to famous Soviet aviation engineers of the late 1930s.

Mikhail Gurevich was born on 12 January 1893 in the village of Rubanshchina, Kursk province, located in the centre of the European part of the Russian Empire. The head of the family, Joseph Gurevich, was engaged in the repair and adjustment of equipment at the Kharkov and Kursk provinces' wineries. This business turned out to be profitable enough to provide good conditions for the family's existence. Mikhail, the only child of the Gurevich couple, was surrounded by care and love. His parents created favourable conditions for the development of a capable son and spared no expense in getting him the best education that could be found in this province. In 1910, after successfully graduating from Okhtyrka Men's Gymnasium, Mikhail was admitted to the mathematics department of Kharkov Imperial University without exams. When analyzing this event, it should be taken into account that, in the Russian Empire, the admission of persons of Jewish nationality to universities was strictly limited. The fact that Gurevich overcame this administrative barrier testifies to the outstanding mathematical abilities of the future aircraft designer, which were combined harmoniously with hard work and a high motivation to study.

However, it soon became clear that Mikhail was not only concerned about studying at the university. He could not help noticing the vices of the thoroughly rotten tsarist regime. For participating in student protests against police brutality and restrictions on freedom of speech, Mikhail Gurevich was arrested and administratively expelled from Kharkov province. After being expelled from Kharkov Imperial University, the path to get an education in the Russian Empire was closed for him. Mikhail could only continue his studies abroad.

In 1912 Mikhail Gurevich entered the University of Montpelier, one of the most prestigious universities in France. He spent his free time at the local airfield, where he watched with interest the flights of French aviation pioneers Henri Farman, Alberto Santos-Dumont, Louis Blériot and others. However, at this stage of his life, the talented young man was not yet ready for an unambiguous choice of profession.

In 1914, having successfully passed the exams and finished the second year of university, Mikhail went to his parents for the summer holidays. However, the beginning of the First World War destroyed all plans for the future. The talented young man could no longer return to France to continue his studies and the path to education was again closed for three long years. To ensure his existence, Mikhail took a number of temporary jobs, none of them corresponding to his ideas about his future profession.

The 1917 revolution turned the Russian Empire into a republic. Russian citizens had received broad rights and freedoms. The previous total prohibitions of the tsarist regime were lifted. Mikhail Gurevich had the opportunity to continue his studies and the future famous Soviet aircraft

State Aviation Plant No. 1.

designer entered Kharkov Technological Institute's Faculty of Mechanics where, later, an aircraft building department was organized. Due to the civil war and the total economic crisis caused by the Bolsheviks, the terms of study at the institute were extremely stretched. Mikhail Gurevich received a design engineer's diploma only in 1925. During his studies, he became seriously interested in designing gliders which demonstrated excellent flight characteristics at competitions. However, the path to design work again turned out to be very long. For several years after graduation, the talented aviation engineer was forced to vegetate in minor positions, engaged in the design of industrial ventilation.

In 1929 Gurevich moved from Kharkov to Moscow where he soon got a chance for self-realization in the chosen direction. After passing rigorous exams, he became a member of the design bureau of the French aircraft designer Paul Aimé Richard. The acute shortage of qualified engineering personnel forced the Bolsheviks to invite foreign aviation specialists to work in the USSR. During this period, the future creator of the LaGG-3, Semyon Lavochkin, also worked at the same Richard design bureau.

After 1931 Gurevich worked at the Kochergin Design Bureau. His first independent project was the creation of an armoured ground-attack aircraft, the TSH-3. Despite the good results shown by the aircraft during tests, no decision was made on its mass production.

In 1936, together with a group of Soviet aviation engineers, Mikhail Gurevich was sent on a long business trip to the United States. The trip was carried out within the framework of an agreement on the licensed

Fighter I-200 (MiG-3) No. 1.

production of the DC-3 aircraft in the USSR. The implementation of the contract involved the transfer to the Soviet Union of the entire complex of innovative production technologies developed at Douglas Aircraft. After returning from the United States in summer 1937, Gurevich participated in the organization of serial production of the DC-3 aircraft at Soviet aviation plants.

At the end of 1937, aircraft designers Andrey Tupolev and Vladimir Myasishchev were arrested on Stalin's orders. Their design bureau was liquidated, and many members of their team were repressed by the NKVD. Although the future creator of the MiG-3 fighter escaped arrest and Gulag, he was left without his favourite job. The disgraced aircraft designer was saved from the threat of oblivion by Nikolai Polikarpov, who invited him to his design bureau. Thus, Gurevich became an integral part of the 'King of Fighters' team. So highly did Polikarpov appreciate the talented designer's potential that he appointed Gurevich to the responsible post of head of the department of the general views and preliminary design. Under his leadership, experienced engineers turned the calculations of aerodynamic and strength calculations into sketches of the appearance of the future aircraft.

Despite his pronounced design talent, Mikhail Gurevich always remained in the shadow of bright leaders. He sorely lacked the firmness of character to become head of his own design bureau. Any serious obstacles stopped him, and the necessity, in some cases, to criticize subordinates harshly was beyond his strength. Knowing about the harassment of Polikarpov, Gurevich did not stand up for him but dutifully took the position of deputy to Mikoyan, who was thirteen years younger, and in terms of work experience simply not comparable with him.

Of course, this is a full-fledged project!

From the moment Stalin approved the I-200 project, a feverish race began. The pace of work, the resources allocated and the optimism about the flight data of the future fighter were fantastic. On 25 December 1939 the Red Army Air Force commission considered and approved the aircraft's layout. The next day, in accordance with the order of Artyom Mikoyan, the best Soviet aircraft designers began to develop and produce working drawings of the I-200. In the People's Commissariat of Aviation Industry of the USSR, the project also received full support. On 31 December People's Commissar of Aviation Industry Mikhail Kaganovich ordered that production of the I-200 be considered a priority and included serial production of the 'wonder fighter' in the plan for 1940.

However, despite the obvious success, the situation for Voronin, Dementiev and Mikoyan continued to be very alarming. The partners understood that they had entered into a very dangerous game with Stalin. They were literally responsible with their heads for the success of the new fighter which, in conditions of a catastrophic lack of time, directly depended on the speed of implementation of the project. The usual procedure for creating a new aircraft involved constructing an experimental sample, on which all design solutions were tested. Sometimes, taking into account the problems identified, it was necessary to create several prototypes one after another. This was followed by fresh long-term tests. It was according to this scheme that Yakovlev acted when creating the Yak-1 fighter. However, the implementation of the I-200 project lagged behind its competitors (Yak-1 and LaGG-3) by at least six months. Following the usual protocol of testing prototypes would lead the partners to an inevitable defeat. Such a situation would certainly have baffled a German or British aircraft designer. However, Soviet specialists, fulfilling Stalin's insane orders, were used to working in conditions of complete disregard for norms, rules and protocols. Soon, a way out of the impasse caused by the lack of time for implementation of the project was found. It consisted in rejecting the construction and testing stage of experimental prototypes of the aircraft. This very risky decision would save a few precious months but required full confidence in the design of the fighter, which so far existed only on paper. All the partners' doubts were dispelled by the specialists of the Central Aerohydrodynamic Institute (TsAGI). They conducted several tests of aircraft models in a wind tunnel in record time and gave a positive assessment of the flight qualities of the future MiG-3. Confidence in the success of the 'wonder fighter' led to the chief designer Artyom Mikoyan and Director of State Aviation Plant No. 1 Peter Dementiev deciding to build five pre-production copies of the I-200 (MiG-3) fighter without preliminary prototype testing.

However, even such an extraordinary step was not enough to defeat Yakovlev. A significant gain in time could only be obtained by the accelerated introduction of a new fighter into mass production. As a rule, it was at this stage that the biggest problems arose and, consequently, much time was lost. Knowing about this vice, Voronin, Dementiev and Mikoyan took unprecedented measures to overcome it. Long before the construction of pre-production copies and the conduct of state tests, large-scale preparations for serial production of

Fighter I-200 (MiG-3) No. 2.

the future fighter began at State Aviation Plant No. 1. When organizing this work, there was an unusual feature that is totally uncharacteristic of the Soviet aviation industry. For the first time, aircraft designers and specialists in the organization of production, at least temporarily, overcame the usual disunity resulting from opposing interests. This turned out to be possible since, during the implementation of the I-200 project, aircraft designers and production organizers had a common goal, formed a single team and were interested in helping each other. Thus, instead of the usual swearing and mutual accusations, there was joint work and consideration of the needs of both sides.

The chances of success were increased by the application of new principles and technologies for the design and production of aircraft, borrowed from abroad and used for the first time on such a scale when creating a Soviet fighter. The main role in this process was played by Mikhail Gurevich, who had extensive experience in business trips to American aviation enterprises. In accordance with the principles of mass production, the airframe of the MiG-3 was divided into complete structural and production units during the design. The detachable wing consoles, the fuselage divided into parts and the single-column landing gear with very simple kinematics allowed for parallel assembly of the units on different stands and convenient assembly on the conveyor. In turn, aviation technologists provided for the maximum simplification of production processes for fighter parts through the widespread introduction of casting and hot stamping. A small number of very simple connections made it possible easily and quickly to replace faulty components and assemblies, even in the field. All these measures were to significantly speed up future serial production of the fighter, as well as facilitate the operation of the aircraft in aviation regiments.

Mikoyan is surrounded by the leading engineers of his team: Tretyakov and Litvinov.

Thus, at the beginning of 1940, everyone who participated in the creation of the new Stalinist fighter was convinced that they were dealing with the 'wonder fighter', which had no equal in world aviation: the best project, the best engineers and managers, the best Soviet fighter production plant. All the pretentious epithets used to describe the fighter created the illusion of an indispensable great success for the project participants. The premonition of an early victory over competitors was spinning heads. Finally, the will of the 'Great Leader' would connect with the intelligence of the Red aircraft designers and the hands of the Red workers. Very soon, the best Red fighter in the world would be created with which the Red Army would make all of Europe Red. So thought many creators of the future MiG-3. The second half of 1941 showed how mistaken they were.

Stalin is satisfied with the new fighter!

The change of leadership of the People's Commissariat of Aviation Industry of the USSR, which happened at the behest of Stalin on 10 January 1940, accelerated the process of implementing the I-200 project. The power-hungry

Director of State Aviation Plant No. 1, Pavel Voronin, became Deputy for the organization of serial production of aircraft of the new People's Commissar of Aviation Industry Aleksey Shakhurin. Chief Engineer Peter Dementiev was promoted to the position of Director of State Aviation Plant No. 1.

By the beginning of 1940 the situation was developing in different directions for the main competitors Voronin, Dementiev and Mikoyan. Yakovlev, after being appointed by Stalin, became the Deputy for Experimental Development of the new People's Comissar – not only retaining, but strengthening his position. Lavochkin, after the dismissal of People's Commissar of Aviation Industry Mikhail Kaganovich, lost his high patron and implemented the LaGG-3 (I-301) project with great difficulty.

Meanwhile, the implementation of the I-200 project was carried out at record pace. The first flight machine was handed over for factory tests on 31 March 1940. On 5 April, the honoured 'Stalin's Falcon' Arkady Ekatov lifted the I-200 No. 01 into the air for the first time. The results of this and subsequent flights of the 'wonder fighter' showed that the efforts of its creators were not in vain. The flight characteristics and take-off and landing properties of the plane obtained during the tests practically coincided with the calculations and corresponded to almost all the tactical and technical requirements of the Red Army Air Force. During the factory tests, an increase in speed was achieved with each flight.

On 24 May 1940, pilot Arkady Ekatov, in the first pre-production aircraft reached a speed of 648.5km/h at an altitude of 6,900 metres. Information about the Artyom Mikoyan fighter reaching a record speed was immediately

MiG-3 fighter at a field airfield.

reported to Stalin. Satisfied with the success, the 'Red Lord' ordered urgently, before conducting state tests, the start of mass production of the wonder fighter. Stalin's will was implemented immediately. On 25 May the Defence Committee at the Council of People's Commissioners of the Soviet Union adopted a document 'On the organization of mass production of the I-200 aircraft at State Aviation Plant No. 1 and the cessation of production of the BB-22 aircraft'. This decision by Stalin meant complete victory of the triumvirate of Voronin, Dementiev and Mikoyan over their competitor Yakovlev. State Aviation Plant No. 1 was cleared completely of both the Yakovlev BB-22 two-engine short-range bomber, being produced there, and of any possibility of producing a Yak-1 fighter. All the production capacity of the largest aircraft factory in the USSR, specializing in the building of fighters, was focused on the early release of the I-200. In accordance with the increased production programme of the aviation plant, it was to produce 125 Mikoyan 'wonder fighters' in 1940.

The best of the experienced domestic aircraft

Factory tests of the I-200 were completed on 25 August 1940. In total, 109 flights were performed with a total duration of 40 hours and 49 minutes. The main difficulties for the Mikoyan team arose with engine cooling. During the tests, water and oil radiators were changed many times. Despite the actions taken, the problem of engine overheating and unbearable heat in the cockpit accompanied the MiG-3 until the end of production. However, Stalin was in a hurry to get a new generation of fighters for the implementation of his far-reaching plans and demanded that the process be speeded up. To satisfy the desire of the 'Red Lord', other extraordinary measures were taken, violating all the accepted norms and rules.

Again, as in the case of preparation for mass production, a strange unanimity and consistency was found between the usually conflicting representatives of the industry and the military. The Mikoyan team, which had almost unlimited resources, presented two of the most refined pre-production copies of the I-200 at once for state tests. In turn, the representative of the military, the Red Army Air Force Research Institute, provided two of its best test pilots who could test both copies of the I-200 in parallel.

Thanks to such careful preparation, state tests of the I-200 were carried out in record time (from 28 August to 12 September 1940) and ended with

MiG-3 fighter tests at the Red Army Air Force Research Institute for the possibility of manually starting the engine, May 1941.

satisfactory results. At the conclusion of the state tests, approved by the Chief of the Red Army Air Force, Lieutenant General Pavel Rychagov, it was noted:

> the I-200 AM-35A aircraft designed by engineers Mikoyan and Gurevich produced by State Aviation Plant No. 1 by its speed, equal to 628km/h, is the best of the experienced domestic aircraft and is not inferior to the same type of foreign aircraft at altitudes above 5,000m.[3]

Make the plane pleasant to piloting!

On 13 September 1940, the day after the end of the state tests of the I-200, a meeting of the Technical Council of the Red Army Air Force Research Institute was held. The creators of the fighter, Artyom Mikoyan and Mikhail Gurevich, were invited to it to discuss the test results. The meeting was led, as always, by the extremely demanding Head of the Red Army Air Force

3 TSAMO RF, Foundation Red Army Air Force Research Institute.

Research Institute, Alexander Filin. The meeting began with a discussion of the advantages of the new fighter. The leading test pilot Stepan Suprun noted that the I-200 'proved to be the full aircraft in state tests. The aircraft withstood them well.' Thus, the I-200 was the only fighter of the 'New Type' that passed the state tests 'from the first presentation' and with a good result. Competitors Yak-1 (I-26) and LaGG-3 (I-301) were provided for state tests repeatedly and passed them satisfactorily only on the second attempt.

Representatives of the customer (military) emphasized that, during the factory and state tests, not a single aircraft was lost, not a single pilot was injured. Further, 'given the urgent need to supply Red Army Air Force units with type I-200 fighters', the Technical Council of the Red Army Air Force Research Institute recommended testing these aircraft in aviation regiments as soon as possible.[4]

Then the discussion of the shortcomings identified during the state tests of the I-200 fighter began. This unpleasant dialogue led to the fragile agreement between delegates of State Aviation Plant No. 1 and representatives of the Red Army Air Force being destroyed. The head of the Red Army Air Force Research Institute, Filin, made a number of comments to Mikoyan, which, according to the military, should have been eliminated during the serial production of the fighter, namely:

a) to increase the longitudinal stability and at the same time make it easier to control, make the plane pleasant to piloting;
b) increase the lateral stability;
c) install the fuel tank protector in the fuel tanks located in the wing centre section;
d) install slots, new wheels sized according to the standards of the People's Commissar of Defence Industry and pneumatics on the tail wheel (instead of airless tyres);
g) install two additional easily removable 7.62 mm ShKAS machine guns or 12.7 mm BS machine guns;
h) increase the fuel reserve, bringing the flight range in the normal version to at least 1,000 kilometres when flying at 0.9 maximum speed.[5]

4 TSAMO RF, Foundation 35. Inventory 11287, Case 575, Sheet 196.
5 RGAE, Foundation 8044, Inventory 1, Case 338, Sheet 12.

MiG-3 fighter with suspended rocket-powered projectiles RS-82.

Artyom Mikoyan was outraged by what he thought were Filin's quibbles. Very emotionally, he objected to the implementation of the military's proposals. A particularly big dispute arose because of Filin's demand to increase the range, which required significant changes in the plane's design. Mikoyan argued that such a long range was not provided for in the initial requirements. Despite the emotional reaction of the chief designer of the I-200, Filin did not change his position regarding the new fighter's shortcomings. Mikoyan was forced to agree with the requirements of the Red Army Air Force Research Institute, although he was in no hurry to specify the exact time-frame for eliminating the problem made by the military. Later, the young chief designer, confident in Stalin's support, ignored most of those comments. Further events would show that Artyom Mikoyan's decision to abandon work on increasing the range of the I-200 was unwise and short-sighted.

'Cuttlefish' for Stalin

3 October 1940. One of the premises of the Experimental Design Department of State Aviation Plant No. 1.

The best team of the Mikoyan Design Bureau was concentrating on eliminating numerous problems in the I-200. According to the memoirs of leading aircraft designer Nikolai Matyuk, the Director of State Aviation Plant No.1, Peter Dementiev, entered the room where aircraft designers

Yakov Seletsky and Nikolai Andrianov were located. By the director's concerned look, those present realized that he had not come to them to wish them good night and send home those who had stayed until late in the evening. Nikolai Matyuk recalled the details of an unpleasant evening conversation between aircraft designers and director:

> 'If you do not suggest how to bring the high-speed range of the I-200 to 1,000 km, then the fighter can be removed from mass production,' Dementiev addressed the audience without further ado.
>
> 'And when is this solution required?' one of us asked.
>
> 'Tomorrow morning,' the Director replied.
>
> After that, Peter Dementiev politely said goodbye to everyone and left.
>
> Obviously, it is impossible to increase the range without placing an additional fuel tank ... . By the morning, we managed to 'push' an unusual-shaped gas tank into the fuselage under the pilot's cabin; for this we had to move the water radiator and the aircraft control system units.

This episode clearly shows a typical picture of the 'solution' of complex design problems when creating a new generation of fighters. By a resolution of the People's Commissariat of Aviation Industry of the USSR and the Air Force leadership of 2 October 1940, it was decided to increase the range of all newly-designed fighters introduced into mass production. Although more than two weeks had passed since the Technical Council of the Red Army Air Force Research Institute, at which the new military requirement was announced, Artyom Mikoyan continued to ignore this problem. With the threat of stopping serial production of the I-200 becoming real, the Director of State Aviation Plant No. 1, Peter Dementiev, who had no less authority than the formal Chief Designer Artyom Mikoyan, took over the quest for a solution to the problem.

The unusually-shaped fuel tank, which had to be created by Soviet aircraft designers to carry out the will of the incompetent Stalin, was wittily dubbed 'cuttlefish'. Such forced humour reflected the bitter sense of hopelessness characteristic of all Soviet engineers who were trapped by the ruthless totalitarian regime. Once again, talented specialists were forced dutifully to fulfil the whim of a stupid and incompetent 'Red Tsar'.

On 29 October 1940 the first flight of the so-called 'improved' I-200 fighter, with an increased capacity of fuel in the internal tanks, took place. In the cockpit was the highly-experienced test pilot, Arkady Ekatov. The flight was successful. However, endless violations of the regulations, ignoring technical standards and feverish haste could not but affect the flight characteristics and safety of the I-200. With each such 'improvement', the flight characteristics of the already overrated new fighter fell. Problems relating to the AM-35A engine were growing like a snowball.

1941. 'It is impossible to claim that the aircraft is of good quality ... .'

1940 ended with a huge success for the team of Voronin, Dementiev and Mikoyan. In just one year, they were able to advance from drawings to mass production of the new 'wonder fighter'. Stalin, the chief referee of the fight with Yakovlev, appreciated their efforts highly. In addition to the already mentioned appointment of Voronin to the post of Deputy People's Commissar of Aviation Industry, all the main participants in the project also received high awards from Stalin. Chief Designer Artyom Mikoyan and his deputy Mikhail Gurevich received the Order of Lenin. State Aviation Plant No. 1 received the State Stalin Prize for mastering the serial production of the I-200 fighter and was also awarded the Order of Lenin.

'Stalin's Falcon', Arkady Ekatov.

On 9 December the I-200 fighter was officially renamed the MiG-1 (Mikoyan and Gurevich – the First). A variant of the fighter with increased range and flight duration was designated MiG-3. According to the 1940 results, the Mikoyan fighter took first place in terms of output among the Stalinist fighters of the 'New Type'. Of the 111 I-200 aircraft manufactured this year, ninety-two were of the MiG-1 type, and nineteen of the MiG-3 type.

However, 1941 brought new problems for aircraft designers and MiG-3 manufacturers. The military tests revealed many very dangerous engine defects, including seizing in flight. There were serious problems in other aircraft systems as well. The official representative of the Red Army Air Force, Mikhail Frantsev, wrote in a report for March 1941:

> It is impossible to claim that the aircraft is of good quality, since until now it has significant defects:
>
> - the engine has a throttle response at an altitude of more than 6,000m;
> - systematic failure of the engine due to spark plugs;
> - oil pressure drop at height;
> - the pressure drop of gasoline at a height ... .[6]

The first large-scale negative reviews about the quality of the new fighters came from aviation regiments which noted numerous small and medium-sized malfunctions in the MiG-3. However, until the end of February 1941, accidents with the deaths of pilots were avoided. In the worst case, a flight accident ended with an emergency landing and a crashed plane.

The first victims of MiG-3

With the growth of serial production, the quality of MiG-3 manufacturing naturally decreased, which caused an increase in the number of flight accidents. Initially, the high accident rate was associated with chronic defects of the most complex unit of the fighter, the AM-35A aircraft engine. The first examples of Alexander Mikulin's engine, assembled manually by experienced workers, worked satisfactorily. However, serial engines produced by low-skilled workers in an incredible hurry showed completely unsatisfactory results. Factory pilots who tested new fighters before transferring them to military units were the first to put their lives in danger. For example, in February 1941, when testing the new MiG-3, factory pilots made seventeen forced landings due to various engine malfunctions. Unfortunately, the first victims soon appeared. On 28 February 1941, Captain Sergey Afanasyev was killed in a MiG-3 crash. He had managed to air test five fighters that day. His sixth flight turned out to be fatal.

6 RGAE, Foundation 8164, Inventory 1, Case 338, Sheet 145.

The engine stalled. While trying to turn around and land the MiG-3 at the factory airfield, Afanasyev broke into a spin. The investigation did not reveal the exact cause of the disaster. According to experienced colleagues of Afanasyev, 'Stalin's Falcon' was the victim of a bad throttle response on the AM-35A engine.

The creators of the MiG-3 did not have enough time to pay attention to the human casualties caused by the new fighter's chronic defects. The Mikoyan team worked feverishly, trying at any cost to fulfil Stalin's whim to increase the range of the MiG-3. Moreover, aircraft designers at State Aviation Plant No. 1 and the experts of the Red Army Air Force Research Institute had completely different ideas on measuring the flight range of the modified fighter. Thus, a serious conflict between Mikoyan and the Head of the Red Army Air Force Research Institute, Alexander Filin, broke out at a meeting of the Technical Council of the Red Army Air Force Research Institute on 13 September 1940 and reached a new level of confrontation.

Stalin, who encouraged such a confrontation of his 'sons', did not interfere, leaving the rivals to sort things out on their own. Two influential and principled opponents spared no time and effort to prove their case. Artyom Mikoyan was convinced that his engineers not only fulfilled the requirement for a range of 1,000 kilometres, but also exceeded it. As evidence, he cited the results of factory tests of the MiG-3 with a 'cuttlefish' fuel tank installed under the pilot's seat. However, Alexander Filin did not recognize the results of factory tests. He believed that the tests were carried out in violation of the accepted methodology and demanded new tests of the range of the fighter according to the standards and with the control of the Red Army Air Force Research Institute. It was during a series of such tests that a disaster occurred and drew special attention to the problem of flight safety on the MiG-3 fighter.

The death of Arkady Ekatov

13 March 1941. Crimean Peninsula. Kacha military airfield near the city of Sevastopol.

In the morning, plant test pilot Arkady Ekatov habitually took a seat in the cockpit of MiG-3 fighter with the factory number No. 2147, a plane that had already been flown. During the test flight, he had to climb to 8,000 metres and determine specific fuel consumption at that altitude. The take-off took place normally. However, during the climb, when the engine was running at high speeds, something fatal happened. Eyewitnesses reported that, without reaching the desired height, the plane suddenly entered a steep dive. Further, the fall, which lasted several tens of seconds, was uncontrollable. To the horror of experienced observers, they could not notice any attempts by the pilot to restore control or leave the doomed plane. Shortly before the collision with the ground, the fighter's right wing collapsed from extreme overloads. Then there was a terrible explosion, fire and smoke.

When examining the crash site, a deep crater was found. The plane went into the ground to a depth of five to six metres. Extracting the wreckage of the plane and the remains of the pilot entailed a lengthy excavation. The force of the impact was so great that even the metal parts of the fighter were very badly damaged, and most of the fuselage and wings were fragmented and scattered over a large area. The only thing that the members of the commission investigating the disaster could reliably establish was that the engine was working until the moment of the collision with the earth. Thus, the most likely cause of the crash was loss of control of the aircraft as a result of sudden loss of consciousness or death of the pilot. This circumstance led

Place of Arkady Ekatov's death.

the commission to a dead end. It seemed unlikely that an experienced pilot who regularly underwent strict medical examinations could suddenly have a heart attack or stroke. It was also not possible to get any evidence to support this theory. Such was the state of the pilot's body that it was impossible to determine the reason for his apparent inactivity during the fighter's rapid dive. The only thing that could be established exactly was the time of the disaster: the hands of Ekatov's wristwatch, bent almost in half, recorded the moment of the plane hitting the ground to the second.

However, this time Stalin's commission failed to hush up the case, identifying the disaster as an accident related to the human factor. The crash of Ekatov's fighter had been preceded by a series of MiG-3 accidents and those of other aircraft with the AM-35A engine. This indicated clearly that aviation accidents occur due to the fault of technology. The most likely cause of the death of the 'Stalin's Falcon' was destruction of the supercharger blades of the AM-35A engine. The supercharger, designed to increase the flight altitude of the aircraft, like much other MiG-3 equipment, was a completely new and poorly-tested unit. The huge speed of rotation created a high load on the supercharger blades, which compressed air for the engine. Design errors, a violation of the processing technology, or a change of the grade of steel from which the part was made could lead to its spontaneous destruction in flight.

The commission investigating the death of Ekatov suggested, although this was not the only theory, that the pilot was killed either by a detached supercharger blade, or was burned by a jet of steam that escaped from the expansion tank of the engine cooling system, pierced by this flying blade, and lost consciousness from pain shock.

Although Ekatov was not as famous as Chkalov, information about the death of another 'Stalin's Falcon' in tests of fighters of the 'New Type' was reported to Stalin. It was impossible to hush up the problem with the supercharger. Another Stalin commission went to Aircraft Engine Plant No. 24 (Moscow), where the serial production of aircraft engine and supercharger for MiG-3 took place. The culprit for the defective manufacturing of the unit was found very quickly. It turned out to be the Director of Aircraft Engine Plant No. 24 Vladimir Dubov. For the delivery of a defective supercharger, he was removed from his post immediately and sent to direct the construction of the aircraft engine plant – a stand-in for Aircraft Engine Plant No. 24 in the city of Kuibyshev. Such leniency in punishing the man responsible for the deaths of several 'Stalin's Falcons' was easily explained. Dubov, absolutely loyal to Stalin, tried sincerely to fulfil the order of the 'Father of Nations' to accelerate the production of new aircraft. He could not be responsible for all the vices of the Stalinist aviation industry. In addition, experienced managers in the conditions of a constant increase in the number of aviation industry enterprises were sorely lacking.

Meanwhile, the new management and engineers of Aircraft Engine Plant No. 24 were looking for ways to fix problems with supercharger. During this time, flights of MiG-3, TB-7 aircraft with the AM-35A, as well as experimental aircraft with the engine, were prohibited. The solution was found in the shortest possible time. The motors were equipped with a new mechanical device for controlling the supercharger blades, which made it possible to reduce the likelihood of their destruction during flight.

'Too many flight accidents with MiGs … .'

Despite the huge number of defects, the serial production of the MiG-3 grew. In parallel, endless improvements were carried out. According to the report of the official representative of the Red Army Air Force in the first quarter of 1941, the following main changes were made to the MiG-3 design:

- the capacity of fuel tanks has been increased to 461kg and thus the flight range has been increased;
- the fighter's firepower has been strengthened thanks to the introduction of two 12.7mm UBK machine guns with 150 rounds of ammunition per barrel, located on the wing;
- new water and oil systems have been introduced, the design of which is approved by the Central Aerohydrodynamic Institute (TsAGI);
- reinforced wing flap;
- the engine exhaust pipes are reinforced;
- improved reliability of oxygen equipment;
- the transition to bakelite plywood for the wing skin instead of BS-1 plywood, which was used earlier;
- a more reliable OP-ZU water radiator was installed;
- basically, a satisfactory throttle response of the motor is provided at altitudes up to 5,000m'.[7]

7 TSAMO RF, Foundation Red Army Air Force Research Institute, Inventory 485609, Case 108, Sheets 5-51.

Pilots in the parking lot of the MiG-3 fighter.

The work on improving the MiG-3 while it was already in mass production was like a vicious circle of endless problems. The requirements imposed by the military led to the emergence of new difficulties and more endless improvements and changes. Installing an additional fuselage fuel tank changed the aeroplane's centre-of-gravity position, which often led to failure of the aircraft in a spin.

Designers tried to solve this problem by installing automatic slats, the presence of which also caused new difficulties. An attempt to increase the fighter's firepower by installing underwing machine guns also worsened the stability and controllability of the aircraft. An important consequence of solving endless problems was the constant increase in the fighter's weight: the weight of the MiG-3 exceeded the weight of the LaGG-3 and, by even more, the Yak-1. Moreover, with increased fuel tanks and machine guns installed, the fighter turned into an inert and clumsy target. Realizing the acute problem with the weight of the fighter, the Mikoyan team began a campaign to lighten it by equipping some MiG-3s with fuselage tanks of reduced volume.

Workers and engineers at State Aviation Plant No. 1 were exhausted, trying to introduce numerous 'improvements' during production. Making changes on completed fighters made it necessary to create special field factory teams which carried out repairs and modifications of fighters already in military units.

By 1 June 1941 a total of 1,094 MiG-3 fighters had been produced. It turned out to be the most massively produced of the 'New Type' fighters before the German attack on the USSR. However, the MiG-3's flight characteristics and, especially, its manufacturing quality were very low. 'Too many flight accidents with MiG-3s' was the disappointing conclusion reached by the leadership of the People's Commissariat of Aviation Industry of the USSR following the results of the production of the fighter in the first half of 1941.

Chapter 7

'We fly in coffins!'
Dogfight with own plane

10 April 1941. Baltic Military District. Military airfield of the city of Kaunas.

On the airfield, the MiG-3 duty link (three fighters) from the 31st Fighter Aviation Regiment of 8th Mixed Aviation Division, under command of Lieutenant Aksyutin, was in a state of readiness for take-off. Soon, information was received from ground observers at the airfield command post that an unidentified twin-engine aircraft at high altitude had violated the air border and was continuing to fly deep into the territory of the USSR. After receiving an order to intercept the intruder, a trio of MiG-3 fighters flown by Lieutenant Aksyutin, Junior Lieutenant Akimov and Junior Lieutenant Yevtushenko soared into the endless sky.

With great difficulty, the pilots managed to find an unidentified aircraft on a white contrail. A German reconnaissance aircraft, presumably a Ju 86 P,

MiG-3 fighter with underwing 12.7mm UBK machine guns.

was flying at an altitude of more than 11,000 metres. Due to the lack of radio communication, each of the pilots tried to intercept the intruder aircraft independently. The MiG-3 pilots began the long process of climbing.

The MiG-3 Junior Lieutenant Akimov was the first to climb to an altitude of 11,000 metres. However, it turned out that the German scout was flying much higher. When trying to perform nose-up pitching, the Akimov fighter fell into a spin. He left the spin by switching to dive. An attempt to abruptly withdraw the MiG-3 from dive led to a further spin. Junior Lieutenant Akimov again repeated all the actions to withdraw the fighter from spin. However, this time he moved the control handle smoothly, which made it possible to successfully transfer it to horizontal flight at an altitude of 5,000 metres. Having barely recovered from such deadly manoeuvres, Akimov no longer thought about chasing after violators of air borders. Fuel was running low, and he sent the fighter towards his airfield. However, the adventures of Junior Lieutenant Akimov did not end there. When landing, he noticed that the left undercarriage landing gear spontaneously fell out, while the right undercarriage landing gear remained retracted. After several attempts, the pilot managed to release the right undercarriage landing gear and safely land the fighter at his airfield.

Cabin of MiG-3 fighter.

Meanwhile, the hunt for the ultra-high-altitude German scout continued. The most successful actions to intercept the intruder aircraft were performed by the commander of the duty link, Lieutenant Aksyutin. An experienced pilot, he got close enough to the German plane that he was able to identify its nationality. For a moment, he clearly saw a cross on the fuselage and a swastika on the vertical stabilizer of a twin-engine reconnaissance aircraft. However, after a few seconds, Aksyutin's MiG-3 abruptly broke into a spin. Then the pilot's hard struggle for his own life began. Fortunately, the height margin allowed several recovery attempts to be made before the plane hit the ground. Three times Lieutenant Aksyutin took the fighter out of a spin, but each time the MiG-3 stubbornly fell into it again. Another desperate attempt led to the seat belts breaking off due to extreme overload. Aksyutin was thrown out of the cockpit, the uncontrolled plane crashed into the ground, but the pilot landed safely with a parachute.

The details of what happened to the third plane and its pilot are unknown. Junior Lieutenant Yevtushenko was killed when his MiG-3 crashed. Apparently, he was less experienced and less lucky than his comrades and could not get his fighter out of the deadly spin.[1]

Similar problems associated with an unexpected breakdown into spin were also observed when pilots of military units mastered LaGG-3 and Yak-1 fighters. The number of cases of fatal 'battles' between MiG-3 pilots and their own aircraft turned out to be significantly higher only because there were relatively more Mikoyan fighters in military units. Numerous problems in organizing mass production of its LaGG-3 and Yak-1 competitors meant that they simply had entered Red Army Air Force service in sufficient numbers at the beginning of 1941.

After all the 'improvements', the MiG-3 was characterized by pronounced longitudinal and transverse instability, leading to an unexpected stall in spin. Soon the pilots and technicians felt all the 'advantages' of this 'wonder fighter'. Produced with great effort and transferred to the Red Army Air Force, the fighters needed long and dangerous training study for pilots; flying the MiG-3 required the highest level of pilot qualification. The pilot retraining programme, reduced to a minimum, did not allow even a satisfactory level of training to be obtained. Experienced pilots experienced great difficulties when retraining on the MiG-3 due to its fundamental

1 TSAMO RF, Foundation Red Army Air Force Research Institute, Inventory 502941, Case 30, Sheets 228-34.

difference from the I-16 that had become familiar. The worst thing was with the preparation for young pilots who had just finished training in flight schools. As a result of the general training, they had only a few hours of solo experience of the Polikarpov U-2 trainer. Getting into the cockpit of the MiG-3, young pilots faced sudden death.

However, even such accelerated training was not always available to pilots of new fighters. Stalin's ambitious plans were aimed at increasing the Red Army Air Force by a hundred aviation regiments at once in 1941. It was planned that after the new fighters entered the military units, fighters of the 'Old Type' were to be transferred to training units to train new pilots. Due to constant delays in the delivery of new aircraft, all these 'well-thought-out' plans failed completely. Thus, due to constant haste and contradictory orders from the Red Army Air Force leadership on the eve of the German attack, the pilot retraining system for fighters of the 'New Type' was in a state of chaos.

Quantity corresponds to quality

22 June 1941 became a watershed, allowing the separation of Stalin's dreams from the results of their implementation. The failure in flight characteristics and the terrifying quality of the new generation of Soviet fighters was obvious to everyone who had at least some knowledge of aviation. However, perhaps the quality of the new Soviet fighters was somehow compensated for by their numbers?

As already noted above, in 1938, Stalin felt alarmed about his beloved aviation industry and made great efforts to stimulate the creation and strategic re-equipment of the Red Army Air Force with fighters of the 'New Type'. Due to limited resources and time, the leader's main attention was focused on creating a new generation of universal Soviet fighters. It was planned to mass produce them at the fantastic rate of 20,000 planes per year. It was these compact aircraft, designed by the new Stalinist aircraft designers and made, mainly from wood, by young low-skilled workers, that were supposed to make up for the shortage of bombers, ground-attack aircraft and reconnaissance aircraft in the Red Army Air Force.

There was a tremendous growth in the quantitative indicators of the Soviet aviation industry. In the first half of 1941, aircraft factories produced more than fifty aircraft per day. At aviation and aircraft engine plants, the number of workers was 174,400 people, the production area was more than

MiG-3 fighters assembly at State Aviation Plant No. 1.

22 million square metres and 26,711 metal-cutting machine tools were used. In total, 466,400 people worked in the aviation industry, taking into account enterprises producing various components for aircraft during the period.

However, the real consequences of Stalin's vicious attention to the problems of the Red Army Air Force turned out to be terrible. Working in a state of constant emergency, the Soviet aviation industry was finally disorganized. Young managers, selected and appointed personally by Stalin to replace 'enemies of the people', were exhausted, trying to fulfil the insane orders of the 'Father of Nations'. To achieve the non-existent figures of German daily aviation production, impossible production plans for Soviet fighters were increased several times. The attempt to achieve, if not superiority, then at least parity with a potential opponent in the field of aircraft production by intensifying work in existing plants was not crowned with success. The bet on an emergency increase in production capacity through the construction of new aviation plants also ended in complete collapse.

Stalin's optimistic plans turned out to be completely impossible. By 22 June 1941 a little more than 2,000 fighters of the 'New Type' were released during the entire production period. Moreover, only the MiG-3 was in noticeable numbers in military units. Most of the Lavochkin and Yakovlev aircraft were either at the factory sites waiting for military acceptance or in disassembled form, packed in crates for delivery to aviation regiments.

Thus, the main burden of the confrontation with the Luftwaffe fell on fighters of the 'Old Type', I-16 monoplanes and I-15 and I-153 biplanes. At the same time, since the production of spare parts for fighters of the 'Old Type' was stopped by Stalin's order, their repair was extremely difficult.

Fighters of the 'New Type' join the fight

On 22 June 1941 Hitler dealt a crushing blow to the strategic plans of the 'wisest of the wise'. He was literally a few days or weeks ahead of his friend Stalin. The 'Red Lord' had been preparing for a major aggressive war for many years with the aim of capturing the whole of Europe. Peasants and workers had been turned into slaves and the Red Army had become the largest land army in the world in terms of the numbers of soldiers and the number of tanks. Stalin's favourite 'commanders': Zhukov and Timoshenko, played war games on maps, practising the offensive on Western Europe, with childish enthusiasm. All the games ended with the complete defeat of the Germans and the capture of East Prussia, Romania, Hungary, etc.

However, Stalin's gigantic aviation project was completely unprepared for a defensive war with the Luftwaffe, which was at the peak of its form. The children's ideas of the 'Red Lord' about the power and technical perfection of his new fighters collapsed during the first months of fighting on the Eastern Front of the Second World War. A frightened and depressed

Pilot Safronov near the I-16 fighter with the side inscription, 'For Stalin!'.

Stalin, who barely overcame the shock of the defeat, was forced tearfully to ask yesterday's enemies, Britain and the United States, to send fighter aircraft to his rescue.

Meanwhile, with thousands of fighters of the 'New Type' fighters built before the war and produced in large quantities after it began, Stalin's incompetent commanders continued to sacrifice to the Luftwaffe. No one just knew what to do with the new fighters. Since there had not been time to make any serious tests of fighters of the 'New Type' in aviation regiments before the war, the planes had to be tested directly in frontline conditions. The leadership of the Red Army Air Force had been pleasing Stalin's imagination for many years with 'perfect' and 'scientifically' based latest tactical techniques for the use of Soviet aviation. However, it turned out that, in a real war with a strong enemy, they had nothing to offer 'Stalin's Falcons' except for the suicidal ramming of enemy aircraft. There was simply no planning or centralized management of the Red Army Air Force after 22 June. Fighters were used chaotically, 'tactics' were developed spontaneously in the process of endless improvisations and 'experiments' at all levels of the aviation command.

As an example, we can consider the typical practice of using fighter aviation regiments in the period from 1941 to 1943, which allows us to see several of the most striking symptoms of the complete intellectual and organizational impotence of Stalin's aviation command.

It all started with the fact that fighter aviation regiments that had just been re-equipped from the I-16 to the LaGG-3 or Yak-1 were immediately thrown into battle. Once at the front, the regiments (especially formed according to the reduced wartime staff of twenty aircraft and twenty pilots)[2] initially acted in accordance with their direct purpose, that is, in the role of frontline fighters with the task of fighting for 'air supremacy' in a given area. However, very quickly, especially in areas where the Luftwaffe was active, fighter aviation regiments suffered serious losses and lost more than half their aircraft.

2 The Red Army Air Force fighter aviation regiments were first created in 1938 and became the main tactical unit of fighter aviation. The standard fighter aviation regiment included sixty-three aircraft with sixty pilots. After the crushing defeat of the Red Army Air Force by Luftwaffe aircraft in 1941, Stalin ordered the quantitative composition of fighter aviation regiments to be reduced three times. On paper, the number of fighter aviation regiments increased; in reality, the Red Army Air Force held on under the onslaught of the enemy with reduced forces.

After that, the second stage came: the implementation of 'mixed' tasks, when a relatively large number of sorties were achieved by intensification: each fighter made two to three sorties per day. Then the number of combat-ready fighters was reduced to several planes, and the tasks performed were increasingly moving away from the original ones, such as weather reconnaissance, ground attack, bomber escort, etc. Thus, the 'life' of the regiment was artificially stretched, but the combat capabilities were reduced to one link (three fighters). This led to the fact that there were many fighter aviation regiments operating at the front, but each performed only three to five sorties a day.

Then, for one or one and a half months, poorly-trained pilots were 'eliminated' in the course of a cruel selection. In each fighter aviation regiment, a certain backbone of the best pilots was formed and made a feasible contribution to the air war with small forces. Later, during the re-formation and staffing, it was these survivors who became an elite, on whose experience the next generations of 'Stalin's Falcons' were trained. However, until the end of the war, despite all efforts, even the improved fighters of the 'New Type' were not able to resist the Luftwaffe fighters on equal terms.

'Fathers' and 'children'

Usually, the lack of experience of young aircraft designers chosen by Stalin is indicated as a key factor in the failure of the new generation of Soviet fighters. If the same huge opportunities were provided to aircraft designers of the old generation, the result would be completely different. For example, among the 'experts' of Soviet aviation, the myth is popular about the criminal underestimation of the late developments of Nikolai Polikarpov, the I-180 and I-185 aircraft. Allegedly due to the intrigues of young competitors against the former 'King of Fighters', these 'outstanding' fighters remained at the level of experimental samples. However, readers know from the previous chapters that, despite his undoubted talents, Nikolai Polikarpov cannot be called a successful aircraft designer. His I-15 and I-16 fighters, created specifically for mass production in the conditions of the archaic Soviet aviation industry, suffered from a large number of irreparable defects. Other representatives of the older generation who remained at large by the end of the 1930s, Sergey Ilyushin and Pavel Sukhoi, also tried to develop new high-speed fighters. However, they did not advance in their

A typical picture of 1941. German soldiers are studying a Soviet fighter that landed on the fuselage.

work beyond drawings and layouts. In addition, as the crushing failure of the Il-2 ground-attack aircraft and Su-2 light bomber showed, even in the case of the creation and mass production of new fighters designed by Sergei Ilyushin or Pavel Sukhoi, the result could be disappointing. An important proof of this thesis is the fact that the MiG-3 prototype was created by the Polikarpov team with the direct participation of the former 'King of Fighters'. This fighter, modified later by the team of Mikoyan and Gurevich, turned out to be no better than the aircraft created by young competitors Lavochkin and Yakovlev.

Stalin's bet on unknown engineers was indeed associated with a great risk. However, it is difficult to blame Yakovlev and especially Lavochkin for a lack of experience. In his work, newcomer Artyom Mikoyan relied on a representative of the older generation, Mikhail Gurevich, and an experienced team of former Polikarpov engineers. In addition, the oldest of Stalin's three favourite aircraft designers, Semyon Lavochkin, who was already 38 years old at the time of the creation of the LaGG-3, can only be indirectly connected to the young aircraft designers. Thus, youth and lack of experience cannot be considered a significant factor in the failure of fighters of the 'New Type'. The bitter truth of the Soviet aircraft industry is that the talents and experience of Stalin's aircraft designers did not play a significant role in the success of the future fighter. Weakened by Stalin's repressions, the older generation of Soviet aircraft designers was not able to compete with young aircraft designers and create a fighter with better characteristics than those designed by Lavochkin, Yakovlev and Mikoyan. Engineers and managers turned out to be slaves of the all-powerful totalitarian Stalinist system and were forced to act in accordance with its pathological features.

'Now a lot of young aircraft designers have appeared … .'[3]

Much more difficult is the answer to the question, why were there exactly three young aircraft designers? There is no doubt that such an amazing result was influenced by many different reasons. In the author's opinion, in the conditions of radical changes in the Soviet aviation industry, the psychological factor of relations between Stalin and the main actors of the race for the creation of a new fighter played a leading role.

Nikolai Polikarpov was given a monopoly in the design of fighters in the middle of the 1930s when the focus of Stalin's attention was Andrei Tupolev's bombers; and fighters were considered by the 'Great Leader' as an important addition to them. Stalin's choice of the I-16 for mass production did not deprive Tupolev of a leading position in the aviation industry. Polikarpov's main 'competitor' could focus on designing more prestigious bombers. In addition, the 'King of Fighters', unlike Tupolev, had never demonstrated claims to absolute power in the aviation industry. Thus, although Polikarpov also had serious competitors, the situation of rivalry between the leading aircraft designers of the mid-1930s did not result in an acute confrontation.

At the end of the 1930s the situation in the Soviet aviation industry changed fundamentally. Andrei Tupolev, who angered Stalin, and his team were sent to prison. Nikolai Polikarpov was left at large but, as a result of the strongest emotional shock, he lost interest in professional activity. The

3 The words of People's Commissar for Defence of the Soviet Union, Kliment Voroshilov, from the minutes of the Main Military Council of the Red Army Commission of 5 May 1940.

former leaders were replaced by a new young generation that was eager to seize power in the rapidly developing aviation industry of the USSR.

The failure of bomber production forced Stalin to change the development strategy of the Red Army Air Force towards the dominance of universal single-engine fighters. Thus, the fullness of power in the aviation industry came to be determined by the degree of control over the production of this type of combat aircraft. Under such conditions, Stalin's choice for the vacant position of 'King of Fighters', Alexander Yakovlev, was perceived by the clique of aviation industry bosses as a disaster. The authoritarian nature and claims of the creator of the Yak-1 to total dominance in the entire aviation industry did not leave young managers Pavel Voronin and Peter Dementiev any chance of existence. A war between the pair of managers claiming leadership in the industry and Yakovlev was inevitable. As a result of the confrontation, the young leaders of a powerful group of aviation bosses were able to create an alternative to the Yak-1 fighter in the shortest possible time. However, paradoxically, the greatest advantages from the fight of Stalin's

Fighter Aviation Regiment armed with MiG-3 fighters produced at State Aviation Plant No. 1 take the oath to Stalin, Winter 1941.

young favourites were received by aircraft designer Semyon Lavochkin. Despite the loss of support in the top management after the resignation of People's Commissar of Aviation Industry Kaganovich and the break with Gorbunov and Gudkov, the Lavochkin LaGG-3 designer stubbornly continued his work. Thanks to his abilities, hard work and a share of lucky chance, this talented aircraft designer and deeply decent person was also among the winners. The result of this unprecedented struggle of the end of the 1930s was the emergence of several new leaders of the Soviet aviation industry at the same time.

Analyzing the psychological manifestations of the characters of Alexander Yakovlev and Artyom Mikoyan, it can be argued that they manifested themselves more as managers than aircraft designers. Being the heads of large design teams, they were focused on promoting their aircraft and organizing their mass production. Yakovlev showed these qualities earlier; he was more assertive and selfish. Mikoyan had always been the youngest among his competitors and had to work harder than anyone to prove his professional maturity. He, as a successful manager, fully revealed himself eventually in the era of jet aviation and defeated Yakovlev. Semyon Lavochkin did not have such pronounced managerial qualities nor ambitions to dominate the Soviet aviation industry. However, thanks to his purposefulness and ability to build conflict-free relationships with his subordinates and rivals, he was able to emerge victorious from the numerous intrigues of his competitors.

Although Stalin's emotional preference was an important factor determining success in the competitive struggle, the very specifics of the design activity set a very strict framework for the professional selection of applicants for the title of 'King of Fighters'. This factor was decisive in the fact that the posts of chief designers were undoubtedly held not only by talented engineers but extremely strong-willed people. Lavochkin, Yakovlev and Mikoyan had proved in practice that they could work in conditions of 'a sharp reduction in the terms of design, construction, testing and introduction into a series of experimental aircraft.'[4] Undoubtedly, there were other gifted engineers in the USSR, but in the conditions of the pathological Stalinist regime they had very little chance of self-realization. At best, they were waiting for a job in the design bureaux of Stalin's new favourites, and, at worst, oblivion and death.

4 RGASPI, Foundation 17, Inventory 162, Case 27, Sheet 11.

'Chief Designer, Chief Engineer, what are we going to do?'

January 1941. Gorky City. Aviation Plant No. 21.

Deputy People's Commissar of Aviation Industry Peter Dementiev arrived at the plant for another check of the executive order to start serial production of the LaGG-3 fighter. He had recently been appointed to this position for the successful introduction into mass production at State Aviation Plant No. 1 of the MiG-3 fighter. Dementiev's arrival was prompted by the serious concern of the leadership of the People's Commissariat of Aviation Industry regarding the implementation of the plan for organizing serial production of the LaGG-3. According to it, Gorky Aviation Plant No. 21 was supposed to produce the first LaGG-3 fighter in February 1941. However, the plant's management was sceptical about the recently arrived team of engineers led by Semyon Lavochkin.

During 1940 the plant consistently received orders to deploy serial production of I-180, I-21 and I-200 (MiG-3) fighters. After a while, all these orders were cancelled. Finally, in November 1940, the plant was obliged to prepare for the serial production of the Semyon Lavochkin fighter. Exhausted by the constant change of the main production facility, Director of Gorky Aviation Plant No. 21 Vasily Voronin was in no hurry to fulfil the order. He expected the very likely cancellation of the order for the serial

Artyom Mikoyan, Alexander Yakovlev and Sergey Ilyushin.

production of the LaGG-3 and did not want to waste valuable resources and the time of his workers. Only the personal intervention of two deputies of the People's Commissar, Pavel Voronin and Peter Dementiev, forced the plant management to stop sabotage and organize real work to prepare for the release of LaGG-3.

To speed up production, the plant management placed orders for the production of large batches of semi-finished components for the assembly of the fighter at the large city's plants: the Gorky automobile plant 'Molotov' (GAZ) and the Krasnoye Sormovo Shipyard No. 112. However, this 'acceleration' paradoxically led to another delay in the production of the LaGG-3. It turned out that the drawings according to which the parts were made were temporary and that significant changes had already been made to them by the time the first fighters were assembled. As a result, the entire batch of semi-finished components, to produce which much time and money was spent, was rejected and went to the scrap metal warehouse.

During a regular telephone meeting with Moscow, Director of Gorky Aviation Plant No. 21 Vasily Voronin reported the incident to the leadership of the People's Commissariat of Aviation Industry and accused Chief Designer Semyon Lavochkin of unprofessionalism. Stalin's young top managers reacted with lightning speed to an unfortunate incident that could significantly complicate serial production of the LaGG-3 in Gorky. Aircraft designer Evgeny Adler described the details of the arrival of the high Moscow authorities at the plant in his memoirs:

> Deputy People's Commissar of Aviation Industry Peter Dementiev, who arrived at the plant, immediately ran through the workshops according to his habit, and found a strange thing. On the machine tools, parts were cut out of solid blanks in large numbers.
>
> Furious and perplexed, he rushed to the Chief Engineer Plant with question: 'Where are your stampings and forgings?'
>
> 'All rejected.'
>
> 'Why?'
>
> 'Due to changes made by the Chief Designer.'
>
> 'Where is he?'
>
> 'On the plant.'
>
> When Semyon Lavochkin, who came to the office, began to deny the massive introduction of serious design changes to the drawings, Dementiev demanded to drag all the forgings

Aircraft designer, Pavel Sukhoi.

and stampings to this office and deal with these semi-finished products in the presence of the Chief Designer.

The Head of Production selected one of the semi-finished components from the pile and read a piece of paper tied to it with information about the cause of the rejection: 'This semi-finished component was rejected according to the change sheet from such and such a date sent by Lavochkin Design Bureau. Such-and-such a size was changed to such-and-such ... as a result, a complete rejection was established.

'Semyon Alekseevich, is this true?'

'Yes, it was done for such and such a reason.'

Then the procedure was repeated endlessly, and the rejected semi-finished components were placed to the left. If the aircraft designer managed to challenge the very fact of issuing such a change sheet, or, despite the recognition of the change, it was still possible to make the part from the ordered semi-finished component, it was placed to the right. By two o'clock in the morning, the last useless semi-finished component was put on the left and there was a dead silence. On the left was a mountain of rejected items due to the fault of aircraft designers, on the right a pathetic bunch of suitable semi-finished components.

Suddenly Dementiev, clutching his bald head with both hands, jumped up as if on springs, and ran around the office with the words: 'You are deceivers … You have deceived the Government … You have deceived the People … You deceived the Army … You have deceived the Country ... an unprecedented bloody war is underway. People are drowning in blood. And here they are playing with toys. They forgot their honour and conscience! Chief Designer, Chief Engineer, what are we going to do? Although no. That's enough for today. Go to bed, everyone. And tomorrow, at nine, everyone will come to me. If such a beautiful plant as the twenty-first stumbled on LaGG-3, then what can we expect from others?[5]

The axe as a means of managing the plant

March 1941. Gorky City. Aviation Plant No. 21.

Despite daily operational meetings and regular visits to Gorky Aviation Plant No. 21 by Pavel Voronin and Peter Dementiev, serial production of the LaGG-3 aircraft unfolded very slowly. Numerous problems associated with the development of new production technologies for the plant and the lack of qualified workers led to a chronic lag behind the planned indicators. This failure looked especially contrasting against the background of the continuing mass production of the 'outdated' I-16 fighter. In contemporary reports, the low quantitative indicators of the LaGG-3 output were compensated for by excellent output indicators of the I-16, which was in full production. Thanks to this, the plant was able to receive sufficient financial resources from the state. The money was transferred to the plant accounts only after delivery of the finished aircraft to the actual customer, the Red Army Air Force, and allowed the regular payment of employee salaries. Thus, at the beginning of 1941, at Gorky Aviation Plant No. 21 there was a deadlock situation, typical of the Soviet aviation industry. The workers and engineers of the plant were not interested in stopping production of the I-16, which fed their families, and switching to a half-starved existence with the piece production of the labour-intensive LaGG-3. Neither persuasion nor orders from the Moscow authorities helped in this situation. It took very

5 Adler, E.G., op. cit., p.51.

Light bomber Su-2.

drastic measures by Deputy People's Commissar of Aviation Industry Pavel Voronin to stop manufacture of the outdated I-16.

Lavochkin's deputy Leonid Zaks recalled the details of another visit to the Pavel Voronin plant:

> One morning we came to the workshop, and another I-16 appeared from the gate. Voronin ran up to the fire equipment, grabbed an axe hanging there and began to strike at the plane. Disfigured it completely. It was a terrible sight – the Deputy People's Commissar was chopping down a new combat aircraft with his own hands. Voronin turned to the workers with tears in his eyes, 'Well, we don't need I-16s anymore!'

Only a completely deadend situation could force the balanced and democratic Pavel Voronin to take such a desperate step. Soviet aviation industry top management had no other means to force the employees of Gorky Aviation Plant No. 21 to fulfil Stalin's edict to stop production of the I-16. Could the helplessness and incompetence of the aviation industry top management be the main reason for the failure of the creation of Soviet fighters of the 'New Type'?

Slavery as a factor in the management of the military industry

At the beginning of the 1930s the implementation of accelerated industrialization became a fixed idea for Stalin. The top management positions in the industry were occupied by people who were totally loyal to the 'Red Lord'; most were fanatical Bolsheviks. All their 'experience' in organizing and managing production was reduced to working as a locksmith or blacksmith. Total incompetence, and sometimes an adventurous nature, helped them believe in the possibility of implementing Stalin's ambitious plans in a poor agrarian country. Bolshevik enthusiasm, *Shturmovshchina*, and adventurism became the main methods of their 'work'. In the early stages of creating the military industry, when Stalin's attention was focused on quantitative indicators – plants under construction, aircraft produced – such leaders were quite satisfied with the 'Father of Nations'.

The first results of accelerated industrialization in the form of endless failures of all types of combat aircraft discouraged and alarmed Stalin. He reacted to the failures of his beloved aviation with another wave of bloody repression and the universal replacement of senior leaders. The endless executions stopped when Stalin felt that the people he had chosen to occupy top management positions in the aviation industry needed, in addition to loyalty, intellectual ability and high competence. As a result, the last representative of the older generation of 'ardent' Bolsheviks in the leadership of the aviation industry was the former locksmith Mikhail Kaganovich. Then the total replacement of the previous cadres with a new young generation, who had received higher professional education under the Bolsheviks, began. Although it is difficult to call Aleksey Shakhurin, who replaced Kaganovich as People's Commissar of Aviation Industry,

Semyon Lavochkin, Alexander Yakovlev and Artyom Mikoyan, end of the 1940s.

competent in the functioning of aviation enterprises, he differed sharply from his predecessor in having higher education. In addition, solving the main problems was entrusted to his deputies, bright representatives of the new generation of managers of the industry: Pavel Voronin and Peter Dementiev. Thus, for the first time, Stalin appointed people with high levels of professional competence and real experience of managerial work to top managerial positions in the industry. However, even Voronin and Dementiev's organizational qualities and frenzied energy could not change the administrative system of economic management created by Stalin. In the absence of motivation for workers and engineers to work, the administrative measures were ineffective. Thus, in the author's opinion, although the new leadership of the People's Commissariat of Aviation Industry of the USSR had a share of responsibility for the failure of the creation of 'New Type' fighters, they were not the main culprits.

By the middle of 1940, the forced labour system created by Stalin had been completed. The decree of the Supreme Soviet of the USSR of 26 June 1940 deprived workers in industrial plants of their last labour rights and attached them to the plant where they were working at that time. Any possibility of transferring an employee to other plants without permission from the plant director was excluded. Weekends were cancelled, and a seven-day working week was introduced. For any violation of labour 'discipline', the worker was punished severely. Repeated violation was punishable by long-term imprisonment.[6]

On the eve of the planned great war, Stalin's last resource for improving the efficiency of the defence industry in general and aviation in particular was slave labour.

The reason for the failure is the enemies!

Blaming 'the enemies' was a direct consequence of Stalin's paranoia. A psychopath who has got to the very top of power is always looking for reasons for his own failures in the sophisticated machinations of his enemies. The search for, and exposure of, 'enemies of the people' was

6 Collection of laws of the USSR and decrees of the Presidium of the Supreme Soviet of the USSR, 1938-1944, Moscow, *Vedomosti of the Supreme Soviet of the USSR, 1945*, pp.141-2.

relevant throughout Stalin's bloody dictatorship. Numerous 'saboteurs' were also discovered in the aviation industry, beloved by the 'Red Tsar'. Perhaps the most striking 'enemy' who made the greatest 'contribution' to the failure of the 'New Type' Soviet fighters was the head of the Red Army Air Force Research Institute, Alexander Filin.

At the beginning of the 1930s, this famous 'Stalin's Falcon' was one of the best test pilots in the USSR. While working at the Red Army Air Force Research Institute, Filin participated in the tests of many aircraft: Polikarpov I-5, I-15, I-16, Yakovlev UT-1, Tupolev ANT-25 and others. Together with his colleagues, he developed universal methods of combat aircraft flight tests, participated in various record-breaking flights and grand Stalin's parades. In addition, Filin paid close attention to ensuring flight safety, developing measures to reduce accidents during the operation of military aircraft. He was the first to summarize the available empirical data and create instructions for the recovery of several types of aircraft from spin. The appointment of Filin to the position of Head of the Red Army Air Force Research Institute finally consolidated his status as a conceptual leader, creating great opportunities for his influence on the development strategy of the Red Army Air Force. In this position, 'Stalin's Falcon' proved to be an effective leader and consistent supporter of the development of the concept of new requirements for combat aircraft. Unlike most of his intellectually limited colleagues from the Red Army Air Force command, who believed that speed and guns decided everything, Filin drew deeper conclusions from the air campaigns in Spain, on Khalkhin Gol and Finland. He advocated the mandatory equipping of fighters with good radio communication, devices for flying at night and in difficult weather conditions, and other important equipment. His concept was confirmed by tests at the Red Army Air Force Research Institute of Bf 109 E, Do 215 B, and Bf 110 C aircraft purchased in Germany.

Aircraft designer, Nikolai Polikarpov, in the last years of his life.

Alexander Filin's professional and personal qualities were most

clearly manifested during the key events of the dramatic company for the development, testing and launch into mass production of 'New Type' fighters. He consistently demanded testing of prototypes of new fighters with radio communication equipment installed, pilot armour protection and other modern equipment. That uncompromising attitude provoked an acute conflict between Filin and Stalin's new favourites, and ultimately changed completely the nature of his relationship with the 'Father of Nations'.

The elevation of Filin to Head of the Red Army Air Force Research Institute, in addition to his professional qualities, was undoubtedly due to Stalin's sympathy. However, as already noted, being the 'son' of the paranoid Stalin was no less dangerous than being his blood enemy. Sometimes the process of Stalin's transition from paternal love to fierce hatred took a very short time. People's Commissar of Aviation Industry Aleksey Shakhurin writes in his memoirs:

> Once, after discussing some aviation issue with Filin, Stalin invited him to dinner. I still remember the beautiful, pale face of Alexander Ivanovich, a slender figure, an attentive look of blue eyes and a smile. At lunch, Stalin asked Filin about flight work, planes. He was interested in his health ... then, asking what fruits Filin likes, he ordered to take some fruit and several bottles of wine to his car. Stalin looked at him all the time with a cordially and friendly expression.
>
> And a few weeks later, it was worth one aircraft designer to report: 'Comrade Stalin, Filin slows down the test of my fighter, makes all sorts of claims' and there was a sharp turn in the fate of Filin.
>
> 'How so?' Stalin asked.
>
> 'Yes, Filin points to shortcomings, but I claim that the plane is good.'
>
> Beria, who was present, muttered something to himself. It was possible to understand only one word: 'Bastard ... '
>
> And a few days later it became known that Filin was arrested ... .[7]

7 Shakhurin, A.I., op. cit., p.51.

During the 'investigation', which lasted more than six months, Alexander Filin was charged with an anti-Soviet conspiracy. On 23 February 1942, Stalin's 'enemy' was shot.

Another favourite of Stalin could not escape the 'father's' anger either. On 5 January 1946, Aleksey Shakhurin was removed from the post of People's Commissar of Aviation Industry and arrested. On 11 May 1946, he was found guilty by the Military Collegium of the Supreme Court of the Soviet Union and sentenced to seven years in Gulag.

The Stalinist 'court' accused Aleksey Shakhurin of:

> for a long time produced aircraft and engines with large structural and production defects and, in collusion with the Soviet Air Force command, supplied them to the Red Army Air Force, as a result of which a large number of accidents and catastrophes occurred in aviation units, pilots died, and many defective aircraft that could not be used in battles with the Germans accumulated ... .

Only after Stalin's death in 1953 was Shakhurin released and rehabilitated. All the titles and awards taken away after his arrest were returned and he was appointed to the post of Deputy Minister of Aviation Industry.

The trial of the leadership of the Red Army Air Force

9 April 1941. Moscow. A meeting of the Political Bureau of the Central Committee of the Communist Party of the Soviet Union, the Council of People's Commissioners of the Soviet Union and the leaders of the People's Commissariat of Defence of the Soviet Union.

It was one of the endless meetings on aviation problems that worried Stalin so much. The main difference between this and many other meetings was that it was conducted personally by Stalin. The stated topic of the meeting 'On accidents and catastrophes in Red Army aviation' suggested a 'trial' of the perpetrators of the collapse of discipline in the Red Army Air Force. Stalin acted in his usual role of 'chief judge'. After a brief speech, reduced to the usual statement of the importance of re-armament and increasing the combat readiness of the Red Army Air Force, the 'Red Lord' drew the attention of the audience to some egregious violations of discipline by military personnel, leading to an increase in accidents in aviation.

Propellers completion line at Gorky Aviation Plant No. 21.

Then the floor was given to Stalin's chief 'specialist' on Red Army Air Force matters, Secretary of the Communist Party of the Soviet Union (Stalin's deputy in the party) Georgy Malenkov who, acting in the usual role of 'prosecutor', read out an extensive report on the state of aviation. According to his habit, during Malenkov's speech, the 'chief judge' thoughtfully smoked a pipe and walked along the long table at which numerous participants of the meeting were sitting. At the end of his accusatory speech, Malenkov said:

> The facts say that due to low discipline, on average, two to three aircraft are lost every day in accidents and catastrophes, which is 600 to 900 aircraft per year. The current leadership of the Red Army Air Force has proved unable to lead a serious struggle to strengthen discipline in aviation and reduce accidents and catastrophes.[8]

8 RGASPI, Foundation 17, Inventory 163, Case 1308, Sheet 210.

Assembly line I-16 at Gorky Aviation Plant No. 21. In the foreground is the assembly of training aircraft UTI-4.

After these words an uneasy silence hung over the meeting. The aviation representatives shifted in their chairs. Chief of the Red Army Air Force Lieutenant General Pavel Rychagov wiped the sweat from his forehead with a hand trembling with excitement, which had appeared profusely during Malenkov's report. Stalin, maintaining his equanimity, invited those present to take turns to speak on the essence of the problem. Members of the Communist Party Central Committee gave confused explanations for the causes of the accidents, generally reduced to insufficient party control and a small number of Communists among Red Army Air Force servicemen. Finally, came the turn of the representatives of military aviation, who were sitting in a compact group on one side of the huge table. Stalin stopped pacing the room and, frowning, stared at the Chief of the Red Army Air Force, Pavel Rychagov, waiting for an explanation. The 29-year-old Rychagov impetuously jumped up from his seat and said loudly: 'The accident rate will be great, because you make us fly in coffins!'

This shout was completely unexpected for everyone present, including Stalin. There was a deathly silence. Only Pavel Rychagov was standing, his face purple with excitement. A few steps away stood a pale 'Red Lord'. The truth expressed in person had a stronger effect on Stalin than even a strong slap in the face could give. For the first time in many years, in front

Workers of Kazan Aviation Plant No. 22 study the aircraft engine, at the start of the 1940s.

of numerous servants, the 'Great Leader' lost his composure. Admiral Ivan Isakov, who was at the meeting, described this scene in his memoirs:

> Stalin stopped and was silent. Everyone was waiting for what would happen. He stood for a moment, then walked past the table, in the same direction in which he was walking. He reached the end, turned around, walked the whole room back in complete silence, turned around again and, taking the pipe out of his mouth, and slowly and in a low voice filled with undisguised anger, he said in response: 'You shouldn't have said that!'
>
> And he went again. He reached the end again, turned around again, walked across the room, turned around again and stopped almost at the same place as the first time, said again in the same quiet voice: 'You shouldn't have said that,' and, after a tiny pause, added, 'The meeting is adjourned.'
>
> And he was the first to leave the room.

Above: Female workers in one of the workshops of Aviation Plant No. 126 (Komsomolsk-on-Amur).

Left: 'Red Lord' Joseph Stalin and his chief executioner, Lavrentiy Beria.

Below: A typical meeting at Stalin's.

Stalin's chief 'specialist' on Red Army Air Force issues, Georgy Malenkov.

Rychagov's words had the effect of an exploding bomb. For many years, no one dared tell Stalin the truth. The 'Red Lord', who was used to learning about events hidden from him from private conversations with his 'agents', was completely shocked. The meeting, carefully prepared by Stalin, was totally disrupted. The old theory about the collapse of discipline and hooligan pilots who constantly crashed his favourite planes in accidents was refuted by one phrase of yesterday's boy. The 'son', whom Stalin appointed on a whim to be of chief of the Red Army Air Force, accused him directly of the very deliberate sabotage that was usually attributed only to 'enemies of the people'! The usual picture of the world, which the 'Red Emperor' practised so diligently throughout all the 1930s, collapsed in front of numerous witnesses. It turned out that the main enemy of the Red Army Air Force was Stalin.

General Pavel Rychagov surrounded by pilots.

It took the 'Great Leader' several days to recover. Three days after the disrupted meeting, Pavel Rychagov was removed from his post and that of Deputy People's Commissar for Defence of the Soviet Union, 'as undisciplined and unable to cope with the duty of Chief of the Air Force of the Red Army.' Then events unfolded outside the box. Stalin, who had lost face, did not dare to immediately deal with a man who humiliated him publicly in front of his servants. Pavel Rychagov was allowed to live for almost seven more months. He was arrested by NKVD officers only on 24 June 1941. During interrogation, Stalin's executioners tortured Rychagov terribly, trying to force him to give false testimony against other top air force commanders. However, despite the monstrous measures of physical influence and unprecedented psychological pressure, this surprisingly brave man responded to the Stalinist executioners with a categorical refusal.

By order of Stalin's main executioner, Lavrenty Beria, the famous 'Stalin's Falcon', the hero of the Spanish Civil War Pavel Rychagov was shot on 28 October 1941 in the village of Barbysh near the city of Kuybyshev (now Samara).

Conclusion

The Soviet history of the Second World War, written in the era of a totalitarian regime, reflected all its features. It was a solid set of patriotic myths that have no connection with reality. Most events of the war were distorted beyond recognition or even made up from beginning to end. Archives with original documents were available only to selected, specially verified KGB 'historians' who presented only the version of the war acceptable to the Soviet regime. After the collapse of the Soviet Union, the process of declassifying archives and granting wide access to information gradually began to reveal the terrible truth of the crimes of the Soviet regime. One, of course, was the incompetent leadership of the Red Army, which caused so many victims amongst the Russian people. However, the consequences

Soviet poster celebrating 'Stalin's Falcons'.

Voting for the immediate execution of all 'enemies of the people'! Moscow, 1938.

of decades of lies of Soviet propaganda had a very strong impact on both Russian and world historical science. As a result, not only Russian but, unfortunately, many European and American historians found themselves believing the Soviet myth.

The history of Soviet fighter aircraft did not escape this fate. The tale of Stalin's Falcons, which allegedly shot down dozens and even hundreds of Luftwaffe planes, was persistently drummed into the heads of generations of Soviet people. These heroes flew on Soviet fighters, whose technical characteristics were many times superior to their German counterparts. German aces were afraid of meeting them in the sky. This primitive propaganda cliché became a model for describing the actions of Stalin's fighter aircraft. Any information that did not fit into this template was compensated for by manipulation of facts and outright lies from Soviet 'historians'.

Soviet history writes evasively about the defects in design and quality of aircraft production during the war, carefully manipulating the thesis that the alleged defeat of Soviet aviation in 1941 and 1942 was the result of a sudden attack by the Germans with several other equally unconvincing reasons.

Stalin's propaganda persistently held that, every year of the war, the quality of Soviet fighters and the skill of their pilots increased. The official Soviet myth even named specific battles in which significant Luftwaffe forces were allegedly defeated. For example, the version about the conquest of the sky by Soviet fighters over the Kuban bridgehead (Kubanbrückenkopf) in 1943 is still being promoted.

That many real Soviet aces fought on British Hurricanes and Spitfires and American Airacobras and Kittyhawks is a fact that official Soviet history tried not to mention.

Almost all Soviet aircraft designers were declared 'enemies of the people' on the absurd charge of having links with foreign intelligence services. The death penalty or slow death in a Gulag was replaced by slave labour in a prison under the strictest supervision of the NKVD. About what 'planes' aircraft designers created in prison under the threat of death for two weeks or sometimes even for a few days showed the terrible losses of Soviet aviation. This indisputable fact was a closely guarded secret until the collapse of the Soviet Union.

About the conditions under which Soviet fighters were produced using virtually slave labour of prisoners, as well as the ruthless exploitation of

Consequences of the Luftwaffe air raid. 15th Fighter Aviation Regiment. The surroundings of the city of Kaunas.

More consequences of the Luftwaffe air raid – the surroundings of the city of Minsk.

A burnt-out MiG-3 fighter.

women and adolescents, official history also remained silent or modestly pointed out the military necessity of such barbaric measures.

The list of such 'dark' aspects of the creation and operation of Soviet fighter aircraft can be continued for a long time. And the main exposure of the myth of Stalin's Falcons is that, until the end of the war, literally until the end the battle of Berlin, Soviet fighters could not effectively resist the Luftwaffe, even taking into account the fact that German planes were then very rarely seen in the sky.

References and Sources

Adler E.G., *Earth and sky. Notes of an aircraft designer*, Moscow, 'Russian Aviation Society' (RUSAVIA). 2004.

Degtev D.M. Zubov D.V., *LaGG-3. Fighter, attack aircraft, scout. Wood against metal*, Moscow, Eksmo-Yauza, 2018.

Khvoshchevsky G.I., *Pages of the history of Aviation Plant No. 39 named after Menzhinsky: from Moscow to Irkutsk: a chronicle and documentary history*, Irkutsk, Publishing house of LLC 'Printing house 'Irkut', 2012.

Kondrat E.F., *We got a restless century: A documentary story*. Moscow, DOSAAF, 1978.

Kostyrchenko G.V., '*From the history of the formation of the Soviet aviation industry*', Aviation industry. 1988. No. 12.

Kuznetsov S.D., *The First Yak*, Moscow, Favorite book. 1995.

Maslov M.A., *Fighter I-16. Skittish 'Donkey' of 'Stalin's Falcons'*, Moscow, 'Yauza', 'Collection', EKSMO, 2008.

Mukhin M.Y., *Aviation industry of the USSR in 1921-1941*, Moscow, Nauka, 2006.

Nevezhin V.A., *Stalin's table speeches: Documents and materialsm*, Moscow, AIRO-XX. 2003.

Petrov I.F., '*I was carrying out Stalin's task*', Rodina, 1992, No. 5.

Petrov I.F., '*I consider it my duty to tell you. The war began before the war*', Inventor and innovator, 1986, No. 4.

Rabkin I.G., *Time, people, planes*, Moscow, Moskovsky rabochy, 1985.

Russian Air Force. Unknown documents (1931-1967). Moscow, Publishing house 'Bulletin of the Air Fleet', 2003.

Shakhurin A.I., *Wings of Victory. Memoirs*, Moscow, Politizdat, 1990.

Shumikhin V.S., '*Were shot on take-off*', Soviet warrior, 1989. No. 1.

Slugin V.E., *We started with difficulties*, Working Life, 1997, No. 18, 20.

Stepanov A.S., '*The mission of General Petrov: the influence of the German factor on the development of the Red Army Air Force on the eve of the Great Patriotic War*', History of aviation, 2001, No. 2.

Yakovlev, A. S., *The purpose of life: Notes of an aircraft designer*, Moscow, Politizdat, 1987.

Yakubovich N.V., *Aviation of the USSR on the eve of the war*, Moscow, Veche, 2006.

Zefirov M V., *Aces of the Second World War: Luftwaffe Allies: Estonia. Latvian. Finland,* Moscow, AST, 2003.

Collection of laws of the USSR and decrees of the Presidium of the Supreme Soviet of the USSR. 1938-1944, Moscow, Vedomosti of the Supreme Soviet of the USSR, 1945.

Archives

Central Archives of the Ministry of Defence of the Russian Federation (TSAMO RF)

TSAMO RF. Foundation 35. Inventory 11287. Case 24. Sheet 15.

TSAMO RF. Foundation 35. Inventory 11287. Case 575. Sheet 196.

TSAMO RF. Foundation Red Army Air Force Research Institute. Inventory 485623. Case 20. Sheets 2 - 19.

TSAMO RF. Foundation Red Army Air Force Research Institute. Inventory 485609. Case 108. Sheets 5 -51.

TSAMO RF. Foundation Red Army Air Force Research Institute. Inventory 502941. Case 30. Sheets 228-234.

Russian State Archive of Socio-Political History (RGASPI)

RGASPI. Foundation 558. Inventory 11. Case 151. Sheet 57.

RGASPI. Foundation 17. Inventory 162. Case 27. Sheet 11.

RGASPI. Foundation 17. Inventory 163. Case 1308. Sheet 210.

State institution Central archive of the Nizhny Novgorod region (GU TSANO)

GU TSANO. Foundation 2066. Inventory 9. Case 51. Sheet 17.

GU TSANO. Foundation 2066. Inventory 9. Case 171. Sheet 43.

GU TSANO. Foundation 2066. Inventory 9. Case 171. Sheet 33.

GU TSANO. Foundation 2066. Inventory 6. Case 570. Sheet 12.

GU TSANO. Foundation 2066. Inventory 6. Case 563.

GU TSANO. Foundation 2066. Inventory 6. Case 586.

GU TSANO. Foundation 2066. Inventory 6. Case 630.

GU TSANO. Foundation 2066. Inventory 6. Case 638.
GU TSANO. Foundation 2066. Inventory 6. Case 640.
GU TSANO. Foundation 2066. Inventory 6. Case 653.
GU TSANO. Foundation 2066. Inventory 6. Case 654.
GU TSANO. Foundation 2066. Inventory 6. Case 655.
GU TSANO. Foundation 2066. Inventory 6. Case 656.
GU TSANO. Foundation 2066. Inventory 6. Case 678.
GU TSANO. Foundation 2066. Inventory 6. Case 682.
GU TSANO. Foundation 2066. Inventory 6. Case 694.
GU TSANO. Foundation 2066. Inventory 6. Case 695.

Russian state archive for scientific-technical documentation (RGANTD)
RGANTD (Samara branch). Foundation P-217. Inventory 3-1. Case 65.

Russian State Military Archive (RGVA)
RGVA. Foundation 29. Inventory 34. Case 365. Sheet 160 – 162.

Russian State Archive of Economics (RGAE)
RGAE. Foundation 8044. Inventory 1. Case 338. Sheet 12.
RGAE. Foundation 8164. Inventory 1. Case 338. Sheet 145.

Index